The Big Bob Gibson BBG Book
by Chris Lilly

"Bare Naked Brisket Rub"

Big Green Egg
cookbook

enjoy!

Big Green Egg®
cookbook

Celebrating the Ultimate Cooking Experience

Foreword by Ed Fisher

Recipes by Sara Levy
Text by Lisa Mayer
Photographs by Mark O'Tyson

Andrews McMeel Publishing, LLC
Kansas City · Sydney · London

Big Green Egg Cookbook: Celebrating the World's Best Smoker & Grill
Recipes © 2009 Big Green Egg, Inc. Photographs © 2009 Mark O'Tyson.
All rights reserved. Printed in China. No part of this book may be used or
reproduced in any manner whatsoever without written permission except in
the case of reprints in the context of reviews.

Andrews McMeel Publishing, LLC
an Andrews McMeel Universal company
1130 Walnut Street, Kansas City, Missouri 64106

www.andrewsmcmeel.com

ISBN: 978-0-7407-9145-1

13 14 15 16 17 SDB 11 10 9 8 7

Library of Congress Control Number: 20099341318

For additional information about Big Green Egg products and the company, or
to find Big Green Egg dealers near you, visit www.biggreenegg.com.
BIG GREEN EGG and EGG are registered trademarks of The Big Green Egg, Inc.
EGGhead, EGGheads, EGGfest, and EGGcessories are trademarks of The Big
Green Egg, Inc. The particular green color and overall configuration of the
cooker in this color are also trademarks of The Big Green Egg, Inc.

Produced by Donna Myers, DHM Group, Inc.
Packaged and designed by Jennifer Barry Design, Fairfax, California
Recipe development and food styling: Sara Levy
Food styling and recipe testing assistance: Bree Williams and Bryan Hartness
Design and art direction assistance: Leslie Barry
Layout production: Kristen Hall
Copyediting: Leslie Evans

Attention: Schools and Businesses
Andrews McMeel books are available at quantity discounts with bulk purchase
for educational, business, or sales promotional use. For information, please
e-mail the Andrews McMeel Publishing Special Sales Department:
specialsales@amuniversal.com

contents

"If you are new to the world of cooking on a Big Green Egg, welcome and congratulations! You have some great culinary adventures in your future." —Ed Fisher

Foreword

We might as well break it to you right now: your kitchen oven is about to become a high-priced storage cabinet. So versatile is the Big Green Egg that you may never want to use your indoor appliances again.

If you are new to the world of cooking on a Big Green Egg, welcome and congratulations! You have some great culinary adventures in your future. We know this book will help you master the basics, move on to some new cooking sensations, and quickly join the legions of enthusiasts for whom cooking in their EGG is not just their favorite way to prepare a meal, but a lifestyle built around great-tasting food, friends, family, and camaraderie!

This dedicated band of followers, affectionately known as EGGheads, considers the EGG more than just a grill. To them it is The Ultimate Cooking Experience, much like a Harley is more than just a motorcycle—it's the ultimate motorcycle. And as many Harley owners live, sleep, and

breathe the Harley lifestyle, so too do many passionate EGG owners embrace their EGGs as a way of life.

If you already are one of these seasoned EGGheads, you know what we mean. We thank you for your support and loyalty to this cooking marvel. Your fervent passion for the EGG is among the reasons for its growing success over the past three decades. We recognize your tremendous contributions to the evolution of our product, including ideas for new products and features, and we are appreciative of your support. After all, no one knows the EGG better than those passionate enough to use it day in and day out.

Like most of us, you probably have grilled, smoked, roasted, and baked your way to culinary bliss in the Big Green Egg. But what you'll find new here are fabulous recipes, nearly 170 of them, that take cooking with an EGG to a whole new level. From modern twists on tried-and-true barbecue favorites to exotic, gourmet dishes with sophisticated flavors, you'll find inventive menus to add pizzazz to your culinary repertoire.

Could there be anything better than cooking good food in the great outdoors? We don't think so. The mix of fresh air, spicy wood smoke, and the zesty aroma of food cooking over the coals is an intoxicating elixir that will not only get your mouth watering but also light the desire to cook every meal in the EGG all year long.

So stoke up the fire, don the apron, and take up the tongs. A very tasty adventure awaits.

Happy EGGing,
Ed Fisher, Chairman and Founder
Big Green Egg, Inc.

The Big Green Egg creates food that is moister, more flavorful, and far superior to food cooked on an ordinary barbecue grill

Introduction

The Big Green Egg: A Newfangled Grill with a Long History

What exactly is a Big Green Egg, and why have so many come to embrace it as The Ultimate Cooking Experience?

In a nutshell, a Big Green Egg is a modern evolution of a type of elliptically shaped barbecue originally called a "kamado." While it still may be somewhat of an unusual appliance by today's standards, evidence of enclosed, rounded earthen cooking vessels has been found by archaeologists in the ruins of practically every ancient civilization since cavemen (or, more likely, cavewomen) figured out that meat tasted a whole lot better when it was cooked over a fire.

These oblong clay cookers were first used in China during the Qin Dynasty (221 B.C.–207 B.C.). The Japanese adopted these domed cooking vessels in the third century C.E. and called them "kamados," which has been translated to mean oven, stove, heater, or fireplace. Initially, pots were hung over the fire inside the kamado, and eventually a slatted cooking grid was fitted inside for grilling and roasting meats. Versatile even then, the base of the unit also provided heat to the house.

Throughout the centuries there were a number of variations on the theme, including stationary indoor kamados, portable outdoor kamados (could this be the first-ever barbecue grill?), and even "mushi-kamados" used exclusively for cooking rice. Not able to get enough of a good thing, wealthy Japanese often had two or more kamados lined up inside the home to prepare meals.

Now, skip ahead to World War II. U.S. servicemen first encountered kamados in Japan, loved cooking in them, and brought them home when they returned to America after the war. They discovered that the rounded shape and clay walls of the cookers retained both heat and moisture in a way that a regular grill couldn't. The kamados were an unusual but exciting alternative to the barbecue grills of the day, and early fans were soon hooked on the added flavor and juiciness the "new" cooker gave to foods.

How the Modern Big Green Egg Was Hatched

Ed Fisher was one of the first people in the United States to catch on to the fun and flavor of kamado cooking. After eating a meal prepared in a kamado grill in the early 1970s, Fisher declared it the "best food he had ever eaten" and made it his mission to perfect these ancient cookers and get them into backyards everywhere. In fact, so convinced was he of the benefits of this quirky barbecue that he began importing these rudimentary clay kamados from Asia and selling them out of an Atlanta storefront in 1974.

These early models, made of the same fire clay and design that had been used for thousands of years, produced great results and began to attract a following. However, as Ed quickly learned, the material used in these kamados becomes brittle and will crack if it gets too hot, or after a few years of use and exposure to the elements.

Not satisfied with the short-lived materials and marginal thermal properties of a typical kamado grill, Fisher made a decision

to create the very best outdoor cooker, period. Although the overall shape and heat-retention properties of the kamado were part of his equation, the objective was to move far beyond the inferior fire clay and low-grade ceramics that were offered by others, and produce the most technically advanced, highest quality ceramic cooking device ever "hatched" . . . and did he ever succeed!

Partnering with advanced ceramic manufacturing experts and composite materials engineers, Fisher's company launched a product that incorporated new types of ceramics originally developed by NASA for the space program. This sophisticated material, proprietary to the Big Green Egg, is the highest grade of composite used in any cooker—it is impervious to the elements, has excellent insulating properties, and is incredibly durable, able to withstand extreme heat, cold, heavy use, and all kinds of weather conditions without cracking or incurring other damage. And the moment Fisher saw how far superior his product was, he immediately and without hesitation decided that the EGG would be backed by a best-in-class limited lifetime warranty (practically unheard of in barbecue grills) on all of the ceramics!

From this point forward, the Big Green Egg left all other kamado cookers behind and stood alone as the only outdoor cooker of its type—the Big Green Egg.

But What Came First . . . the Name or the EGG?

While working on a strategy to generate awareness of this revolutionary new invention, Fisher would often comment how much the product resembled an oversized egg. And perhaps subconsciously inspired by Dr. Seuss's whimsical story, he decided to make the egg-shaped

cooker fun and distinctive by coloring it green. Thus, the Big Green Egg was born and named, with a look and moniker he hoped would be very memorable for prospective customers. Right he was. Once someone sees the Big Green Egg, or hears the name, he or she might chuckle, but is not likely to forget it.

With virtually no sales staff or advertising in the early days of the company, Fisher relied on dedicated fans of the EGG to spread the word as members of his unofficial sales force. Once they cooked a few meals of their own, these enthusiasts wanted everyone to experience food prepared in the Big Green Egg, and convinced untold numbers of neighbors and friends to try it and buy one.

Faithful owners were also Fisher's first research and development team, regularly returning to his store to suggest ideas for new product features and useful tools and enhancements, now known as EGGcessories.

Never content to rest on their laurels, the team at Big Green Egg has painstakingly developed dozens of additional improvements over the years to keep making the EGG better and better . . . a process that continues today in a never-ending quest to improve performance, durability, and the cooking experience.

The Big Green Egg is foolproof and fuel efficient and can cook anything from fish and steak to pizza and pie. It really does it all.

How to Speak EGGlish:

EGGstraordinary: The way food tastes cooked in the EGG.

EGGceptional: The quality of EGG products.

EGGcessories: All the fabulous cooking gear for the EGG.

EGGheads: People who love this cooker.

EGGfests: Cooking festivals for all who love the EGG.

EGGstravaganza: A meal cooked entirely in the EGG.

For instance, a proprietary, permanent nontoxic glaze ensures the signature green color will not fade or discolor over time or under any outdoor conditions. The patented draft door and air flow control system offer precise and easily regulated temperature ranges. Other updates include a convenient spring-band hinge system that makes the lid easier to open and close, and heavy-duty stainless steel or cast-iron cooking grids, to name just a few. And, of course, the sizes, which grew to five—from the fun and portable Mini to the "invite the neighborhood" XLarge—and are all made to the same exacting standards.

Other improvements are invisible—subtle improvements in the technology that goes into the manufacturing process, upgrades in specifications and materials, and so on.

Bottom line, when you look at outdoor grills and cookers, you should know that while there are many brands and kamado-style grills being offered today—many still calling themselves "kamados"—there is only one, original Big Green Egg. While others may claim to be similar, the

Big Green Egg really is a different product entirely and is far superior to any kamado grill on the market today.

The Big Green Egg is available only through a dedicated and knowledge-able network of Authorized Dealers in over twenty-five countries. Big Green Egg headquarters in Atlanta, Georgia, is not far from the small store where the company was founded all those years ago.

The Big Green Egg: Better Than a Barbecue . . . by Design

The Big Green Egg creates food that is moister, more flavorful, and far superior to anything cooked on an ordinary metal barbecue. A bold statement, we know, but it's true. While metal grills may be satisfactory to quickly grill a burger or boneless chicken breast over high heat, their design and materials are limiting when it comes to smoking, roasting, or baking a variety of foods.

What makes the Big Green Egg so different? For one, unmatched heat retention properties—thanks to thick ceramic walls that insulate and hold heat inside the grill while it remains cool to the touch on the exterior. A proven design, updated with modern engineering, circulates the heat within the cooker and controls temperatures with precision. The dome-shaped lid remains closed during all cooking and allows heat to radiate from the top as well as from the coals below the cooking grid. And finally, the properties of the ceramic material, together with the tight seal of the lid, hold

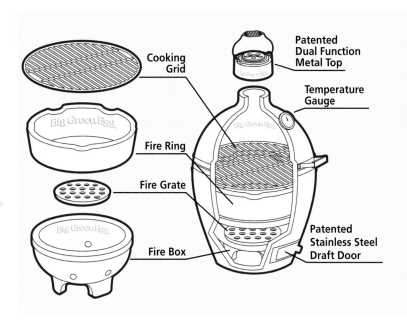

moisture in food, lock in natural flavors and juices for better taste, and prevent or minimize food shrinkage.

Another key difference between the Big Green Egg and other types of grills is the EGG's all-natural, lump charcoal fuel that gives food cooked on the EGG its distinctive flavor and texture. Entirely different from briquettes or other heat sources, our premium, select lump charcoal contains no additives, chemicals, or petroleum by-products. As a result, it burns clean with less ash and adds a delicate wood smoke flavor to food.

One more benefit: Not only does lump charcoal light quickly, but it also enables the EGG to cook faster than other barbecue grills, conserving both fuel and time. And who doesn't need more of that?

The EGG is an efficient multitasker, too, eliminating the need for several outdoor appliances to match the EGG's ability to perform a wide variety of outdoor cooking tasks.

An EGG can sear at 750°F/400°C temperatures like an infrared grill, slow-smoke over a 200°F/93°C charcoal and wood fire like an old-fashioned smoker, and roast and bake to crusty perfection like a brick oven—in fact, pizza prepared in an EGG is considered by many to be superior in taste and texture to the ones baked in the pizza ovens of Italy! And, because the heat is retained, circulated, and radiated so evenly, a cumbersome rotisserie is never needed to achieve evenly browned, rotisserie-like results. To learn more about mastering these specific cooking techniques, see pages 24–25, visit BigGreenEgg.com, or scan using your SmartPhone

This Cooker Has Actually Spawned a Culture

It's unusual, dare we say unheard-of, that a cooking appliance would inspire a whole culture and way of life. Can you imagine an organized and extremely passionate band of followers for the microwave called The Micromaniacs or electric cooktop enthusiasts called The Electric Rangers? We can't either. But that's exactly what the EGG has inspired.

So unique and so exceptional is this ceramic cooker that, one by one, like-minded EGG enthusiasts began to find one another via the Internet. They were eager to share recipes, new techniques, and praise for the EGG with others who, like themselves, considered the Big Green Egg the secret to culinary success.

United in their desire to promote and celebrate cooking in the EGG, the group evolved and expanded. They communicated online more frequently and began calling themselves "EGGheads." Before long they were asking, "Wouldn't it be fun to get together in person to meet one another and celebrate the EGG?" It proved such a good idea that they came away feeling they had just attended a big family reunion. The annual gathering continues even today, only on a much larger scale than the original, relatively intimate get-together.

EGGheads

Even if you have heard the term EGGhead in relation to the Big Green Egg, you may still be wondering, what the heck is that? Think Trekkies to *Star Trek*, Deadheads to the Grateful Dead, Cheeseheads to the Green Bay Packers, and HOGs to Harley motorcyclists. EGGhead is the affectionate term for a passionate devotee of the EGG.

To call them enthusiastic would be an understatement. Zealous, fervent, dedicated, obsessive, and anything else along those lines much more accurately describes the level of interest and enthusiasm these folks have for this distinctive method of cooking. Most would rather cook in their EGG, brag about cooking in it, chat online about what they are cooking in it, or plan the next thing they will cook in this ceramic wonder than do practically anything else.

But it's not a private club with limited membership; those who are already members take every opportunity to "EGGvangelize" barbecuers everywhere and welcome them into the extended family.

The EGGhead Forum

Many EGGheads maintain a close friendship and communicate regularly online via the EGGhead Forum EGGheadForum.com. This lively web spot attracts postings from potential EGG buyers doing research, from EGG newbies who request assistance and advice on elementary topics, and from veterans who have owned EGGs for decades and wish to share their latest EGG triumph with other like-minded compatriots. Even retailers of the EGG refer prospective buyers to the Forum for information and feedback on the product.

Many Forum regulars consider each other extended family members. The Forum's motto is "Everyone is welcome," and it's true.

How do I smoke cheese? What's the best wood chip to use with lamb? Have you ever made elk jerky? These are just a few of the topics bantered about by the online chat group. The Forum is a great place to learn insiders' secrets to success and to adopt great techniques and new recipes to try on your own. EGGheads love to share, whether it is opinions, advice, or their favorite recipes.

The EGGhead Forum has been very influential in the development, popularity, and success of the EGG. A testament to the power of word-of-mouth recommendations, many a tire-kicker has been inspired to buy an EGG after visiting the Forum. In addition, ideas for enhancements to the EGG and even EGGcessory products have their roots in the threads of online discussions over the years.

hot tip:
You can access the EGGhead Forum at EGGheadForum.com or by visiting the Big Green Egg website at BigGreenEgg.com and clicking on the link to the EGGhead Forum.

EGGtoberfest and EGGfests

More than fifteen years ago, this band of EGGhead Forum friends was looking for a way to meet in person to show off their cooking skills and signature dishes and to finally put faces with names that had become familiar. Over a series of online chats, the idea for EGGtoberfest was born. When Ed Fisher heard about the plans, he decided to host the event and provide EGGs for cooking in recognition of the early EGGheads' importance to the company. No one dreamed this would grow into an annual event.

But the weekend was so successful that since 1998 people have gathered from all over the globe on the third weekend in October to cook, taste, share recipes, and soak up the camaraderie of other Big Green Egg enthusiasts at EGGtoberfest. Held in Atlanta, Georgia, the event is an unbridled, unabashed celebration of the "Ultimate Cooking Experience."

One hundred people attended the first EGGtoberfest and fired up 15 EGGs to cook all kinds of delicacies. The following year, the event doubled in size, and 50 EGGs were used to cook for 200 attendees. On the fifteenth anniversary of this event, over 3,000 people from thirty states and as far away as England, Mexico, and Canada tasted their way through dishes prepared by more than 375 cooks who fired up 220 EGGs. The weekend-long "EGGstravaganza" gets bigger, better, and more fun every year.

The festival's agenda also includes a series of demonstrations, prize giveaways, and lots of family fun. But, unquestionably, food is the highlight of EGGtoberfest weekend. EGGheads take the opportunity to strut their stuff and show off a little (okay, sometimes a lot). These volunteer cooks provide all the food they serve to attendees at their own expense.

All food for the event is prepared exclusively in EGGs, and while the menu changes from year to year, it always includes traditional favorites interspersed with imaginative offerings not typically thought of as barbecue fare. You'll find classic barbecued ribs, brisket, and pulled pork sharing the spotlight with such inventive dishes as Jerked Grouper with Papaya Jam, Twice EGGed Potatoes, Spicy Grilled Chicken Soup, and Apple Crostatas. Sometimes the food represents the geographic region of the chef who is cooking it, like a fresh-caught whole Alaskan salmon or Tex-Mex stuffed jalapeño peppers. Other dishes have a little one-upmanship in mind. Moose satays, ostrich steaks, barbecued turkey necks, and turducken—a boneless chicken stuffed into a duck, which in turn is stuffed into a turkey—are clearly made to impress.

The success and popularity of the annual EGGtoberfest has inspired dozens of local EGGfests, including one in the Netherlands. Like the original, these local EGGfests are fun-filled gatherings of EGG fans doing what they love best—cooking in an EGG and sharing stories, techniques, and delicious food with each other and the hundreds of people who attend.

Some local EGGfests are family friendly, low-key, and laid-back, with little formality or fanfare. Others feature a more structured schedule of activities throughout the weekend, complete with events like Iron Chef–style cook-offs, vendor displays, guest celebrity chefs, and a roster of educational seminars such as Cooking the Thanksgiving Turkey Outdoors or Plank Cooking for Added Flavor. You won't leave one of these festivals without learning something new and tasting something you've never tried before!

hot tip:
EGGtoberfest and many regional EGGfests provide a great way to get a feel for EGG culture. To find out more about EGGtoberfest or any of the regional EGGfests across the country, visit BigGreenEgg.com and click on Events.

This Recipe Collection

Generally speaking, EGGheads are not a very by-the-book lot. As kids, they might have been the ones least likely to color between the lines. Likewise with the art of cooking in the EGG, devotees are inclined to stretch the boundaries, often developing dishes that are way beyond what most people consider barbecue fare.

These creative types are the inspiration behind the recipes in this book. The innovative flavor combinations, ingredients, and techniques showcased here define new parameters for EGG cooking. We believe the most seasoned EGGheads will get ideas for gourmet fare they've never before tried in the EGG, yet the recipes are not so complicated or highbrow that they won't appeal to budding EGG artists. For every meal and every occasion, you'll find recipes to inspire you and make your mouth water.

To start the day, how about a Spicy Spanish Frittata with Chorizo, Apple Pancake, or Tropical Breakfast Muffins for breakfast? All are prepared in the EGG.

In the Baked Goods chapter, there is a United Nations–style collection of bread recipes, including lavash, naan, pita, and pizza dough, along with such all-American favorites as buttermilk biscuits and two differently flavored cornbreads, as well as Prosciutto, Fontina & Arugula Stromboli with Spicy San Marzano Sauce, which defies classification.

Having a dinner party? You might want to start your meal off with appetizers like Chilled White Gazpacho with Grilled Shrimp Relish; Mission Figs with Mascarpone, Honey & Chopped Walnuts; or Smoked Trout Dip with Spinach & Artichokes.

For the main course, how about Stuffed Pork Chops with Poblano Cream Sauce, Beer-Brined Chicken, or Beef Kabobs with Chimichurri? There are extensive chapters on pork, beef, and poultry, each with numerous recipes to choose from.

Hungry for pizza? Skip the basic Margherita style and try Greek Pizza with Yogurt-Mint Sauce or Quail Egg Pizza with Prosciutto & Arugula. In the mood for seafood? How about Thai Sea Bass in Banana Leaves or Cedar-Wrapped Scallops with Orange Beurre Blanc? Vegetarians will enjoy the Vegetable Reuben Sandwich, Dutch Oven Vegetable Fried Rice, and Root Vegetable Pot Pie.

Hope you saved room for dessert! You'll definitely want to try the Roasted Peaches with Pecan Praline Stuffing, Red Chile & Lime Shortbread Cookies, and Apple-Walnut Crostata with Caramel Sauce, among other temptations.

You'll also find favorite EGG recipes from members of the Big Green Egg extended family as well as celebrity chefs and restaurateurs.

Prepare to get hungry.

Get Acquainted with EGGs and EGGcessories

What started with a single-size EGG has now grown into a family of five models and an extensive complementary line of accessory products, each specially designed for the EGG. Used in tandem, EGGs and EGGcessories make an incredibly versatile and convenient cooking experience. The Big Green Egg comes in five sizes with a model to suit the needs of every backyard chef, even ones who like to take their cookout on the road.

XLarge
Cooking Grid Diameter: 24 inches/61 centimeters
Cooking Area: 452 square inches/2,919 square centimeters
Weight: 227 pounds/103 kilograms
Holds 2 (20-pound) turkeys, 24 burgers, 11 whole chickens, 12 steaks, or 14 racks of ribs vertically
Easily accommodates meals for large families and cookouts with all your friends

Large
Cooking Grid Diameter: 18.25 inches/46 centimeters
Cooking Area: 262 square inches/1,688 square centimeters
Weight: 155 pounds/70 kilograms
Holds 1 (20-pound) turkey, 12 burgers, 6 whole chickens, 8 steaks, or 7 racks of ribs
Most popular size and a favorite to handle the cooking needs of most families and gatherings of friends

Medium
Grid Diameter: 15 inches/38 centimeters
Cooking Area: 177 square inches/1,140 square centimeters
Weight: 114 pounds/52 kilograms
Holds 1 (18-pound) turkey, 6 burgers, 3 whole chickens, 4 steaks, or 4 racks of ribs
Perfectly sized for smaller families and couples

Small
Grid Diameter: 13 inches/33 centimeters
Cooking Area: 133 square inches/856 square centimeters
Weight: 77 pounds/35 kilograms
Holds 1 (12-pound) turkey, 4 burgers, 1 whole chicken, 2 steaks, or 1 rack of ribs
Perfect for individuals or couples and even tailgating

Mini
Grid Diameter: 10 inches/25.4 centimeters
Cooking Area: 78.5 square inches/507 square centimeters
Weight: 39 pounds/18 kilograms
Holds 2 chicken breasts, 2 pork chops, or 1 steak
Ideal solution for grilling on apartment balconies or for picnicking, tailgating, camping, and boating

EGGcessories

Simply put: EGGcessory products help you create endless possibilities for your dinner plate. Roasting a turkey to golden brown, succulent perfection? Cooking authentic trattoria-style pizza with a crispy crust and a hint of  wood smoke? Baking a moist and delicious cake? All are easily accomplished in the EGG with the right gear.

Other EGGcessories help increase the amount of cooking space, make cleanup a snap, and allow you to monitor whatever you're cooking from a remote location. Here is a rundown of some essential EGGcessories, a number of which you'll find used in the recipes in this book:

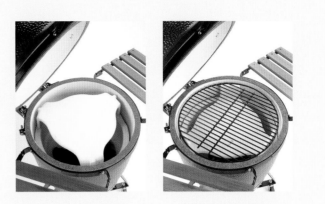

The Plate Setter in the "legs down" and "legs up" positions.

The Basics: For the Sake of Convenience

Charcoal Tools: How do we spell convenience? With gadgets like an Ash Tool to stoke, sift, rearrange coals, and pull ashes into the Ash Pan, a Grill Gripper to raise the cooking grid to add more fuel, and an Ash Pan to help remove ashes after the fun is over.

Nest: The easiest way to raise the EGG to a good work height and be able to move it about the patio is by placing it in a wheeled metal base called an EGG Nest.

Side Shelves: Need a spot to rest tongs, platters, or a bowl of sauce? Two styles of fold-down side shelves fit on the EGG and provide handy, easy-to-clean work surfaces beside the grill.

hot tip:

Big Green Egg painstakingly sources our natural lump charcoal to ensure that it contains no fillers, nitrates, chemicals, anthracite coal, limestone, treated wood, or petroleum products. Pure and natural Big Green Egg charcoal is carbonized wood with NO additives whatsoever. What do *you* want to cook with?

Surround Tables: For an upscale, built-in look, attractive wooden surround tables for the EGG are the way to go. Made of durable cypress wood from responsibly managed forests, the workstations bring the cooker up to a standard counter height and provide plenty of prep and serving surface.

Ventilated Covers: The durable EGG is tough enough to withstand the harshest weather, but you'll want to keep your baby clean anyway. Heavy-duty weatherproof covers shield the cooker from the elements while vents let it breathe. Covers are available to fit EGGs in Nests as well as in tables.

Cooking Tools of the Trade

Plate Setters: What jelly is to a peanut butter sandwich and frosting is to a cupcake, the Plate Setter is to the Big Green Egg; without it, the EGG is only half as versatile. In fact, the Plate Setter is practically essential to helping the EGG achieve its full potential.

Perhaps the most versatile EGGcessory ever, a Plate Setter is a flat, ceramic disk with three legs that acts as a heat shield. It is the best way to accomplish any type of cooking in the EGG where you don't want direct exposure to the flame and heat. The Plate Setter can be used to turn your EGG into a brick oven for baking bread, pizza, and desserts, a convection oven for roasting meats and vegetables, or a smoker for making down-home barbecue. Use it in conjunction with other EGGcessories, such as a Drip Pan, V-Rack, Grill Extender, or Vertical Roaster, and you have the tools to accomplish anything in your EGG that you can do in your indoor oven. For more information on cooking with a Plate Setter, see page 26.

Baking Stones: To make pizza, bread, and other baked goods, heavy-duty, ceramic Pizza/Baking Stones will help you achieve authentic brick-oven results. The thick round disks come in three sizes, as well as deep dish and half-moon configurations.

Cast Iron Grids: What's the secret to world-class grill marks? A Cast Iron Grid. Heavyweight Cast Iron Grids get very hot and retain heat for an awesome steakhouse-style sear. A Cast Iron Grid can be used as an alternative to the stainless steel grid that comes with the EGG.

Dutch Oven: Great for simmering stews, soups, and chili, preparing baked beans, or even baking cobblers, this 5 quart/4.7 liter, heavy-duty Dutch Oven is a valuable tool to have in your accessory arsenal. It truly enables you to cook an entire meal on the grill at once.

Grill Extenders: Cooking for a crowd? Grill Extenders are the perfect way to double or triple the size of your cooking surface by creating a second or even third cooking tier above the main cooking grid. Thanks to heat circulation within the EGG, food cooks to perfection whether it's on the main cooking grid or a higher level.

Half Moon Raised Grids: If you are cooking the whole meal in the EGG, you may find not only that you need more space but also that you need to cook some foods over direct heat while simultaneously cooking other foods over indirect heat. Half Moon Raised Grids make this possible by dividing the cooking area into separate direct- and indirect-cooking zones. There are many combinations and configurations for a versatile Half Moon Raised Grid. Used as is, it provides a second level for direct cooking over half the surface of the EGG, so you can grill pork chops over the flame on the lower cooking grid and vegetables on the Half Moon Raised Grid above them. Or use half the stainless steel grid for direct grilling, and on the other side, with a Half Moon Baking Stone, and a Half Moon Drip Pan in place, you can take advantage of a double layer of indirect heat to bake biscuits in a pan on one tier and sweet potatoes on the second tier.

Thermometers: Thermometers are an important part of every Big Green Egg cooking experience. Indispensable meat thermometers should be used whenever possible, not only to achieve rare, medium-rare, medium, or well-done meat as desired but also to determine internal temperatures for food safety too. An external thermometer, which comes built in as a standard feature on the Big Green Egg lid, measures the cooking temperature inside the EGG.

Food should always be cooked to temperatures high enough to destroy any food-borne bacteria. A programmable Dual Probe Wireless Remote Thermometer lets you monitor both meat and cooking chamber temperatures from your poolside or garden or the comfort of your easy chair. It conveniently signals when food is done, so you don't have to lift the lid to peek and let heat escape unnecessarily. An Instant Read Digital Food Thermometer inserted in the thickest part of the meat gives a quick read on its internal temperature. Other thermometer options include the Quick Read Pocket Thermometer, a Traditional Quick Read Thermometer, and a Traditional Stick and Stay Thermometer.

hot tip:

Take advantage of the extra
cooking surface gained with Grill
Extenders and Half Moon Raised Grids
and cook two meals at once. Enjoy one
dinner tonight and refrigerate the
other to reheat tomorrow night for
a fast home-cooked meal with a
cooked-over-the-coals taste that's
much better than fast food. Saves
time, money, and fuel.

Vertical Roasters: More convenient than a rotisserie, the Vertical Roaster, available in several styles and sizes, fits inside the cavity of a chicken or turkey and suspends it vertically to produce even browning. The Vertical Roaster can be used in tandem with a Drip Pan to catch drippings or hold juice, beer, wine, or other liquids to infuse the bird with flavor and juiciness from the inside out. It also makes carving the bird much easier.

V-Racks: Depending on your menu, this double-duty gadget will turn out perfectly roasted meats or enough ribs to feed a small army. Use it right side up to hold beef or pork roasts, or two chickens, and combine with a Drip Pan beneath to catch drippings for gravy. Or invert, and it holds racks of ribs vertically between the slats. The design of the EGG ensures that heat circulates perfectly throughout the grill, providing a convection effect and cooking multiple racks of ribs to pit-barbecue tenderness.

Fuel: What to Use and How to Light It

Ceramic cookers are fueled by charcoal, but not all charcoal is created equal. Natural lump charcoal is the recommended fuel for the Big Green Egg. An understanding of what makes this type of fuel so superior requires knowledge of what makes natural lump charcoal different from traditional charcoal briquettes.

Natural lump charcoal is made from a variety of 100 percent hardwoods that are turned into charcoal the old-fashioned way: by charring the wood in a closed oxygen-free kiln or pit. What emerges is lumpy, irregularly shaped pieces (hence the name *lump*) of pure carbon, called charcoal.

Unlike most standard briquettes, natural lump charcoal is 100 percent natural, so only the authentic wood smoke flavor comes through to enhance the taste of food. Natural lump charcoal burns hotter than traditional briquettes, and because there are no by-products, it burns clean.

Another benefit of natural lump charcoal is that it is very fuel efficient. It requires less charcoal than briquettes, lasts longer, and produces very little ash to clean up. After you have finished cooking, the fire can be extinguished by closing the dampers and cutting off the air supply. Any remaining charcoal can be relit for the next cookout.

Most traditional charcoal briquettes are made from scrap lumber that has been charred, ground to a powder, and combined with ground coal, limestone, starch binders, fillers, and petroleum-based additives to make them easier to light. The mixture is then compressed into the familiar pillow-shaped briquettes we all know. The large pile of ash remaining after a cookout fueled by traditional briquettes is composed mainly of these leftover additives. All-natural briquettes are available in some organic stores and are acceptable to use if you can find them.

Self-lighting charcoal briquettes should never be used in a ceramic cooker. The petroleum additives can penetrate the ceramic surface and permanently impart an off flavor to foods.

Cooking temperatures can be precisely controlled to within a few degrees, even for long cooking periods.

Lighting Your Fire

Most people find the ritual of lighting the fire a satisfying process that adds to the enjoyment and naturalness of cooking in a ceramic cooker. But whether you consider it a necessary chore or part of the fun, the good news is—it's fast, easy, and virtually hassle-free.

The Golden Rule to remember: Never use lighter fluid. The petroleum-based liquid can permanently penetrate the porous ceramic interior of the EGG and thereafter impart a chemical off taste to food. Rather, there are two equally fast and all-natural options for lighting the fire.

Option 1: Natural Charcoal Starters
These little blocks of compressed sawdust are coated with a natural paraffin wax. To use, fill the Fire Box of the EGG with natural lump charcoal. With the lid open, slide the draft door completely open. Nestle one or two Natural Charcoal Starters into the charcoal and light with a match or long-handled lighter. After eight to ten minutes, or when several coals are burning, close the lid and adjust the top and bottom dampers to regulate the temperature; when the desired temperature is reached, you are ready to cook.

Option 2: Electric Charcoal Starter
If you have access to an electrical outlet, an Electric Charcoal Starter is a simple and surefire way to light the charcoal. Fill the Fire Box of the EGG with natural lump charcoal, burying the Electric Charcoal Starter's coil into the charcoal. As the coil turns red hot, it will ignite the coals in approximately seven minutes. To remove the Starter, disconnect it from the power source, and holding it only by the handle, carefully place on the positioning bracket to air cool. Close the lid of the EGG and adjust the dampers to reach the desired temperature.

Adjusting the Temperature

Precise cooking temperatures can be achieved easily by monitoring the exterior temperature gauge and adjusting the draft openings accordingly. For lower temperatures, reduce the airflow by minimizing the openings of both the Dual Function Metal Top and the Draft Door in the base. To boost temperatures, open the dampers wider. Keep in mind that the greater the Draft Door openings, the higher the temperature. With a little practice, cooking temperatures can be controlled to within a few degrees, even for long cooking periods.

Regulating temperature is easy by monitoring the external gauge and adjusting the air flow in the Dual Function Metal Top and the Draft Door in the base of the EGG.

hot tip:

The secret to the extraordinary food cooked on the Big Green Egg centers on heat retention, air circulation, and temperature control. The lid should be left down while cooking to allow heat to radiate off the top as well as off the coals. Leaving the lid open reduces the Big Green Egg to an ordinary, inefficient barbecue grill that allows foods to dry out.

Adding More Fuel During Cooking: You can cook for many hours when the Fire Box in the EGG is fully loaded with natural lump charcoal—more time if your cooking temperatures are lower, less time if temperatures are higher. Because the EGG is so fuel efficient, it is rare that you would roast or smoke something that would take more than one load of charcoal. If necessary, however, you may add charcoal during the cooking process.

The best way to do this is to remove the food and lift the cooking grid with a Grill Gripper. Then you can add more natural lump charcoal around the outside edges of the burning coals, which will be lit by the existing fire. Readjust the dampers to recover the desired cooking temperature.

Extinguishing the Fire: To put out the fire, simply close both dampers completely to shut off airflow. This will extinguish the fire and preserve any unused charcoal for the next cookout. Remember, because of the thick ceramic walls, which retain heat inside the cooker, it may take a while to cool down and for coals to be fully extinguished. Never use water to put out coals inside your EGG. Wait at least twenty-four hours or longer until all the ash is completely cooled before removing it from the EGG.

Restarting the Fire: You will notice that some of the natural lump charcoal from your previous cookout was not burned and remains in the Fire Box. This charcoal can be reused next time you fire up your EGG. Before relighting the fire, stir or rake the coals across the Fire Grate using the

Ash Tool, allowing any ash to fall through the holes in the Grate and into the bottom of the EGG. Then add more charcoal to the leftovers to fill the Fire Box and light as described on page 20.

If you have been cooking at temperatures above 300°F/148°C, be very careful when opening the lid of your EGG. First raise the lid an inch or two and pause to "burp" it before raising the lid completely. This will allow the sudden rush of oxygen to burn safely inside the cooker without causing a "flashback" that could startle or injure you.

Cooking with Wood Flavor Enhancers

Cooking with wood chips, chunks, pellets, and planks adds a whole new dimension of flavor to foods without adding a single calorie or gram of fat. Think of cooking woods as seasonings. Just as each herb or spice in your spice rack imparts a different flavor to foods, each variety of wood, from apple to mesquite to hickory and beyond, seasons food with its unique flavor.

As you experiment with aromatic woods, you will master the art of mixing and matching them with certain foods to suit your preferences. You may even want to combine two or more varieties of wood to create a distinctive blend of smoke flavors. And remember that any given wood will

Think of cooking woods as seasonings—each variety of wood, from apple to mesquite to hickory and beyond, seasons food with its unique flavor.

Variety	Flavor	Best with
Hickory	Pungent, smoky, bold, hearty	Southern-style barbecue, pork, beef, poultry
Mesquite	Rich, tangy, strong; can turn bitter with too much smoke	Southwestern-style dishes, beef, duck, lamb, pork
Pecan	Light, nutty, mellow	Pork, poultry, game birds
Alder	Mild, delicate	Salmon, shellfish, poultry
Apple	Subtle sweetness	Poultry, pork, sausages, ham, bacon
Cherry	Mild, fruity; adds a rosy color to foods	Duck, game birds, beef, pork, lamb, poultry
Maple	Mild, sweet, subtle, all-purpose	Chops, steaks, ribs, pork, beef, poultry, seafood, vegetables, fruits
Whiskey Barrel Oak Chips	Distinctive whiskey flavor	Pork, beef (especially steaks), poultry

Soak wood chips (for at least 30 minutes) and wood chunks (for at least 2 hours) before adding them to the fire.

A handful of wood chips, shown scattered in a spiral pattern on top of the coals, adds a distinctive smoky aroma and flavor to foods.

hot tip:

The type of aromatic wood
you choose to provide the smoke
flavor is a matter of preference.
Although experienced barbecue chefs
do not all agree on whether to soak
wood in water before adding it to the
fire, soaking helps wood to smolder
rather than burn quickly, releasing
a swirl of smoke that envelops
and permeates the food.

react differently with one food than another. There are no rules here, so have fun trying new combinations. Just remember to stick with hardwoods such as apple, alder, cherry, maple, pecan, oak, hickory, and mesquite and stay away from softwoods like pine and cedar (with the exception of western red cedar), which release tar and resins that can impart a bitter taste to foods.

Wood Chips and Chunks: Made especially for the EGG, our cherry chips, pecan chips, hickory chips, or apple chips can be placed on the charcoal once the desired cooking temperature is achieved. For a more intense smoky flavor, the chips can be soaked in water for at least thirty minutes, and wood chunks for two hours, before adding to the charcoal fire. This will allow the wood to smolder rather than incinerate quickly, so it will release the smoky aromas and flavors to permeate food. Instead of water, use wine, beer, or fruit juice to soak the wood to add another flavor dimension. Because of the efficient design of the EGG, a little smoke enhancement goes a long way; a handful of chips should be enough to boost the flavor of most meals. Experienced outdoor chefs sometimes wrap long-cooking meats in foil after a few hours of smoking if they prefer a milder smoke flavor.

Wood Planks: The technique of cooking on wood planks originated with Native Americans. They discovered that fish and meats turned out not only incredibly moist but also imbued with smokiness from the smoldering plank. Today,

plank grilling is a popular restaurant technique that is easy to re-create at home in your ceramic cooker. Wood planks are increasingly used for cooking everything from steaks, chops, and fish to vegetables and desserts.

To use, submerge the plank in water to soak for at least one hour. Then, place it on the hot cooking grid for a few minutes, flip the plank, and position the food directly on the heated side, cooking without turning until the food is done. Serving directly from the plank at the table makes a dramatic presentation.

Grilling planks may be reused if they are not overly charred and blackened. Scrub the used plank with a brush and hot water and allow it to dry. When reusing, soak and preheat it again according to the above directions, using the same side as before for food. After two uses, break up the charred plank (it is now natural hardwood charcoal) into smaller pieces and add them to your next charcoal fire. If using the plank for indirect cooking, you may get more than two uses out of it.

Now You're Cooking

More than just a grill—although it grills exceptionally well—the Big Green Egg offers versatility unrivaled in the world of barbecues or even indoor cooking appliances, for that matter. Smoke? Superbly. Bake? Beautifully. Roast? Outrageously. An EGG offers cooking flexibility, flavor, and juiciness second to none.

Here is a sampling of what you can accomplish in the EGG.

Direct Grilling: Think hot and fast. For direct grilling, food is placed over the fire and cooked by direct exposure to the flame and heat. Generally, foods that are tender, less than two inches thick, and boneless are good candidates for direct grilling. It is the ideal way to cook steaks, chops, burgers, boneless chicken breasts, kabobs, fish fillets, many vegetables, and other quick-cooking foods. And with a Wok Topper, a specially designed wok pan, in place directly over the hot fire, you can even make a tasty stir-fry.

Direct grilling over intense heat at 700°F/370°C is hot enough to sear the exterior surface of the meat to form a delicious crust, much like cooking on a restaurant-style infrared grill. Juices are locked inside and any drippings sizzle on the coals, evaporating into flavor-filled smoke that is redeposited back onto the meat, adding more taste.

Because of the ingenious design of the EGG and the fact that grilling is always done with the lid closed, flare-ups and hot spots are virtually eliminated.

For some foods, you will want to start out searing over high temperatures and then reduce the heat by adjusting the dampers to finish cooking.

Indirect Grilling and Roasting: In indirect grilling and roasting, the food is not directly exposed to the flames and heat of the fire. Rather, a shield such as a Drip Pan or Plate Setter is placed beneath the food to deflect the heat. Food is cooked by convection heat—actually the heated air—and radiant heat, which reflects off the coals, side walls, and lid of the cooker.

Using a Drip Pan is ideal for indirect cooking of pork or beef roasts or whole chickens. Place the Drip Pan directly beneath food to catch drippings and deflect heat. To use the Plate Setter for indirect cooking, refer to "The Plate Setter: The Most Versatile Accessory" on page 26.

Indirect grilling or roasting is best for larger cuts of meat such as turkeys, chickens, roasts, and hams, which take longer to cook. In general, use this method to cook anything thicker than two inches or with a bone, such as chicken pieces; otherwise the exterior will be charred before the interior is cooked through. One exception to this would be bone-in steaks, such as T-bone or porter-house, which are best grilled directly over the fire.

While indirect grilling and roasting are possible on other types of barbecue grills, because of the insulating properties of the ceramics and the elliptical design of the EGG, food cooks much faster, with even browning and moister results. In addition, once the dampers are adjusted to the desired temperature, the charcoal fire will burn steadily for hours without requiring frequent tending or replenishing.

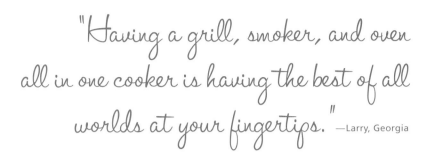

Baking: With the addition of a Plate Setter and a Pizza/Baking Stone, your ceramic cooker becomes a classic brick oven that bakes fantastic breads, biscuits, pies, pizzas, cobblers, cookies, and cakes. The combination of precise temperature control and heat retention, with the properties of the ceramics in the EGG itself and the Pizza/Baking Stone, create the perfect environment for baking. As pizza cooks, moisture is drawn to the Stone for an authentic, crispy, brick-oven-style crust that is impossible to recreate in an indoor oven or on an ordinary barbecue grill.

A variety of ovenproof bakeware may be used to bake in the EGG. Depending on the type of baking dish used, you may need to adjust the cooking time and temperature. It is important to note that paper muffin cups and parchment paper should not be used when baking in the EGG, as they may burn.

Smoking: Cooking slowly over low heat infused with wood smoke is what smoking—and what some call "real barbecue"—is all about. Cooking "low and slow" is the only way to break down connective tissue and tenderize tough (and typically less expensive) cuts of meat like beef brisket, pork shoulder, pork butts, and spare ribs. For smoking these kinds of foods, cooking times are measured in hours rather than minutes. But boy, is it worth it! The result is succulent, fall-off-the-bone tenderness with the tangy, complex combination of spices, smoke, and natural meat flavors—exactly like pit barbecue. Of course, you can also smoke other types of foods that do not fit the standard profile. Fish, turkey, nuts, vegetables, and even cheeses do not need to be tenderized with slow cooking, but they taste even better when kissed with the essence of wood smoke.

True smoking temperatures generally range from 225°F/107°C to 275°F/135°C. Once you get the hang of it,

it's a piece of cake to adjust the draft openings to set the proper temperature. But unlike a true pitmaster, who must work hard to maintain those low temperatures steadily throughout the extended smoking period, an EGG can retain heat at precise temperatures for many hours of cooking with little attention required.

Resist the urge to peek under the lid to check the progress while you are smoking. Every time you raise the cover, you release precious heat and smoke and extend your cooking time. Simply check the reading on the external thermometer and follow the timing in the recipe. As long as the temperature stays within the desired range, your results will be predictable every time—and usually faster than in a traditional metal smoker, which is affected by external weather conditions such as wind and temperature.

Unlike some metal smokers that require a water pan to create steam to keep foods from drying out, food smoked in an EGG retains its moisture. There is no need for a water pan or the hassle of continually refilling one.

A Plate Setter is particularly useful when smoking because it acts as a barrier between the food and the direct heat of the fire but allows the hot air and smoke to flow around the food. In addition, it eliminates the need to turn food during the smoking process.

If you are preparing your EGG for a very long, slow smoke, you can alternately layer the lump charcoal with wood chips to ensure sufficient smoke flavor throughout the extended process. First, pour a layer of charcoal into the Fire Box, then sprinkle a small handful of wood chips over the top. Add another layer of charcoal and another handful of chips, alternating until the layers reach the top of the Fire Box. This should provide enough heat and wood smoke to last for a long period of smoking at 250°F/121°C.

There is no other way to achieve the fantastic flavor, moistness, and juiciness of food cooked in a Big Green Egg.

The Plate Setter: The Most Versatile Accessory

If you could own only one accessory product for your Big Green Egg, this would be the one. A Plate Setter is probably the most practical and versatile multipurpose tool around, allowing you to make the most of your EGG by being able to do indirect cooking, smoking, roasting, and baking.

A Plate Setter looks like a ceramic baking stone with three legs. To use it as a brick-oven baker, place it on the fire ring with the legs facing up, and add the cooking grid. Place a Pizza/Baking Stone on top of the cooking grid, and you can bake pizza, bread, biscuits, and cookies or other desserts on the stone. Although the direct heat from the fire is blocked, the hot air is able to circulate under and around the Plate Setter and about the interior of the EGG in a convection pattern.

To roast, smoke, or grill indirectly in your ceramic cooker, the Plate Setter acts as a barrier between the food and the direct heat of the charcoal fire, cooking food as if it were in a convection oven. You may place your cooking grid on the three upturned ceramic legs and place food directly on the cooking grid. Or you may put food in a V-Rack, Vertical Roaster, or other type of cooking rack placed on the cooking grid. A Drip Pan can even be positioned beneath food directly on the Plate Setter to catch drippings or hold juice, wine, beer, stock, or other liquids to infuse foods with another layer of flavor.

The Plate Setter can also be used in conjunction with one of several Grill Extender options to gain a second and even a third tier of cooking surface. Because of the unique design of the EGG, the convection effect ensures that food browns as perfectly on the upper rack as it does on the main cooking grid.

Ready to Roll

In a world of high-tech gadgets and electronic bells and whistles, a ceramic cooker is a low-tech throwback that is relatively simple compared with other barbecues. In spite of that, or perhaps because of it, this type of cooker has withstood the test of time and is more popular today than ever before. Even people who surround themselves with the latest high-tech gadgets are reconnecting with the old-fashioned ritual of building and lighting the fire and taming the temperature, now made even easier thanks to modern design improvements. They are embracing the organic connection to the way people have cooked for centuries: real food over a real fire in a cooker made from the earth. They understand that there is no other way to achieve the fantastic flavor, moistness, and juiciness of food cooked in a heavy-duty Big Green Egg ceramic cooker.

We hope that you find these recipes as satisfying for the soul as for the stomach—and that you have a whole lot of fun and good eating in the process.

enjoy!

eggceptional!

appetizers

recipes

Eggplant Fries
with Spicy Romesco Sauce

When you think of cooking or grilling in the EGG, frying might not be the first thing that comes to mind. These eggplant fries will change that! They are crisp on the outside and tender on the inside. Be prepared, however, for these are so good they may not make it to the table!

Ingredients

6 cups all-purpose flour
1 cup confectioners' sugar
½ cup cornstarch
2 tablespoons garlic powder
2 tablespoons table salt
2 cups buttermilk
2 cups whole milk
1 (2-pound) eggplant, peeled
8 cups vegetable oil
Kosher salt
¼ cup grated Parmigiano-Reggiano cheese
¼ cup chopped fresh flat-leaf parsley
1 cup Romesco Sauce (page 201)

Equipment: Porcelain coated grid, Dutch Oven
Set the EGG for direct cooking with the porcelain coated grid.
Preheat the EGG to 375°F.

Mix the flour, sugar, cornstarch, garlic powder, and table salt in a medium bowl and blend well. Using a whisk, combine the buttermilk and milk in a medium bowl. Cut the eggplant into finger-size wedges.

Pour the oil into the Dutch Oven and set on top of the grid to preheat. Have ready a rimmed sheet pan lined with paper towels. Heat the oil until it reaches 350° to 400°F, or test to see if the oil is ready by adding one eggplant wedge to the oil—if it starts to boil, the oil is ready.

Toss the eggplant in the flour mixture, dip in the buttermilk mixture, then return the fries to the flour mixture to coat well. Working in small batches, carefully add the eggplant to the oil. Close the lid of the EGG and fry for about 5 minutes, or until light golden brown. Using a slotted spoon, transfer the eggplant to the prepared sheet pan. Repeat the process until all of the fries are cooked.

Sprinkle the fries with kosher salt. Transfer the fries to a platter and dust with the cheese and parsley. Serve immediately with the sauce. **Serves 4**

Bruschetta with White Bean Salad

You will find that this salad plays heavily on earthy flavors. Cannellini beans, which are Italian white beans known for their nutty flavor, are tossed with grilled mushrooms and asparagus, then drizzled with white truffle oil. White truffle oil is an olive oil that has been infused with white truffles, which are often called "white diamonds," as they are one of the most costly and exotic foods in the world. Truffle oil can be found at most specialty markets or gourmet stores. If you can't find truffle oil, substitute extra-virgin olive oil. Serve this salad with Cioppino (page 124) or Shrimp Fra Diavolo (page 278) at a dinner under the stars, and you will feel as if you have been transported to the Italian countryside.

Ingredients

8 ounces asparagus, cut into bite-size pieces
1¼ cups quartered white mushrooms
½ cup shiitake mushrooms, halved
1 tablespoon extra-virgin olive oil
Kosher salt and freshly ground black pepper
1 (15-ounce can) cannellini beans, drained and rinsed

Dressing
1 teaspoon minced garlic
1 teaspoon chopped fresh rosemary
2 tablespoons freshly squeezed lemon juice
1 teaspoon Dijon mustard
1 tablespoon water
½ teaspoon kosher salt
¼ teaspoon freshly ground black pepper
¼ cup extra-virgin olive oil

1 fresh baguette, sliced 1 inch thick diagonally
Extra-virgin olive oil for brushing
White truffle oil
½ cup shaved Parmigiano-Reggiano cheese

Equipment: Porcelain coated grid, perforated grill pan or Wok Topper
Set the EGG for direct cooking with the porcelain coated grid and perforated grill pan or Wok Topper.
Preheat the EGG to 500°F.

Toss the asparagus and mushrooms in the olive oil, season with salt and pepper, and place in the grill pan or wok. Close the lid of the EGG and cook for 4 to 5 minutes, until tender.

Using barbecue mitts, remove the grill pan or wok from the grid, and transfer the vegetables to a medium bowl. Add the cannellini beans and mix well. Set aside.

To make the dressing, mix the garlic, rosemary, lemon juice, mustard, water, salt, and pepper in a small bowl. Using a whisk, slowly add the olive oil, whisking constantly until emulsified. Pour the dressing over the bean salad, toss, and refrigerate.

Brush both sides of the bread with olive oil, place on the grid, and grill the bread for 20 seconds per side, or until golden brown. Using a long-handled spatula, remove the bread and transfer to a rimmed sheet pan. Place each slice of bread on a small plate and top with ½ cup of the bean salad. Drizzle with truffle oil and sprinkle with cheese. Serve immediately. **Serves 8**

Asparagus with Truffle Aioli & Parmigiano-Reggiano

Asparagus become white in color when they are deprived of sunlight during the growing period and cannot produce chlorophyll, which is necessary to give them their green color. They tend to be slightly milder in flavor than the green asparagus. Fresh white asparagus are seasonal and sometimes hard to find. If they are not available, you can substitute green asparagus.

Ingredients

10 ounces white asparagus, peeled
8 ounces green asparagus
2 tablespoons plus ½ cup extra-virgin olive oil
Kosher salt and freshly ground black pepper
1 tablespoon water
1 large egg yolk
1 teaspoon freshly squeezed lemon juice
1 teaspoon white truffle oil
½ cup shaved Parmigiano-Reggiano cheese (1 ounce)

Equipment: Cast Iron Grid
Set the EGG for direct cooking with the Cast Iron Grid.
Preheat the EGG to 400°F.

Drizzle the asparagus with 2 tablespoons of the olive oil and season with salt and pepper. Place the white asparagus on the Grid, close the lid of the EGG, and cook over high heat for 4 minutes. Add the green asparagus and continue cooking for 4 more minutes, turning occasionally. When the asparagus are tender, transfer to a plate and refrigerate for 30 minutes to 1 hour.

Mix the water, egg yolk, and lemon juice in a small bowl. Slowly drizzle the ½ cup of olive oil into the bowl, whisking constantly. Whisk the truffle oil into the sauce and season with salt and pepper.

Divide the asparagus onto plates and drizzle with the truffle aioli. Top each serving with cheese and serve.
Serves 4

Mission Figs with Mascarpone, Honey & Chopped Walnuts

Figs are seasonal and are available in many varieties. Though this recipe calls for Mission figs, which are a teardrop shape and purple with a crimson interior, you can substitute any type of fresh fig that is available in your local market. These can be served either as an hors d'oeuvre or as a light dessert.

Ingredients

12 fresh Mission figs
1 cup mascarpone cheese, at room temperature
 (8 ounces)
¼ cup chopped walnuts
¼ cup honey

Equipment: Cast Iron Grid, 12 bamboo or metal skewers
Set the EGG for direct cooking with the Cast Iron Grid.
Preheat the EGG to 350°F.

If using bamboo skewers, soak the skewers in water for 30 minutes.

Remove the stems from the figs and cut the figs in half lengthwise. Insert a bamboo or metal skewer in the end of each fig half until the skewer runs through the length of the fig and the fig is secure on the skewer. Place the figs on the Grid, bottom side down. Close the lid of the EGG and grill for 1 to 2 minutes. Carefully turn the figs over, close the lid again, and grill for another 1 to 2 minutes. Do not overcook. Transfer the figs to a rimmed sheet pan and let cool. Remove the skewers.

Using a melon baller or teaspoon, remove a small amount from the center of each fig. Fill the figs with cheese and top with chopped walnuts. Place the figs on a dish and drizzle with honey. Refrigerate until ready to serve.
Serves 4

Roasted Fingerling Potatoes with Crème Fraîche & Caviar

Fingerling potatoes are naturally small, usually elongated, and a little bumpy. They come in a variety of colors, from gold to red to purple. Because of their size, they are superb for hors d'oeuvres, and by topping them with caviar, they become a wonderful beginning to an elegant dinner. If you are unable to find crème fraîche, you can use sour cream in its place or make your own.

Ingredients

2 pounds white fingerling potatoes (about 16)
¼ cup plus 2 tablespoons extra-virgin olive oil
Kosher salt and freshly ground black pepper
1 cup crème fraîche, purchased or homemade (see below)
1 ounce sturgeon caviar
Fresh chives for garnish

Equipment: Cast Iron Grid
Set the EGG for direct cooking with the Cast Iron Grid.
Preheat the EGG to 500°F.

Toss the potatoes in ¼ cup of the olive oil and sprinkle with salt and pepper. Place on the Grid, close the lid of the EGG, and roast for 20 minutes, turning occasionally.

Cut each potato in half and, using a melon baller or teaspoon, scoop out the flesh from the potato, leaving a little around the edges. Discard the flesh or save it for another use. Brush the potatoes inside and out with the 2 tablespoons of olive oil and season with salt and pepper. Place the potatoes, cut side down, on the Grid, close the lid of the EGG, and grill for 3 to 4 minutes, until brown and crisp. Using tongs or a long-handled spatula, transfer the potatoes to a rimmed sheet pan. Let the potatoes cool for 5 minutes.

Place 1 teaspoon of the crème fraîche inside each potato, top with ½ teaspoon of the caviar, and garnish with chives. Serve immediately. **Serves 8**

Homemade Crème Fraîche

In a small saucepan on the stovetop, add 1 tablespoon buttermilk, sour cream, or yogurt to 1 cup heavy cream and whisk with a spoon. Heat almost to the boiling point and then let the mixture stand, covered, in a warm place for 24 hours, or until it thickens. The crème fraîche can then be refrigerated for 4 to 5 days.

Smoked Trout Dip
with Spinach & Artichokes

The nutty flavor of wild rainbow trout is preferred over farm raised, but for this dip, either type will work well. Make sure that you remove all of the bones before adding the trout to the dip. Pita Bread (page 215) would be perfect for dipping.

Ingredients

1 pound rainbow trout, butterflied and bones removed
1 tablespoon plus 1 tablespoon olive oil
Kosher salt and freshly ground black pepper
1 tablespoon minced garlic
1/3 cup minced shallots
16 ounces cream cheese, at room temperature
1/2 cup mayonnaise
1/2 cup sour cream
1/2 cup finely grated Parmigiano-Reggiano cheese
1 (10-ounce) package chopped frozen spinach,
    thawed and drained well
1 cup canned artichoke hearts packed in water,
    drained and chopped
2 tablespoons chopped capers
2 tablespoons freshly squeezed lemon juice
1 cup dried bread crumbs

> **Equipment: Porcelain coated grid, hickory chips, Grill Gripper, Plate Setter, 8-inch square glass or ceramic baking dish**
> **Preheat the EGG to 400°F without the porcelain coated grid.**

Place 1 cup of hickory chips in a large bowl, cover with water, and let soak for 1 hour.

Brush the trout with 1 tablespoon of the olive oil and season with salt and pepper. Scatter the presoaked hickory chips over the preheated charcoal, and place the grid on the EGG. When the chips begin to smoke (about 2 minutes), place the trout on the grid, skin side down, and close the lid of the EGG. Smoke for 7 to 8 minutes, until completely cooked. To check if the trout is done, slide a spatula along one of the back (dorsal) fins to see if the flesh is no longer shiny. Using a long-handled spatula, remove the trout from the heat and place on a rimmed sheet pan. Carefully remove the skin and crumble the trout into bite-size pieces, picking out all the bones. Place in a small bowl and set aside.

Using the Grill Gripper and barbecue mitts, carefully remove the grid and add the Plate Setter, legs down.

Heat the remaining 1 tablespoon olive oil in a small saucepan on the stovetop, add the garlic and shallots, and cook for 3 to 4 minutes, until translucent but not brown. Transfer the garlic-shallot mixture to the bowl of an electric mixer. Add the cream cheese, mayonnaise, sour cream, Parmigiano-Reggiano cheese, spinach, artichokes, garlic-shallot mixture, capers, lemon juice, 1 1/2 teaspoons salt, and 1/4 teaspoon pepper to the mixer bowl and combine the ingredients on low speed until just mixed. Add the smoked trout and combine briefly; do not overmix.

Pour the mixture into the baking dish and cover tightly with foil. Place the dish on the Plate Setter and bake for 30 minutes. Uncover and top with the bread crumbs. Cook for 10 to 15 minutes more, until brown and bubbly. Remove the trout dip from the Plate Setter. Let the dip rest for 10 to 15 minutes before serving. **Serves 8**

Mesquite Lemon-Pepper Wings with Creamy Feta Dressing

. . . .

If you are looking for the perfect food for game day, this is it! These wings have just the right amount of lemon, pepper, and spices to please all of your friends. For an irresistible combo, serve them with Mac & Cheese (page 165) and Kahlúa Coffee Brownies (page 251) for dessert.

Ingredients

Creamy Feta Dressing
½ cup mayonnaise
½ cup sour cream
½ cup feta cheese
2 teaspoons red wine vinegar
1 teaspoon Worcestershire sauce
Kosher salt and freshly ground black pepper

¼ cup lemon zest, lemons reserved
    (about 6 medium lemons)
½ cup extra-virgin olive oil
2 tablespoons granulated garlic
1 tablespoon kosher salt
1 tablespoon freshly ground black pepper
2 pounds chicken wings

Equipment: Cast Iron Grid
Set the EGG for direct cooking with the
    Cast Iron Grid.
Preheat the EGG to 500°F.

Mix the mayonnaise, sour cream, cheese, vinegar, and Worcestershire sauce in a small bowl. Season with salt and pepper, blend well, and refrigerate.

Mix the lemon zest and olive oil in a small bowl and set aside. Mix the garlic, salt, and pepper in a medium bowl. Reserve 1 tablespoon of the garlic seasoning for later use. Toss the chicken with the remaining 3 tablespoons of seasoning.

Place the chicken on the Grid and baste with the olive oil mixture. Close the lid of the EGG. Turn the chicken wings every few minutes, basting often, closing the lid each time. Grill for 15 minutes, or until golden brown and slightly crisp. Season with the reserved garlic mixture and cook for another minute.

Transfer the chicken wings to a platter, squeeze the reserved lemons over the wings, and serve immediately with the dressing. **Serves 4**

Grilled Moroccan Lamb Pops with Spicy Tzatziki Sauce

These zesty lamb pops will be a big hit! But since they are small, you'll want to double or triple the recipe for a larger crowd. They require no utensils; just pick them up, dip them in the yogurt sauce, and enjoy!

Ingredients

Marinade

1 teaspoon minced garlic
2 teaspoons lemon zest
2 tablespoons freshly squeezed lemon juice
1 teaspoon ground cumin
1 teaspoon ground coriander
1 teaspoon smoked paprika
½ teaspoon ground cardamom
½ teaspoon ground cinnamon
⅓ cup extra-virgin olive oil
1 teaspoon kosher salt
½ teaspoon freshly ground black pepper

1 (1½-pound) rack of lamb, cut into individual chops

Spicy Tzatziki Sauce

2 tablespoons hot water
1 teaspoon saffron threads
½ cup plain Greek yogurt
1 teaspoon chopped fresh mint
1 teaspoon freshly squeezed lemon juice
¼ teaspoon kosher salt

Lemon wedges

Equipment: Cast Iron Grid, 9 by 13-inch glass or ceramic baking dish, instant read thermometer
Set the EGG for direct cooking with the Cast Iron Grid.
Preheat the EGG to 500°F.

To make the marinade, combine the garlic, lemon zest, lemon juice, cumin, coriander, paprika, cardamom, cinnamon, olive oil, salt, and pepper in a small bowl and mix well.

Lay the lamb chops flat in a large shallow pan, pour the marinade over, and toss well to coat. Cover with plastic wrap and refrigerate for 6 hours or overnight.

To make the sauce, pour the water into a small cup, add the saffron, and let sit for 10 minutes, then strain, reserving the water. Put the yogurt in a small bowl, add the saffron water, mint, lemon juice, and salt and stir well. Transfer to a small serving bowl, cover with plastic wrap, and refrigerate until ready to use.

Remove the lamb from the marinade, discarding the remaining marinade, and place the lamb on the Grid. Close the lid of the EGG and cook for 2 to 3 minutes on each side, until the instant read thermometer inserted in the center of one of the lamb chops registers 125°F for medium-rare.

Using tongs, transfer the lamb to a platter and garnish with lemon wedges. Serve immediately with the sauce on the side. **Serves 4**

Red Chile Scallops with Cool Mango-Mint Salsa

First rubbed with Red Chile Rub, then topped with a sweet mango salsa, these scallops are like yin and yang, a perfect balance between cool and spicy. When served, the scallops should look like they have been dusted with confetti, so when making the salsa, be sure to finely dice all of the vegetables.

Ingredients

Mango-Mint Salsa
¾ cup diced fresh mango
¼ cup diced red bell pepper
¼ cup diced red onion
¼ cup thinly sliced scallions
2 tablespoons finely chopped fresh mint
1 clove garlic, crushed
2 tablespoons freshly squeezed lime juice
1 tablespoon extra-virgin olive oil
2 teaspoons honey
½ teaspoon kosher salt
¼ teaspoon freshly ground black pepper

1 pound large sea scallops (12)
2 tablespoons Red Chile Rub (page 197)

Equipment: Cast Iron Grid
Set the EGG for direct cooking with the Cast Iron Grid.
Preheat the EGG to 500°F.

Using a wooden spoon, combine the mango, bell pepper, red onion, scallions, mint, garlic, lime juice, olive oil, honey, salt, and pepper in a small bowl and stir well. Set aside.

Season the scallops generously with the chile rub and place on the Grid. Close the lid of the EGG and grill the scallops for about 2 minutes on each side, or until golden and lightly cooked. Transfer the scallops to a platter.

To assemble the dish, place 3 scallops on each plate and top with ¼ cup of the salsa. Serve immediately. **Serves 4**

"Food cooked on the Big Green Egg is more than just grilled food—it's a culinary experience!" —Terry, Nevada

Alder-Smoked Mushrooms with Bacon, Arugula & Walnut Oil

Because of their ability to impart a sweet yet smoky flavor, alder chips are a great choice for smoking these rich and flavorful mushrooms. Alder chips come from the red alder tree, a member of the birch family found in the Pacific Northwest, where Native Americans frequently used them for smoking fish. They are widely used today in the smoked-salmon industry. For this recipe, if large white mushrooms are not available, use your favorite mushrooms and adjust the cooking time.

Ingredients

12 large white mushrooms, gills removed (about 1 pound)
¼ cup olive oil
Kosher salt and freshly ground black pepper

Filling

8 ounces cream cheese, at room temperature
2 tablespoons finely grated Parmigiano-Reggiano cheese
1 cup finely chopped arugula
¼ cup plus ¼ cup panko or bread crumbs
Freshly ground black pepper
12 ounces bacon, finely chopped (about 14 slices)
1 teaspoon minced garlic
2 tablespoons minced shallots

Sauce

1 cup white wine
¼ cup sliced shallots
5 peppercorns
1 bay leaf
½ cup heavy cream
1 cup unsalted butter, cut into cubes
Freshly squeezed lemon juice
Kosher salt

Freshly cracked black pepper
¼ cup walnut oil or olive oil
Chopped fresh chives or flat-leaf parsley for garnish

> **Equipment: Cast Iron Grid, alder chips**
> **Preheat the EGG to 400°F without the**
> **Cast Iron Grid.**

Place 1 cup of alder chips in a large bowl, cover with water, and let soak for 1 hour. Put the mushrooms in a large bowl, add the olive oil, toss the mushrooms in the oil until completely coated, season with salt and pepper, and set aside.

To make the filling, using a wooden spoon, mix the cream cheese, Parmigiano-Reggiano cheese, arugula, and ¼ cup of the panko in a small bowl. Season with pepper and set aside. Cook the bacon in a sauté pan on the stovetop over medium heat, stirring occasionally until almost crisp. Add the garlic and shallots and cook for about 2 minutes, or until the shallots are translucent. Using a slotted spoon,

(continued next page)

Alder-Smoked Mushrooms
with Bacon, Arugula & Walnut Oil *(continued)*

transfer the bacon mixture to the bowl of cream cheese and, using a wooden spoon, stir until completely blended.

Fill each mushroom with 1 to 1½ tablespoons of the cream cheese filling, sprinkle the tops with 1 teaspoon of panko, place on a rimmed sheet pan, and set aside.

To make the sauce, mix the white wine, shallots, pepper-corns, and bay leaf in a small saucepan on the stovetop, cook over medium-high heat, and reduce to about 2 table-spoons. Add the cream and reduce for 4 to 5 minutes, until the cream has thickened. Remove from the heat, add the butter a little at a time, and season with lemon juice and salt. Strain and set aside.

Scatter the presoaked alder chips over the preheated charcoal and place the Grid on the EGG. When the chips begin to smoke (about 2 minutes), place the mushrooms on the Grid and close the lid of the EGG. Cook for 5 minutes, or until the mushrooms are tender.

Transfer the mushrooms to a rimmed sheet pan. Spoon the butter sauce onto individual plates, set two mushrooms on each plate on top of the sauce, season with pepper, and drizzle with the walnut oil. Garnish with fresh chives and serve immediately. **Serves 6**

Greek Pizza
with Yogurt-Mint Sauce

The Greek-themed topping for this pizza is made with deliciously seasoned ground lamb, feta cheese, kalamata olives, and a touch of mint. The Yogurt-Mint Sauce, added just before serving, provides an unexpected burst of flavor. Ground beef can be substituted for the lamb. If you make the Sun-Dried Tomato Pesto for this recipe, you will have about 1 cup left, which can be frozen for later use.

Ingredients

Yogurt-Mint Sauce

1 cup sour cream
½ cup plain Greek yogurt
2 tablespoons chopped fresh mint
¼ teaspoon ground cumin
1 teaspoon freshly squeezed lemon juice
½ teaspoon kosher salt
¼ teaspoon freshly ground black pepper

Lamb

2 tablespoons extra-virgin olive oil
1 pound lean ground lamb
1 tablespoon minced garlic
1 tablespoon dried oregano
1 teaspoon ground cumin
1 teaspoon ground cinnamon
1 teaspoon kosher salt
1 teaspoon freshly ground black pepper

4 pizza dough disks (page 216)
Cornmeal for dusting
½ cup Sun-Dried Tomato Pesto (page 200)
1 cup crumbled feta cheese
1 cup quartered marinated artichokes, drained
1 cup pitted and chopped kalamata olives
1 cup thinly sliced red onions
Olive oil for drizzling

Equipment: Plate Setter, Baking Stone, pizza peel
Set the EGG for indirect cooking with the Plate Setter, legs down, and the Baking Stone on top of the Plate Setter.
Preheat the EGG to 600°F.

To make the sauce, using a spatula, combine the sour cream, yogurt, mint, cumin, lemon juice, salt, and pepper in a small bowl and stir to blend. Transfer the sauce to a squeeze bottle and refrigerate until ready to use.

To cook the lamb, heat the olive oil in a medium sauté pan on the stovetop, add the lamb and garlic, and cook for 2 to 3 minutes, until the meat is browned. Add the oregano, cumin, cinnamon, salt, and pepper and continue to cook for another 2 to 3 minutes, until the meat is thoroughly cooked. Remove the pan from the heat and let cool. Set aside.

To assemble the pizzas, place a pizza dough disk on a lightly floured surface and, using a rolling pin, roll the disk into a 10-inch circle ¼ inch thick. Dust the pizza peel with cornmeal and place the dough disk on the peel. Gently shake the peel back and forth to make sure the dough does not stick. Top the disk with 2 tablespoons of the pesto, ½ cup of the lamb, and ¼ cup each of the cheese, artichokes, olives, and onions. Drizzle with olive oil.

Using the pizza peel, gently slide the pizza onto the Baking Stone. Close the lid of the EGG and cook for 5 minutes. Remove the pizza from the EGG using the pizza peel. Drizzle the sauce over the pizza before serving. Cut the pizza with a knife or pizza wheel into desired portions and serve immediately. Repeat this process with the remaining dough disks. **Serves 4**

Quail Egg Pizza
with Prosciutto & Arugula

You might balk at the idea of using eggs on top of a pizza, but give this a try. Eggs add incredible flavor and texture to the pizza. If you can't find quail eggs, break one large hen egg into the center of the pizza once you have transferred it to the Baking Stone.

Ingredients
4 pizza dough disks (page 216)
Cornmeal for dusting
1 cup Garden-Fresh Tomato Sauce (page 199)
1 pound thinly sliced mozzarella *di bufala*
2 cups chopped baby arugula
1⅓ cups chopped prosciutto
16 quail eggs, or 4 large hen eggs
1 cup grated Parmigiano-Reggiano cheese (4 ounces)
4 teaspoons white truffle oil

Equipment: Plate Setter, Baking Stone, pizza peel
Set the EGG for indirect cooking with the Plate Setter, legs down, and the Baking Stone on top of the Plate Setter.
Preheat the EGG to 600°F.

Place a pizza dough disk on a lightly floured surface and, using a rolling pin, roll the disk into a 10-inch circle ¼ inch thick. Dust the pizza peel with cornmeal and place the dough disk on the peel. Gently shake the peel back and forth to make sure the dough does not stick.

Top the pizza with ¼ cup of the sauce, ¼ pound of the mozzarella, ½ cup of the arugula, and ⅓ cup of the prosciutto. Gently shake the peel back and forth to make sure the dough does not stick.

Slide the pizza onto the hot Baking Stone, crack 4 quail eggs in a circle on top of the pizza, and close the lid of the EGG. Cook for 5 minutes, or until the edges are lightly browned and crisp. Using the pizza peel, remove the pizza from the grill, sprinkle with ¼ cup of the cheese, and drizzle with 1 teaspoon of truffle oil. With a knife or pizza wheel, cut the pizza into desired portions and serve immediately.

Repeat this process with the remaining dough disks.
Serves 4

Shrimp, Artichoke & Pesto Pizza

If this is your first try at making pizza in the EGG, this is an easy recipe to prepare, and the combination of shrimp and pesto is unbeatable. Make sure you have the ingredients to make the pesto on hand. This pizza requires only ½ cup of the pesto, so freeze the rest in ice trays and take the cubes out as needed to season other dishes.

Ingredients

4 pizza dough disks (page 216)
Cornmeal for dusting
1 pound large shrimp, peeled and deveined
½ cup Fresh Basil Pesto (page 201)
2 cups marinated artichokes, drained
2 cups thinly sliced red onions
16 ounces goat cheese
Kosher salt and freshly ground black pepper

Equipment: Plate Setter, Baking Stone, pizza peel
Set the EGG for indirect cooking with the Plate Setter, legs down, and the Baking Stone on top of the Plate Setter. Preheat the EGG to 600°F.

Place a pizza dough disk on a lightly floured surface and, using a rolling pin, roll the disk into a 10-inch circle ¼ inch thick. Dust the pizza peel with cornmeal and place the dough disk on the peel. Gently shake the peel back and forth to make sure the dough does not stick.

Using a paring knife, butterfly the shrimp by cutting them open along the bottom side and opening them up, but leave the two sides connected so that the shrimp will lie flat on the pizza. Top the pizza with 2 tablespoons of the pesto, ¼ pound of the shrimp, ½ cup of the artichokes, ½ cup of the onion, and 4 ounces of the cheese. Season with salt and pepper.

Gently slide the pizza onto the Baking Stone. Close the lid of the EGG and cook for 5 minutes, or until light brown and crisp around the edges. Using the pizza peel, remove the pizza from the heat and let it sit for 2 minutes before cutting. Using a knife or pizza wheel, cut the pizza into desired portions and serve immediately.

Repeat this process with the remaining dough disks.
Serves 4

Chilled White Gazpacho
with Grilled Shrimp Relish

Gazpacho originated in Andalusia, a region in the southern part of Spain. The gazpacho most people are familiar with is a cold, tomato-based, raw-vegetable soup. White gazpacho, better known as garlic soup or ajo blanco, *is from the same region. One common thread is that both of these soups use bread as a thickening agent. Unlike the Spanish version, which is made with white grapes, this version is made with white grape juice and topped with a delicious grilled shrimp relish. Serve this with Seafood Paella (page 277) for a festive Spanish meal.*

Ingredients

3 cups chopped English cucumbers
1 cup grilled and cubed French bread (about three
   ½-inch slices)
1 cup white grape juice
1 tablespoon prepared horseradish
1 teaspoon minced garlic
Kosher salt and freshly ground black pepper
1 cup heavy cream
4 ounces large shrimp, peeled, deveined, and
   tails removed
1 tablespoon extra-virgin olive oil plus extra for brushing
1 avocado, halved, peeled, pitted, and diced
1 tablespoon freshly squeezed lemon juice
¼ cup finely crumbled feta cheese
1 teaspoon chopped fresh mint

**Equipment: Porcelain coated grid,
   bamboo or metal skewers
Set the EGG for direct cooking with the
   porcelain coated grid.
Preheat the EGG to 450°F.**

If using bamboo skewers, soak the skewers in water for 30 minutes.

Combine the cucumbers, bread, grape juice, horseradish, garlic, and 1½ teaspoons salt in the bowl of a food processor fitted with a steel blade. Process for 2 to 3 minutes, until the ingredients are completely pureed and the liquid is smooth and creamy. Transfer the soup to a large bowl and chill for 30 minutes.

In a large bowl using an electric mixer, whip the cream for 1 to 2 minutes, until soft peaks form. Chill the whipped cream for 30 minutes.

Thread the shrimp on skewers, brush with olive oil, and season with salt and pepper. Place the skewers on the grid. Close the lid of the EGG and grill for 2½ minutes on each side. Remove the skewers from the grid and place on a rimmed sheet pan to cool.

Remove the shrimp from the skewers, chop into bite-size pieces, and place in a small bowl. Add the avocado, lemon juice, cheese, mint, and the 1 tablespoon olive oil to the bowl and mix well. Season with salt and pepper.

To assemble, using a rubber spatula, gently fold the whipped cream into the cucumber mixture until combined. Pour the soup into chilled bowls, place a large spoonful of the shrimp relish in the middle of each bowl, and serve. **Serves 4**

Barbecue Chicken Soup

This version of barbecue soup is a cross between Brunswick stew and a traditional soup. It is a meal on its own but can also be served in small portions as a first course. Though the recipe calls for leftover Beer-Brined Chicken, Chutney-Glazed Beef Brisket (page 284) or shredded pork (page 90) would work just as well. For a real treat, serve this with South-western Cornbread (page 217).

Ingredients

12 ounces applewood-smoked bacon, diced
   (about 14 slices)
4 tablespoons Basic Barbecue Rub (page 196)
1½ pounds tomatoes, chopped (about 4 cups)
1½ cups chopped yellow onions
¼ cup minced garlic
1 chipotle pepper in adobo
12 ounces lite lager beer
4 cups chicken stock
2 cups ketchup
¼ cup yellow mustard
½ cup apple cider vinegar
1 cup firmly packed light brown sugar
2 tablespoons Worcestershire sauce
2 cups yellow corn kernels (about 2 ears)
1 pound tomatoes, grilled and chopped (about 3 cups;
   page 170)
3 cups fresh or frozen lima beans, cooked and drained
4 cups chopped Beer-Brined Chicken (page 98)
1 teaspoon freshly ground black pepper

Equipment: Porcelain coated grid, Dutch Oven
Set the EGG for direct cooking with the porcelain coated grid.
Preheat the EGG to 450°F.
Preheat the Dutch Oven on the grid for 10 minutes.

Place the bacon in the Dutch Oven, close the lid of the EGG, and cook until crisp. Using a slotted spoon, transfer the bacon to a small bowl lined with paper towels and set aside. Reserve the bacon fat in the Dutch Oven.

Add the barbecue rub to the bacon fat and cook for 1 minute. Add the tomatoes, onions, garlic, and chipotle and cook for 2 to 3 minutes, until the onions are translucent. Slowly add the beer to the Dutch Oven, stirring with a wooden spoon to deglaze. Add the chicken stock, ketchup, mustard, vinegar, brown sugar, and Worcestershire sauce. Leave the Dutch Oven uncovered, but close the lid of the EGG. Simmer for 30 minutes, or until the soup has thickened slightly.

Remove the Dutch Oven from the heat. Puree the soup using an immersion blender, or carefully spoon it into the bowl of a food processor fitted with the steel blade, process until smooth, and return to the Dutch Oven. Add the corn, grilled tomatoes, lima beans, chicken, and pepper and stir until completely combined. Serve topped with the reserved bacon pieces. **Serves 8**

eggxemplary!

beef & lamb

recipes

Barbecued Beef Ribs

Ribs really benefit from long, slow cooking. After coating the ribs with Basic Barbecue Rub, place them in the V-Rack and let them cook, low and slow. Once they are pull-away-from-the-bone tender, place them on the grid, douse them with Basic Barbecue Sauce, and cook until they are thoroughly browned. What you will end up with are juicy, rich, flavorful ribs.

Ingredients
2 (2½ to 3-pound) racks beef ribs
½ cup Basic Barbecue Rub (page 196)
1 cup Basic Barbecue Sauce (page 192)

Equipment: Plate Setter, V-Rack set
inside 9 by 13-inch Drip Pan lined with
aluminum foil, porcelain coated grid,
instant read thermometer
Set the EGG for indirect cooking with the
Plate Setter, legs up.
Preheat the EGG to 300°F.

Season the ribs on all sides with the rub. Place the ribs in the V-Rack and set the V-Rack in the Drip Pan. Set the Drip Pan on the Plate Setter and close the lid of the EGG. Cook for 2½ to 3 hours, until tender or the instant read thermometer registers 190°F. Remove the ribs.

Add the grid to the EGG, and raise the temperature to 500°F.

Place the ribs directly on the grid and baste with the sauce. Close the lid of the EGG and grill the ribs, turning and basting the ribs every few minutes, for 5 to 7 minutes, until the ribs are well covered with the sauce.

Transfer the ribs to a platter and serve immediately.
Serves 4

Beef Kabobs with Chimichurri

Chimichurri *is a piquant herbed sauce that is often served in Argentina and other Latin American countries as an accompaniment to grilled meats. In this recipe, the tenderloin is marinated in half of the sauce prior to grilling. The other half of the sauce is reserved to use as a dipping sauce. Chimichurri is also terrific served with chicken, lamb, and fish.*

Ingredients
2 pounds beef tenderloin
2 cups extra-virgin olive oil
1 cup red wine vinegar
½ cup freshly squeezed lime juice (4 to 5 limes)
4 jalapeños, seeded and chopped
8 cloves garlic
2 cups firmly packed fresh flat-leaf parsley leaves
1 cup firmly packed fresh oregano leaves
2 teaspoons red chile flakes
Kosher salt and freshly ground black pepper

Equipment: Cast Iron Grid, bamboo or metal skewers
Set the EGG for direct cooking with the Cast Iron Grid.
Preheat the EGG to 450°F.

Trim the beef and cut into 1½-inch cubes. Place in a shallow pan and set aside.

Add the olive oil, vinegar, lime juice, jalapeños, garlic, parsley, oregano, and red chile flakes to the bowl of a food processor fitted with the steel blade. Blend for 30 seconds, season with salt and pepper, then process for another 10 seconds. Pour half of the sauce over the beef, reserving the remainder. Toss the meat in the marinade until completely coated and refrigerate for 4 to 8 hours.

If using bamboo skewers, place the skewers in a pan and cover with water. Soak for 1 hour.

Remove the beef from the marinade and divide it into 4 (8-ounce) portions. Discard the used marinade. Thread the meat on the skewers and then place the skewers on the Grid. Close the lid of the EGG. Turn the skewers every 2 minutes for a total of 8 minutes for medium-rare to medium, making sure to grill the meat on all sides. Transfer the skewers to a platter and let the meat rest for 5 minutes before serving. Serve with the remaining sauce. **Serves 4**

Beef Tenderloin with Béarnaise Sauce

It doesn't get any better than a beef tenderloin covered in classic béarnaise sauce, except when that roast is cooked in the EGG. This is food fit for a king or your favored guests.

Ingredients

1 (5 to 6-pound) beef tenderloin, trimmed and tied
1 tablespoon olive oil
2 teaspoons kosher salt
2 tablespoons freshly ground black pepper

Béarnaise Sauce

1½ ounces tarragon sprigs
1 large egg yolk
½ cup white wine vinegar
1 shallot, thinly sliced
5 black peppercorns
1 cup unsalted butter, melted
1 teaspoon freshly squeezed lemon juice
Pinch of cayenne pepper
Kosher salt and freshly ground black pepper

Equipment: Porcelain coated grid, V-Rack, 9 by 13-inch Drip Pan lined with aluminum foil, instant read thermometer
Set the EGG for direct cooking with the porcelain coated grid.
Preheat the EGG to 400°F.

Brush the beef with olive oil and season with the salt and pepper. Sear the meat on the grid, turning occasionally until browned on all sides. Transfer the meat to the V-Rack, set the V-Rack in the Drip Pan, and put the Drip Pan on the grid. Close the lid of the EGG and cook for 30 to 40 minutes, until the instant read thermometer registers 130°F for medium-rare. Let the meat rest for 15 minutes before slicing.

To make the béarnaise sauce, separate the tarragon leaves from the stems, reserving the stems. Finely chop the tarragon leaves and set aside. Beat the egg yolk in a small bowl and set aside. Place the vinegar, shallot, peppercorns, and reserved tarragon stems in a small saucepan on the stovetop and simmer over medium heat until the liquid is reduced to 2 tablespoons.

Strain the liquid into the bowl with the egg yolk. Place the bowl over a pot of simmering water on the stovetop and slowly add the butter in a thin stream, whisking constantly until thickened. Add the chopped tarragon leaves and stir well. Remove the bowl from the heat and season with the lemon juice, cayenne pepper, salt, and black pepper.

Slice the beef and serve with the sauce. **Serves 8 to 10**

Rib-Eye Steaks
with Shallot & Garlic Butter

The rib-eye is one of the most tender, juicy steaks on the market because it is so heavily marbled. Grilling it fast, over high heat, sears in all of the juices. Whether you are new to ceramic cooking or an old hand, you will not taste a better rib-eye steak than one cooked in the EGG.

Ingredients
4 (1-inch-thick) rib-eye steaks
¼ cup olive oil
Kosher salt and freshly ground black pepper

Shallot & Garlic Butter
8 tablespoons unsalted butter
1 tablespoon finely minced garlic
¼ cup minced shallots
1 tablespoon minced fresh parsley
Kosher salt and freshly ground black pepper

Equipment: Cast Iron Grid
Set the EGG for direct cooking with the Cast Iron Grid.
Preheat the EGG to 550°F.

Using a basting brush, lightly coat each of the rib-eye steaks with the olive oil, season with salt and pepper, and set aside.

To make the garlic butter, melt the butter in a small saucepan on the stovetop. When the butter begins to foam, add the garlic and cook for 2 minutes, being careful not to let the garlic brown. Remove the pan from the heat, add the shallots, and stir. Let the butter cool for 30 minutes. Add the parsley, season with salt and pepper, and mix well. Pour equal amounts of the mixture into 2 small bowls, reserving one for basting and one for serving.

Place the steaks on the Grid, baste with some of the garlic butter, and close the lid of the EGG. Cook for 3 minutes. Turn the steaks over and baste with more garlic butter. Close the lid and continue cooking for 3 more minutes for medium-rare. Discard the remaining basting butter.

Transfer the steaks to a platter and baste them with some of the garlic butter reserved for serving. Let the steaks rest for 5 minutes. Slice across the grain and serve with the remaining garlic butter. **Serves 4**

Burgers with Avocado BLT Salsa

Combine ground round and ground chuck, then place the burgers in the EGG and grill them to the desired doneness. Top them off with an avocado and applewood-smoked bacon salsa and melted Havarti cheese for the best burger you've ever tasted.

Ingredients

1 pound ground chuck
1 pound ground round
2 tablespoons granulated garlic
Kosher salt and freshly ground black pepper

Avocado BLT Salsa

1 cup diced vine-ripened tomatoes
2 cups chopped applewood-smoked bacon, cooked
    until crisp (12 to 14 slices)
½ cup chopped scallions
1 cup diced avocado
½ cup mayonnaise
1 tablespoon freshly squeezed lemon juice
½ teaspoon kosher salt
½ teaspoon freshly ground black pepper

4 poppy seed buns
8 tablespoons unsalted butter, melted
4 slices Havarti cheese
4 leaves butter lettuce (Boston or Bibb)

Equipment: Cast Iron Grid
Set the EGG for direct cooking with the
    Cast Iron Grid.
Preheat the EGG to 600°F.

Combine the ground chuck and ground round in a large bowl. Form the meat into 4 (8-ounce) patties about 1 inch thick. Season with the granulated garlic, salt, and pepper and set aside.

To make the salsa, mix the tomatoes, bacon, scallions, avocado, mayonnaise, lemon juice, salt, and pepper in a large bowl. Cover and refrigerate.

Cut the buns in half horizontally and brush the inside of each half with butter. Place the hamburgers on the Grid, close the lid of the EGG, and cook for 3 minutes per side, for medium-rare. Top each burger with a slice of cheese, close the lid of the EGG, and cook for 30 seconds longer, until the cheese is melted. Transfer the burgers to a plate and let them rest while you grill the buns, buttered side down, until lightly toasted.

To assemble, place each burger inside a bun and top with a lettuce leaf. Place 2 tablespoons of the salsa on top of each burger and serve. **Serves 4**

Italian Meat Loaf
with Smoked-Tomato Chutney

This recipe is not complicated to make. Grilling the tomatoes before turning them into chutney adds a gentle smokiness and intensifies the tomato flavor. It is the perfect accompaniment to this well-seasoned meat loaf.

Ingredients

Smoked-Tomato Chutney
1 pound Roma tomatoes, cored and cut in half
2 tablespoons olive oil
½ cup minced yellow onion
1 teaspoon minced garlic
¼ cup granulated sugar
¼ cup balsamic vinegar
¼ cup chopped fresh basil
Kosher salt and freshly ground black pepper

Meat Loaf
2 tablespoons olive oil
1 cup minced yellow onions
⅓ cup minced red bell pepper
1 tablespoon minced garlic
8 ounces ground chuck
8 ounces ground round
8 ounces ground veal
8 ounces ground pork
2 tablespoons balsamic vinegar
2 tablespoons Worcestershire sauce
½ teaspoon red chile flakes
¾ cup fresh or dried bread crumbs
¼ cup whole milk
2 tablespoons chopped fresh oregano
1 cup finely grated Parmigiano-Reggiano cheese (4 ounces)
½ cup tomato paste
2 large eggs
1½ teaspoons kosher salt
½ teaspoon freshly ground black pepper

Soak 1 cup of hickory chips in a pan of water for 1 hour. Scatter the hickory chips over the preheated charcoal and, using barbecue mitts, place the Plate Setter, legs down, in the EGG.

To make the chutney, smoke the tomatoes for 10 minutes on the Plate Setter, with the lid of the EGG closed. Transfer the tomatoes to a rimmed sheet pan and let cool. Remove and discard the tomato skins, chop the tomatoes, and reserve. Add the olive oil to a medium saucepan on the stovetop. Sauté the onion and garlic for 2 minutes, cover, then cook for 5 minutes. Add the reserved tomatoes, sugar, and vinegar and simmer uncovered for 15 minutes. Transfer the tomato mixture to the bowl of a food processor fitted with the steel blade. Puree the sauce, add the basil, and season with salt and pepper. Set aside.

To make the meat loaf, heat the olive oil in a medium saucepan on the stovetop. Sauté the onions, bell pepper, and garlic for 3 to 5 minutes, until softened. Transfer to a large bowl. Crumble the meat into the bowl, add the vinegar, Worcestershire sauce, red chile flakes, bread crumbs, milk, oregano, cheese, tomato paste, eggs, salt, and pepper. Using a wooden spoon, mix all the ingredients until completely blended.

Scrape the meat mixture into the loaf pan and cover the pan tightly with aluminum foil. Place on the Plate Setter and close the lid of the EGG. Cook for 1 hour and 15 minutes, or until the thermometer reaches 140°F.

Remove the foil and baste the meat loaf with one-half of the tomato chutney. Close the lid of the EGG and cook for 15 minutes more, or until the internal temperature is 160°F. Remove the meat loaf from the EGG and let it rest for 10 minutes.

Slice the meat loaf and serve with the remaining chutney.
Serves 6

"We do not order steak at steakhouses anymore because they do not compare with a steak cooked on the Big Green Egg." —Kevin, Alabama

Skirt Steak Fajitas

Skirt steak is the most traditional and popular cut of meat used to make fajitas. To boost the flavor, marinate the meat for at least eight hours or as long as twenty-four hours if possible.

Ingredients

Marinade
½ cup pineapple juice
¼ cup soy sauce
¼ cup canola oil
¼ cup minced garlic
1 teaspoon ground cumin

2 pounds skirt steak
¼ cup canola oil
1 green bell pepper, sliced ¼ inch thick
1 red bell pepper, sliced ¼ inch thick
1 medium yellow onion, sliced ¼ inch thick
8 to 10 flour tortillas

Toppings (optional)
Shredded semisoft cheese (queso blanco), such as
   Monterey Jack, farmer's cheese, or queso asadero
Sour cream
Salsa
Cilantro
Guacamole

Equipment: Cast Iron Grid, Half Moon Griddle
Set the EGG for direct cooking with the Cast Iron Grid and the Half Moon Griddle on one side of the Grid. Preheat the EGG to 500°F.

To make the marinade, use a whisk to combine the pineapple juice, soy sauce, canola oil, garlic, and cumin in a small bowl. Place the steak in a shallow pan and pour the marinade over the steak. Cover with plastic wrap and refrigerate for 8 hours or overnight.

Carefully pour the canola oil on the Griddle, and add the peppers and onion. Close the lid of the EGG and sauté until tender. While the peppers and onion are still cooking, remove the steak from the marinade and discard the marinade. Place the steak on the exposed Grid, close the lid, and grill for 3 to 4 minutes on each side for medium-rare.

Transfer the steak, peppers, and onions to a rimmed sheet pan. Let the steak rest for 10 minutes. While the steak is resting, place the tortillas on the Grid and grill for 15 seconds on each side. Transfer the tortillas to a sheet of aluminum foil and wrap tightly to keep warm.

To assemble, slice the steak across the grain into thin strips, place in a large bowl, add the peppers and onions, and toss together. Transfer to a platter and serve with the warm tortillas and your choice of toppings. **Serves 4**

Belgian Beef Stew

In some European countries, wheat beers, pale in color, are traditionally called "white beer." The addition of Belgian white beer gives this stew rich, robust flavor. Be sure to add water to the pot periodically to keep the meat from drying out.

Ingredients

1 (2-pound) chuck or sirloin tip roast
6 sprigs thyme
2 bay leaves
Zest of 1 lemon
Zest of 1 orange
12 ounces applewood-smoked bacon, cut into small strips (about 14 slices)
2 cups diced carrots
2 cups diced celery
2 cups diced onions
Kosher salt and freshly ground black pepper
1 tablespoon minced garlic
2 tablespoons all-purpose flour
4 (12-ounce) bottles Belgian white beer
1 teaspoon ground coriander
9 cups water
3 cups diced russet potatoes
2 cups diced Roma tomatoes
2 tablespoons freshly squeezed lemon juice
¼ cup freshly squeezed orange juice
4 tablespoons unsalted butter
½ cup frozen peas
½ cup thinly sliced fresh chives

Equipment: Porcelain coated grid, Dutch Oven
Set the EGG for direct cooking with the porcelain coated grid.
Preheat the EGG to 500°F.

Place the Dutch Oven on the grid to preheat for 10 minutes.

Trim the beef, cut into 1½-inch cubes, and set aside. To make a seasoning sachet, put the thyme, bay leaves, lemon zest, and orange zest on a small piece of cheesecloth, pull up the sides all around, and tie with string. Set aside. Add the bacon to the Dutch Oven, close the lid of the EGG, and cook for 6 minutes, or until crisp. Using a slotted spoon, transfer the bacon to a plate lined with paper towels and set aside. Reserve the bacon fat in the Dutch Oven.

Add the carrots, celery, and onions to the Dutch Oven, close the lid of the EGG, and cook until caramelized and golden brown in color. Remove the vegetables with a slotted spoon and place them in a small bowl.

Allow the Dutch Oven to reheat for about 2 minutes. Season the beef with salt and pepper, and add to the hot Dutch Oven. Close the lid of the EGG, and sear on all sides for about 10 minutes, or until brown. Add the garlic and cook for 1 minute, then add the flour and stir. Slowly add 1 bottle of beer, stirring constantly. Add the rest of the beer, one bottle at a time. Add the reserved sachet and bacon and the coriander and stir well. Cover the Dutch Oven, close the lid of the EGG, and simmer for 30 minutes.

Reduce the heat to 300°F. After 30 minutes, add 3 cups of water, cover the Dutch Oven, close the lid of the EGG, and simmer for 30 minutes. Add 3 more cups of water, cover, close, and simmer for 15 more minutes. Add 1 more cup of water, cover, close, and simmer for another 15 minutes. Add the potatoes, tomatoes, and reserved carrots, celery, and onions. Add the remaining 2 cups of water, cover, close, and simmer for another 30 minutes. Remove the Dutch Oven from the heat. Discard the sachet and add the lemon juice, orange juice, butter, peas, and chives. Season with salt and pepper. Serve immediately. **Serves 4**

Standing Rib Roast

Before cooking the rib roast, it is best if the bones are cut away and reattached tightly to the body of the roast with butcher's twine. Once it is cooked, you can cut the butcher's twine, and the bones will easily fall away, making it much easier to carve. Most butchers will gladly prep the roast for you. Try serving the roast with Twice-Baked Potatoes (page 159) and Grilled Caesar Salad (page 171).

Ingredients

2 tablespoons minced garlic
2 tablespoons minced fresh rosemary
1 teaspoon garlic salt
1 teaspoon kosher salt
1 teaspoon freshly ground black pepper
1 (5-pound) bone-in rib roast

Equipment: V-Rack, 9 by 13-inch Drip Pan lined with aluminum foil, porcelain coated grid, instant read thermometer
Set the EGG for direct cooking with the porcelain coated grid.
Preheat the EGG to 425°F.

Using a fork, combine the garlic, rosemary, garlic salt, kosher salt, and pepper. Stir to blend well. Stand the roast up on a cutting board with the bones facing upward. Using a very sharp knife, cut the bones away from the meat by following the line of the bones. Remove the bones completely, then tie them back on with butcher's twine. Season the roast all over with the herb mixture.

Place the roast, bone side down, in the V-Rack and set the V-Rack inside the Drip Pan. Put the Drip Pan on the grid and close the lid of the EGG. Roast for 20 minutes at 425°F to sear the meat. Reduce the heat to 350°F, and continue cooking for 1 hour and 20 minutes, or until the instant read thermometer registers 135°F for medium-rare. Remove the pan from the EGG and let the roast rest for 15 minutes.

Remove the butcher's twine and discard. Remove the bones and slice the roast to the desired thickness. Serve immediately. **Serves 6 to 8**

Veal Chops with Bercy Butter

Easy-to-prepare veal chops make a superb special-occasion dinner. Hot off the grill, these chops are topped with a dollop of Bercy butter, an effortless-to-prepare reduction sauce that is named after a neighborhood in Paris. For a truly French-inspired dinner, serve these with Braised Leeks (page 185).

Ingredients

4 (1½ to 2-inch) veal loin chops
1 tablespoon olive oil
Kosher salt and freshly ground black pepper

Bercy Butter

1 cup unsalted butter, at room temperature
1 tablespoon chopped fresh flat-leaf parsley
2 tablespoons freshly squeezed lemon juice
½ cup dry white wine
¼ cup minced shallots
2 tablespoons veal demi-glace, or ½ cup beef broth
Kosher salt and freshly ground black pepper

Equipment: Cast Iron Grid
Set the EGG for direct cooking with the Cast Iron Grid.
Preheat the EGG to 500°F.

Brush each veal chop with olive oil and season with salt and pepper.

To make the Bercy butter, blend the butter, parsley, and lemon juice in a small bowl and set aside. Simmer the white wine, shallots, and demi-glace in a small saucepan on the stovetop until the liquid is reduced to about 1 teaspoon. Allow the liquid to cool completely. Place a small strainer over the bowl of butter and pour the reduced liquid through the strainer. Using a fork, mix the liquid and butter until completely blended, then season with salt and pepper.

Place the veal chops on the Grid. Close the lid of the EGG and grill for 8 minutes per side. Transfer the veal chops to a platter and brush generously with Bercy butter. Let the veal rest for 5 minutes, then top with more Bercy butter before serving. **Serves 4**

Napa Cabbage Beef Wraps

This Asian-influenced beef wrap makes a tasty and fun entrée. Try it with a side of the Dutch Oven Vegetable Fried Rice (page 148) or make a mini version and serve as an hors d'oeuvre at a cocktail party.

Ingredients

Marinade
½ cup chopped fresh basil
½ cup chopped fresh mint
½ cup chopped fresh cilantro
½ cup thinly sliced fresh ginger
¼ cup chopped garlic
1 cup canola oil
1 lime, cut into eighths
1 teaspoon kosher salt

2 pounds flank steak

Sauce
½ cup freshly squeezed lime juice (4 to 5 limes)
½ cup water
¼ cup granulated sugar
2 teaspoons fish sauce
½ teaspoon chili garlic sauce
Kosher salt

Kosher salt and freshly ground black pepper
1 head napa cabbage, separated into leaves
1 cup julienned carrots
½ cup thinly sliced radishes
⅓ cup firmly packed fresh basil leaves
⅓ cup chopped fresh mint
⅓ cup chopped fresh cilantro
½ cup thinly sliced shallots

Equipment: Cast Iron Grid
Set the EGG for direct cooking with the Cast Iron Grid.
Preheat the EGG to 500°F.

To make the marinade, combine the basil, mint, cilantro, ginger, garlic, canola oil, lime, and salt in a medium bowl and mix well. Place the flank steak in a large resealable plastic bag, pour in the marinade, seal the bag, and let the steak marinate overnight in the refrigerator. Turn occasionally.

To make the sauce, mix the lime juice, water, sugar, fish sauce, and chili garlic sauce in a small bowl. Season with salt and refrigerate.

Remove the steak from the plastic bag and discard the marinade. Season the steak with salt and pepper on both sides and place on the Grid. Close the lid of the EGG and grill for 5 minutes per side for medium-rare. Transfer to a platter and let rest for 10 minutes.

To assemble, slice the steak across the grain. Place a few slices inside a cabbage leaf and top with carrots, radishes, basil, mint, cilantro, and shallots. Wrap the cabbage leaf around the beef and toppings. Repeat with the rest of the ingredients. Serve with the sauce for dipping. **Serves 4 to 6**

Herb-Crusted Rack of Lamb

Rack of lamb is very easy to prepare and makes a great special-occasion dinner. Sear the lamb on the grid before applying Dijon mustard and any spices, to help seal in the flavor and give the lamb an appealing golden brown color.

Ingredients
2 (1-pound) racks of lamb
2 tablespoons plus 1 tablespoon extra-virgin olive oil
Kosher salt and freshly ground black pepper
½ cup packed fresh flat-leaf parsley
1 tablespoon minced garlic
1 tablespoon minced shallots
¼ cup Dijon mustard

Equipment: Porcelain coated grid, Grill Gripper, Plate Setter, instant read thermometer
Set the EGG for direct cooking with the porcelain coated grid.
Preheat the EGG to 450°F.

Brush the lamb with 2 tablespoons of the olive oil and season with salt and pepper. Place the racks on the grid, fat side down, close the lid of the EGG, and sear for 3 to 4 minutes. Transfer the lamb to a rimmed sheet pan and set aside.

Using the Grill Gripper and barbecue mitts, carefully remove the grid and add the Plate Setter, legs down. Lower the temperature to 400°F.

Combine the parsley, garlic, shallots, and the remaining 1 tablespoon olive oil in the bowl of a food processor. Blend for 15 seconds, then season with salt and pepper. Coat all sides of the lamb with the mustard. Press one-half of the herb mixture firmly onto the seared side of each rack of lamb.

Place the racks of lamb together on the Plate Setter, leaning the ribs into each other so that the bones are intertwined and the meat is standing up on end. Close the lid of the EGG and cook for 30 minutes, or until the instant read thermometer registers 125°F for medium-rare.

Transfer the lamb to a rimmed sheet pan and let the meat rest for 10 minutes before carving and serving. **Serves 4**

Slow-Roasted Leg of Lamb

Sometimes simple is just better. Thin slices of garlic and sprigs of rosemary are inserted into small slits that have been made all over the outside of the lamb. This infuses the rosemary and garlic flavors into the meat as it slow-roasts. Serve with the Grilled Vegetable Ratatouille (page 187) or slice the lamb thinly and use it to make sandwiches with the Pita Bread (page 215).

Ingredients
1 (5 to 6-pound) leg of lamb
5 cloves garlic, thinly sliced
20 (1-inch) pieces fresh rosemary
¼ cup extra-virgin olive oil
1 teaspoon kosher salt
1 teaspoon freshly ground black pepper

Equipment: V-Rack, 9 by 13-inch Drip Pan lined with aluminum foil, instant read thermometer
Set the EGG for direct cooking with the porcelain coated grid.
Preheat the EGG to 300°F.

Using a small paring knife, make 20 (1-inch) cuts evenly all over the lamb.

Stuff each hole with a slice of garlic and a piece of rosemary. Brush the lamb with the olive oil and season with salt and pepper.

Transfer the lamb to the V-Rack and set the V-Rack in the Drip Pan. Put the Drip Pan on the grid and close the lid of the EGG. Roast for 2 to 2½ hours, until the instant read thermometer registers 140°F. Remove the pan from the heat and let cool for 10 minutes.

Carve the lamb, transfer to a platter, and serve immediately.
Serves 6 to 8

eggxtraordinary!

pork
recipes

Chili-Spiced Pork Tenderloin with Caramelized Blackberry Sauce

The addition of a rich blackberry sauce makes this pork tenderloin sufficiently elegant to serve at a dinner party. Your family will no doubt lobby to have it served as a weeknight dinner so they can enjoy it more often. If you are not a fan of blackberries, or if they are not readily available, substitute peach or apricot preserves in the sauce.

Ingredients

2 (1-pound) pork tenderloins, trimmed
Olive oil
1 tablespoon chili powder
Kosher salt and freshly ground black pepper
½ cup granulated sugar
½ cup balsamic vinegar
1¼ cups blackberry preserves
½ cup chicken stock
2 tablespoons unsalted butter

Equipment: Cast Iron Grid, instant read thermometer
Set the EGG for direct cooking with the Cast Iron Grid.
Preheat the EGG to 400°F.

Brush each tenderloin with olive oil and season with the chili powder, salt, and pepper. Set aside.

Add the sugar to a small saucepan on the stovetop and cook over medium heat until the sugar is melted and caramelized. Add the vinegar, preserves, and chicken stock and whisk together. Cover and simmer for 15 minutes, or until the sauce is heated through and the flavors have combined. Remove the saucepan from the heat, add the butter, and stir well. Season with salt and pepper. Set aside.

Place the pork on the Grid and close the lid of the EGG. Cook for 5 minutes on each side. Turning the meat occasionally, cook until the instant read thermometer registers 145°F or the desired doneness. Transfer the pork to a rimmed sheet pan and let rest for 5 minutes.

Slice the pork and serve with the blackberry sauce.
Serves 6

Asian Pork Loin

Allspice, the berry of the evergreen pimento tree, and slices of garlic are inserted in slits in this pork loin to give it a piquant flavor, which is then complemented by a rich, creamy sauce that melds peanut butter, orange juice, and honey. It's a unique combination destined to have diners asking for a second helping—and the recipe.

Ingredients

½ cup honey
½ cup creamy peanut butter
½ cup freshly squeezed orange juice
2 teaspoons chili garlic sauce
1 (3½ to 4-pound) boneless pork loin
7 cloves garlic, sliced into thirds
20 allspice berries
2 tablespoons olive oil

Equipment: Porcelain coated grid, V-Rack, 9 by 13-inch Drip Pan lined with aluminum foil, instant read thermometer
Set the EGG for direct cooking with the porcelain coated grid.
Preheat the EGG to 400°F.

Whisk the honey, peanut butter, orange juice, and chili garlic sauce in a small saucepan on the stovetop. Simmer over medium heat for 5 minutes, or until incorporated. Remove ¾ cup of the sauce for basting. Reserve the remaining sauce.

Place the pork loin on a cutting board and, using a small knife, make 10 (1-inch) slits down the length of the roast. Alternate putting a sliver of garlic and an allspice berry in each slit. Turn the roast over and repeat the process. Brush the loin with the olive oil and the peanut sauce. Place the roast on the V-Rack and put the V-Rack in the Drip Pan. Place the Drip Pan on the grid and close the lid of the EGG. Basting the pork every 15 minutes, cook for 1 hour, or until the instant read thermometer registers 140° to 145°F for medium. Let the roast rest for 15 minutes.

Reheat the reserved sauce. Slice the roast and serve with the sauce. **Serves 6**

Coffee-Rubbed Pork Tenderloin with Yam Puree

Pork tenderloin gets an added boost of flavor when sliced into thick medallions and rubbed with coffee and spices before grilling. Yams are baked in the EGG to bring out their wonderful caramelized flavor before being pureed with aged Gouda, heavy cream, and butter. A bed of yam puree topped with the pork medallions contrasts the sweet and savory, and a coffee sauce pulls all of the flavors together. The yam puree also makes a perfect side for Smoked Turkey (page 108).

Ingredients

2 (1-pound) pork tenderloins
2 tablespoons plus 1 tablespoon ground coffee
1 tablespoon ancho chile powder
Kosher salt and freshly ground black pepper
2 tablespoons canola oil
1 cup peeled and chopped carrots
1 cup chopped yellow onions
1 tablespoon tomato paste
4 cups water
1 tablespoon fresh thyme leaves, chopped
2 tablespoons plus 3 tablespoons unsalted butter
2 pounds yams
1 cup shredded aged Gouda cheese
2 tablespoons heavy cream

Equipment: Cast Iron Grid, instant read thermometer
Set the EGG for direct cooking with the Cast Iron Grid.
Preheat the EGG to 400°F.

Cut 8 (4-ounce) slices from the center portion of the pork tenderloins, and reserve the ends and trimmings for another meal. To make the coffee rub, mix 2 tablespoons of the ground coffee, the chile powder, 2 teaspoons salt, and 1 teaspoon pepper in a small bowl and set aside.

Heat the canola oil in a small saucepan on the stovetop and add the carrots, onions, and pork trimmings. Cook over medium-high heat for 8 to 10 minutes, until brown and caramelized. Add the tomato paste and cook for 2 more minutes. Deglaze the saucepan by adding the water, and use a wooden spoon to scrape all of the vegetables from the bottom of the pan. Add the remaining tablespoon of ground coffee and the thyme and simmer over low heat for 1 hour, or until reduced by half. Pour the sauce through a fine-mesh strainer into a small bowl. Using a whisk, add 2 tablespoons butter into the strained broth, stirring until blended. Season with salt and pepper and set aside.

Wrap the yams with aluminum foil and place on the outside edge of the Grid. Close the lid of the EGG and cook for 30 minutes.

Season the pork medallions with the coffee rub. After the yams have been cooking for 30 minutes, put the pork slices on the middle of the Grid. Close the lid of the EGG and grill the pork for 5 to 6 minutes on each side, until the instant read thermometer registers 145°F. Remove the yams and pork. Let the pork rest while you prepare the yams.

Peel the yams and place in the bowl of a food processor fitted with the steel blade. Add the cheese, cream, and the remaining 3 tablespoons butter and season with salt. Puree until smooth.

Place ½ cup of the yams in the center of each plate and top with 2 medallions of pork. Top with the sauce and serve. **Serves 4**

Ham Steaks with Jalapeño & Cherry Cola Glaze

Don't balk at the idea of using cherry cola in this sauce—when combined with jalapeño peppers, it makes an incredible glaze. The cola's sweetness balances perfectly with the heat of the peppers. The seeds and veins of the jalapeño are what give food heat, so remove the seeds and the veins and use just the pepper if you want a more subtle taste. When handling hot peppers, it's a good idea to wear gloves and avoid touching your eyes until your hands are clean.

Ingredients

1 cup cherry cola
1 cup firmly packed brown sugar
4 red jalapeños, seeded and chopped
1 green jalapeño, chopped with seeds
4 tablespoons cornstarch
4 tablespoons grenadine
4 (4-ounce) ham steaks
2 tablespoons olive oil
Freshly ground black pepper

Equipment: Cast Iron Grid
Set the EGG for direct cooking with the Cast Iron Grid.
Preheat the EGG to 400°F.

Combine the cherry cola, brown sugar, and jalapeños in a small saucepan on the stovetop and simmer for 10 minutes. Using a fork, mix the cornstarch with the grenadine and add to the saucepan. Whisk together and cook for 1 minute, or until thickened. Carefully pour the hot glaze into the bowl of a food processor fitted with the steel blade and process for 30 seconds. Pour the glaze into a small bowl and set aside.

Brush the ham steaks with the oil and season with pepper. Place the ham steaks on the Grid. Close the lid of the EGG and cook for 5 minutes, turn the steaks over, baste with the glaze, and continue cooking for 5 more minutes.

Transfer the steaks to a platter and baste them with the glaze. Pour the rest of the glaze into a dish. Serve the ham steaks immediately with the glaze on the side.
Serves 4

Mojo Pork Ribs with Mango-Habanero Glaze

Ribs really benefit from long, slow cooking. However, for easier entertaining, these can be roasted a day ahead, then refrigerated. When ready to serve, simply brush with sauce and grill. These ribs are paired with a cool cucumber dipping sauce made by pureeing cucumbers and using the reserved strained liquid to make the sauce. Though the sauce contrasts nicely with the spicy ribs, the ribs are also delicious without the sauce.

Ingredients

1½ cups mango nectar
1 cup rice wine vinegar
1 habanero pepper
2 full racks baby back ribs
½ cup dry mojo seasoning

Dipping Sauce (optional)

2 to 3 whole English cucumbers, peeled, seeded, and chopped
½ cup freshly squeezed lime juice (4 to 5 limes)
⅓ cup granulated sugar
½ teaspoon kosher salt

1 cup Basic Barbecue Sauce (page 192)
½ cup chopped fresh cilantro

> **Equipment: Plate Setter, 9 by 13-inch Drip Pan, porcelain coated grid**
> **Set the EGG for indirect cooking with the Plate Setter, legs up.**
> **Preheat the EGG to 300°F.**

Pour the mango nectar and vinegar into the Drip Pan and add the habanero pepper. Cut each rack of ribs in half between the bones and season liberally with the mojo seasoning. Add the ribs to the Drip Pan and cover tightly with aluminum foil. Place the Drip Pan on the Plate Setter and close the lid of the EGG. Cook for 2 hours, or until tender. Remove the Drip Pan from the EGG and set aside.

To make the dipping sauce, place the cucumber in the bowl of a food processor fitted with the steel blade. Process for about 2 minutes, or until the cucumbers have been completely pureed. Place a strainer over a small bowl and pour the pureed cucumbers into the strainer, reserving the liquid until you have 1½ cups of cucumber liquid. Place the liquid in a small bowl and add the lime juice, sugar, and salt. Mix until the sugar has completely dissolved. Refrigerate until needed.

Add the grid to the EGG, and raise the temperature to 450°F. Remove the ribs from the Drip Pan and strain the juices from the pan into a bowl. Skim the fat from the top of the juices, add the barbecue sauce, and mix well.

Place the ribs on the grid. Brush the ribs with the barbecue sauce. Close the lid of the EGG and grill for 5 minutes. Turn the ribs, baste with more sauce, and cook with the lid closed for another 5 minutes, or until the sauce has caramelized. Remove and let cool for 5 minutes.

Remove the cucumber sauce from the refrigerator, add the cilantro, and blend well. Pour the sauce into a small bowl. Place the ribs on a platter and serve with the cucumber sauce. **Serves 4**

Asian Pork Ribs

These ribs are amazing! The Asian flair results from the use of distinctive five-spice powder with Asian Mop and Asian Barbecue Sauce. To ensure pit-barbecue tenderness, the ribs are cooked low and slow like traditional ribs. A dusting of toasted sesame seeds adds a finishing touch. Serve these with Veggie Noodle Stir-Fry (page 147) or Dutch Oven Vegetable Fried Rice (page 148).

Ingredients

2 full racks baby back pork ribs (8 pounds total)
¼ cup five-spice powder
Kosher salt and freshly ground black pepper
1 cup Asian Mop (page 195)
2 cups Asian Barbecue Sauce (page 195)
1 tablespoon white sesame seeds, toasted

Equipment: Plate Setter, V-Rack, 9 by 13-inch Drip Pan lined with aluminum foil
Set the EGG for indirect cooking with the Plate Setter, legs down.
Preheat the EGG to 300°F.

Season the ribs on all sides with the five-spice powder, salt, and pepper.

Place the ribs in the V-Rack and set the V-Rack in the Drip Pan. Place the Drip Pan on the Plate Setter and close the lid of the EGG. Cook for 3 hours, basting with the mop every 30 minutes. At the end of 3 hours, brush with the sauce, and discard any remaining mop. Close the lid of the EGG and cook for 30 minutes, brushing with sauce every 10 minutes. Remove the ribs from the EGG.

Cut the racks of ribs in half, baste the ribs with more sauce, sprinkle with the sesame seeds, and serve. **Serves 4**

Shredded Pork Sandwich with Fennel Slaw

Despite its name, pork butt is cut from the upper shoulder of the front leg of the pig. Slow-roasted pork butt makes an incredible sandwich, but this sandwich goes one step further, enhanced by a topping of crisp fennel slaw. The slaw is so delicious that you may even want to make it as a side dish. It would be equally good with any grilled meat or even served on top of a hot dog!

Ingredients

Fennel Slaw
1 cup mayonnaise
½ cup sour cream
¼ cup red wine vinegar
¼ cup granulated sugar
1 teaspoon celery seed
Kosher salt and freshly ground black pepper
6 cups finely shredded green cabbage
1 cup finely shredded purple cabbage
¾ cup finely shredded carrots
2 cups shaved fennel
2 tablespoons fennel fronds

1 (4-pound) Boston pork butt
½ cup Basic Barbecue Rub (page 196)
1 cup freshly squeezed orange juice
   (1 medium navel orange; reserve the peel)
1 cup Pernod
1 cup red wine vinegar
Kosher salt and freshly ground black pepper

8 kaiser rolls

Equipment: Plate Setter, 9 by 13-inch glass or ceramic baking dish
Set the EGG for indirect heat with the Plate Setter, legs down.
Preheat the EGG to 300°F.

To make the slaw, whisk the mayonnaise, sour cream, vinegar, sugar, and celery seed together in a small bowl. Season with salt and pepper. Mix the cabbages, carrots, fennel, and fennel fronds in a large bowl. Pour the dressing over the slaw and toss until completely blended. Refrigerate until ready to use.

Season the pork all over with the rub and place in the baking dish. Put the orange juice, Pernod, vinegar, and orange peel in a small bowl and stir well. Pour the Pernod mixture over the pork.

Cover the baking dish tightly with aluminum foil. Place the dish on the Plate Setter and close the lid of the EGG. Cook for 3 hours, or until the meat is tender.

Remove the baking dish from the Plate Setter and let the pork cool slightly. Reserve the juices.

Transfer the pork roast to a cutting board. Using two forks, shred the pork roast and place the meat in the baking dish with the reserved juices. Season with salt and pepper.

To assemble, place shredded pork on each bun and top with ¼ cup of the slaw. Serve immediately. **Serves 8**

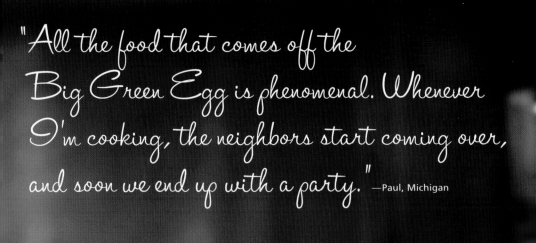

"All the food that comes off the Big Green Egg is phenomenal. Whenever I'm cooking, the neighbors start coming over, and soon we end up with a party." —Paul, Michigan

Carnitas

Carnitas are small bits of well-seasoned pork that are tenderized by simmering them in water before browning them until they are caramelized. This adds deep, bold flavor to the meat. You can use carnitas to make burritos or tacos or wrap them in flour tortillas and top them with cotija, a semisoft cheese often used in Mexican cooking.

Ingredients
1 (4-pound) pork butt (shoulder)
½ cup Tricolor Pepper Rub (page 197)
4 cups water
3 cloves garlic
3 cinnamon sticks
3 bay leaves

Accompaniments (optional)
Flour tortillas
Salsa
1 cup diced yellow onions
1 cup crumbled cotija cheese
½ cup firmly packed fresh cilantro leaves

Equipment: Porcelain coated grid, Dutch Oven
Set the EGG for direct cooking with the porcelain coated grid.
Preheat the EGG to 300°F.

Season the pork all over with the rub. Place the meat inside the Dutch Oven, and add the water, garlic, cinnamon sticks, and bay leaves.

Place the lid on the Dutch Oven, put the Dutch Oven on the grid, and close the lid of the EGG. Cook for 1½ hours. Remove the lid of the Dutch Oven and close the lid of the EGG. Cook for an additional 30 minutes, or until most of the liquid has evaporated and the meat is brown and caramelized. Remove the Dutch Oven from the heat and let cool for 10 minutes.

Cut the pork into large bite-size pieces. Add any remaining liquids to the pork and mix well. Serve with warm tortillas, salsa, onions, cheese, and cilantro.
Serves 6

Italian Sweet Sausage Subs

Traditional Italian sausages with peppers and onions are enhanced with a smoky flavor imparted by grilling over charcoal before topping with provolone cheese on a hoagie roll. But don't confine this tasty combination to sandwiches. Try tossing the grilled mixture with your favorite pasta and sprinkling liberally with grated Parmigiano-Reggiano cheese. For variety, experiment with different types of sausage.

Ingredients

1 red bell pepper
1 green bell pepper
1 red onion
4 (6 to 7-ounce) sweet or hot Italian sausages
3 cups Spicy San Marzano Tomato Sauce (page 200)
4 sausage rolls (hoagies)
8 slices provolone cheese

Equipment: Cast Iron Grid, Dutch Oven
Set the EGG for direct cooking with the Cast Iron Grid.
Preheat the EGG to 500°F.

Cut off the ends of the bell peppers and remove the seeds. Using a small paring knife, cut from the top of one of the peppers to the bottom, on one side only, so that you are able to flatten the pepper into one long piece. Repeat for the other pepper. Slice the onion into ½-inch-thick rounds.

Place the peppers, onion, and sausages on the Grid. Close the lid of the EGG and grill, turning occasionally, for 8 minutes, or until tender and brown. Transfer the peppers, onion, and sausages to a rimmed sheet pan. Place the peppers and onion on a cutting board and, with a knife, cut them into ½-inch strips. Put the peppers, onion, and sausages in the Dutch Oven, add the sauce, and stir. Lower the temperature of the EGG to 350°F.

Put the Dutch Oven on the Grid, uncovered, and close the lid of the EGG. Simmer for 20 to 30 minutes, until the mixture is heated through and the flavors are combined.

Remove the Dutch Oven from the EGG and place 1 sausage in each roll. Top with peppers, onion, and sauce. Place 2 slices of provolone cheese on top of each sausage roll and transfer to a rimmed sheet pan. Place the sheet pan on the Grid with the lid of the EGG closed for 1 minute, or until the cheese is melted.

Serve immediately with the remaining sauce on the side.
Serves 4

Stuffed Pork Chops with Poblano Cream Sauce

Poblano peppers, used in the sauce for these pork chops, are a mild chile pepper that originates in Mexico. These peppers impart subtle heat rather than make a bold statement. The dried version of poblano pepper, ancho chile pepper, is often ground and used as a spice. The stuffing is made from cornbread and sausage. This recipe could also be made using boneless, skinless chicken breasts in place of the pork chops.

Ingredients

Poblano Cream Sauce
2 poblano peppers
1 teaspoon minced garlic
½ cup ham or chicken stock
1½ cups heavy cream
¼ cup yellow cornmeal
1 tablespoon freshly squeezed lime juice
½ cup chopped fresh cilantro

4 double-cut pork chops
1 tablespoon olive oil
4 tablespoons Red Chile Rub (page 197)
1 cup firmly packed Southwestern Cornbread
   (page 217), or store-bought
½ cup chopped smoked chorizo sausage
½ cup chopped fresh cilantro
½ cup ham or chicken stock

Equipment: Porcelain coated grid, Half Moon Baking Stone, instant read thermometer
Set the EGG for direct and indirect cooking with the porcelain coated grid and Half Moon Baking Stone. Preheat the EGG to 450°F.

Place the poblano peppers on the grid. Close the lid of the EGG and cook, turning occasionally, for 3 to 5 minutes, until the peppers are black on all sides. Transfer the peppers to a resealable plastic bag. Seal the bag and let the peppers steam for 5 minutes. Remove the peppers from the bag and place on a cutting board. Using a paring knife, cut the peppers open lengthwise and remove and discard the seeds. Dice the peppers into small pieces. Combine the peppers, garlic, stock, and cream in a small saucepan on the stovetop and simmer for 15 minutes. Using a whisk, add the cornmeal and continue to cook for 7 minutes, or until the sauce has thickened. Remove the saucepan from the heat and add the lime juice and cilantro. Keep warm.

Using a paring knife, cut a 1½ to 2-inch-long pocket along the meat side of each pork chop. Season each pork chop with olive oil and 1 tablespoon of the rub. Crumble the cornbread into a small bowl, add the chorizo, cilantro, and stock, and mix well. Divide the stuffing into quarters and place one-quarter of the stuffing inside the pocket of each pork chop.

Place the pork chops on the grid. Close the lid of the EGG and grill for 3 minutes on each side. Transfer the pork chops to the Baking Stone and close the lid of the EGG. Bake for 12 to 15 minutes, until the instant read thermometer registers 145°F or the desired doneness.

Transfer the pork chops to a platter, top with the sauce, and serve immediately. **Serves 4**

eggxalted!

poultry

recipes

Beer-Brined Chicken

Meats low in fat, such as poultry and pork, may be soaked in a salt solution, which seasons the meat all the way through and adds moisture so that the meat does not become dry during cooking. When brining, make sure that the meat is totally covered with the liquid and that you leave ample time for the process. Brining a whole chicken takes a minimum of twelve hours. This method produces a fall-off-the-bone moist, well-seasoned chicken. Water is the usual liquid in a brine, but in this recipe, lager beer is used instead to impart added flavor. Since the chicken is seasoned from the salt solution, you may omit the salt from the barbecue rub if you like.

Ingredients
8 cups water
1 cup granulated sugar
½ cup kosher salt
24 ounces lite lager beer
1 (5-pound) chicken
¼ cup olive oil
¼ cup Basic Barbecue Rub (page 196)

Equipment: Plate Setter, hickory chips, Vertical Roaster, 8-inch Drip Pan, instant read thermometer
Set the EGG for indirect cooking with the Plate Setter, legs down.
Preheat the EGG to 400°F with the Plate Setter removed.

Combine the water, sugar, salt, and beer in a large stockpot. Stir to dissolve the sugar and salt. Add the chicken to the brine, place the lid on the pot, and refrigerate for 12 hours or overnight.

Place 1 cup of hickory chips in a medium bowl, cover with water, and soak for 1 hour. Spread the hickory chips over the coals, and place the Plate Setter in the EGG.

Remove the chicken from the brine, rinse thoroughly, and pat dry with a paper towel. Discard the brining liquid. Brush the chicken with the olive oil and season with the rub. Place the chicken upright on the Vertical Roaster. Place the Drip Pan on top of the Plate Setter, then place the chicken, on the Vertical Roaster, in the Drip Pan, and close the lid of the EGG. Cook for 1 to 1½ hours, until the instant read thermometer registers 165°F.

Remove the chicken from the EGG and let the chicken rest for 10 to 15 minutes. Carve and serve. **Serves 4**

"The Big Green Egg is the stand-alone champion of smokers. Metal smoker users just don't realize what they're missing!" —Michael, Kansas

Tandoori Chicken

A tandoor is the traditional oven used to cook this typical Indian dish. The tandoor can be charcoal burning or wood burning and can reach almost 500°F. This is where the EGG really shines; with its ability to reach high temperatures, it can reproduce any tandoori dish. Garam masala, a traditional Indian spice blend, is combined with yogurt to marinate the tandoori chicken. Pair it with Naan Bread (page 217) for a perfect Indian meal.

Ingredients

1 cup plain yogurt

¼ cup freshly squeezed lime juice (4 to 5 limes)

2 tablespoons chopped fresh cilantro

3 cloves garlic, crushed

2 teaspoons garam masala

2 teaspoons kosher salt

1 teaspoon red curry paste

1 teaspoon ground cumin

1 red chile pepper (such as cayenne chile pepper, also known as finger chile)

2 tablespoons peanut oil

1 (4 to 5-pound) chicken, quartered

Equipment: Plate Setter, porcelain coated grid, instant read thermometer

Set the EGG for indirect cooking with the Plate Setter, legs up, and the porcelain coated grid on top of the Plate Setter.

Preheat the EGG to 500°F.

To make the marinade, combine the yogurt, lime juice, cilantro, garlic, garam masala, salt, curry paste, cumin, chile pepper, and peanut oil in the bowl of a food processor fitted with the steel blade and process for 30 seconds. Place the chicken in a sealable plastic bag, add the marinade, and toss to coat. Close the bag tightly and refrigerate for 24 hours.

Remove the chicken from the plastic bag and discard the marinade. Place the chicken, skin side up, on the grid. Close the lid of the EGG and grill for 30 minutes, or until the instant read thermometer reaches 165°F.

Transfer the chicken to a platter and serve immediately.

Serves 4

Lemon-Infused Cornish Game Hens

Cornish game hens are full-grown small chickens. They tend to have less meat than a chicken, so if you are serving big eaters, count on using a whole Cornish game hen per person. Try Honey-Roasted Acorn Squash (page 162) as a side.

Ingredients

4 large lemons
⅓ cup chopped fresh rosemary
¼ cup chopped garlic
1 cup extra-virgin olive oil
Kosher salt and freshly ground black pepper
2 (1¼-pound) Cornish game hens

Equipment: Cast Iron Grid, instant read thermometer
Set the EGG for direct cooking with the Cast Iron Grid.
Preheat the EGG to 350°F.

Zest the lemons and measure ⅓ cup. Juice the lemons and measure 6 tablespoons. Reserve the lemons. Combine the lemon zest, lemon juice, rosemary, garlic, olive oil, 1 tablespoon salt, and 1 teaspoon pepper in a medium bowl and mix well. Cut the Cornish game hens in half lengthwise. Place the hens in a resealable plastic bag and add the marinade, reserving ½ cup of the marinade for basting. Marinate in the refrigerator for 12 hours.

Remove the Cornish game hens from the plastic bag, discard the marinade, and season with salt and pepper. Place the hens on the preheated Grid, skin side down. Close the lid of the EGG and cook over low heat for 10 to 12 minutes, until the skin is golden brown. Turn the hens over and baste the skin with the reserved marinade. Close the lid of the EGG and grill for an additional 15 minutes, basting often with the marinade. Remove the hens from the EGG when the instant read thermometer registers 165°F.

Transfer the Cornish game hens to a platter. Squeeze the remaining juice from the reserved lemons over the chicken and let the chicken rest for 5 minutes before serving. **Serves 4**

(See recipe photograph on page 96.)

Chicken & Spinach Salad

Warm bacon drippings do double duty in this classic spinach salad. Crunchy applewood-smoked bacon is crumbled in the salad, and the warm drippings are reserved and used to make the dressing. Not only does this add flavor, but it also slightly wilts the spinach! If you aren't a bacon fan, omit the bacon dressing and use your favorite salad dressing in its place.

Ingredients

8 ounces baby spinach, rinsed and dried
½ cup thinly sliced red onion
½ cup thinly sliced small white mushrooms
2 cups 1-inch cubes French bread
4 tablespoons unsalted butter, melted
4 to 5 slices applewood-smoked bacon
¼ cup minced shallots
1 teaspoon minced garlic
¼ cup red wine vinegar
1 teaspoon Dijon mustard
1 tablespoon granulated sugar
½ cup plus 2 tablespoons olive oil
Kosher salt and freshly ground black pepper
4 (6-ounce) boneless, skinless chicken breasts
4 large eggs, hard-boiled and peeled

Equipment: Cast Iron Grid, perforated grill pan, instant read thermometer
Set the EGG for direct cooking with the Cast Iron Grid and perforated grill pan. Preheat the EGG to 400°F.

Combine the spinach, onion, and mushrooms in a large bowl and set aside.

To make the croutons, in a medium bowl, toss the bread cubes with the melted butter to coat. Place the croutons on the grill pan and cook, turning constantly, until the bread is toasted on all sides. Using barbecue mitts, remove the grill pan from the Grid, and transfer the croutons to a plate and let cool. Add the croutons to the salad.

To make the vinaigrette, cook the bacon in a small frying pan on the stovetop until crisp, then transfer the bacon to a plate lined with paper towels. Reserve the bacon fat in the frying pan. Dice the bacon and add to the salad. Reheat the bacon fat if necessary, then add the shallots and garlic and cook for 2 minutes. Add the vinegar, mustard, and sugar and stir well. Using a whisk, slowly add ½ cup of the olive oil and whisk to blend until emulsified. Season with salt and pepper and set aside.

To grill the chicken, lightly brush the chicken breasts with the remaining 2 tablespoons olive oil and season with salt and pepper. Place the chicken on the Grid. Close the lid of the EGG and cook for 8 minutes per side or until the instant read thermometer registers 165°F. Allow the chicken to cool to warm or room temperature.

To assemble, pour the vinaigrette over the spinach salad, season with salt and pepper, and toss well. Divide the salad between individual plates.

Slice the chicken breasts and arrange 1 breast on top of each salad. Quarter the eggs, and arrange 4 quarters on each plate. Serve immediately. **Serves 4**

Linguini with
Grilled Chicken Breast & Asparagus

This delicious pasta dish has it all: fresh vegetables, lots of flavor, and a delicious sauce. It would be equally good with Maple-Smoked Salmon (page 280) or grilled shrimp in place of chicken. You can also replace the linguini with any pasta you choose. For a complete meal, all you need is a salad and dessert. Try the Grilled Caesar Salad (page 171) and the Roasted Peaches with Pecan Praline Stuffing (page 259). Note that this recipe calls for artichoke hearts rather than bottoms.

Ingredients

4 (6-ounce) boneless, skinless chicken breasts
1 pound asparagus
2 tablespoons plus ¼ cup extra-virgin olive oil
Kosher salt and freshly ground black pepper
2 tablespoons minced garlic
1 (15-ounce) can artichoke hearts, drained and quartered
1 cup dry white wine
2 cups chicken stock
1 cup heavy cream
1 pound linguini, cooked al dente
1 cup dry-packed sun-dried tomatoes
½ cup grated Parmigiano-Reggiano cheese (2 ounces)
3 tablespoons unsalted butter
1 tablespoon freshly squeezed lemon juice
½ cup firmly packed fresh basil leaves, rolled and
  thinly sliced

**Equipment: Cast Iron Grid, Dutch Oven
Set the EGG for direct cooking with the
  Cast Iron Grid.
Preheat the EGG to 400°F.**

Brush the chicken and asparagus with 2 tablespoons of the olive oil, season with salt and pepper, and set the asparagus aside. Place the chicken on the Grid. Close the lid of the EGG and grill for 7 to 8 minutes, turn, and continue cooking for 8 minutes, or until the juices run clear. Transfer to a plate and keep warm. Place the asparagus on the Grid and cook for 2 minutes, turning to cook on all sides. Remove from the Grid and chop into ½-inch pieces. Set aside.

Place the Dutch Oven on the Grid and allow to preheat for 10 minutes. Add the remaining ¼ cup olive oil, the garlic, and artichokes and sauté for 1 minute. Carefully pour the wine into the Dutch Oven while scraping the bottom of the pan with a wooden spoon. Cook for 3 minutes, or until the wine is reduced by half. Add the chicken stock. Close the lid of the EGG and cook for 10 minutes, or until the sauce is reduced by half. Add the cream. Close the lid of the EGG and cook for 4 minutes, or until the sauce is slightly thickened. Add the pasta and cook for 1 minute while gently tossing.

Remove the Dutch Oven from the heat. Add the tomatoes, cheese, butter, asparagus, lemon juice, and basil. Season with salt and pepper. Slice the chicken breasts. Transfer the pasta to individual bowls and top each serving with a sliced chicken breast. **Serves 4**

Chicken & Vegetable Stir-Fry

Stir-frying is a fast, easy, and healthful way to cook and shows just how versatile the EGG can be. Though chicken is used here, you can easily make this dish with just about any meat or vegetable that you have on hand. Just remember that to ensure even cooking, try to cut all of your vegetables about the same size. The Dutch Oven Vegetable Fried Rice (page 148) is a great side to serve with this dish.

Ingredients

2 tablespoons toasted sesame oil
1½ teaspoons plus 1½ teaspoons minced garlic
1½ teaspoons plus 1½ teaspoons minced fresh ginger
2 pounds boneless, skinless chicken breasts, cubed
½ cup rice wine
½ cup light soy sauce
½ cup chicken stock
¼ cup hoisin sauce
2 tablespoons rice wine vinegar
2 tablespoons granulated sugar
2 tablespoons cornstarch
1 teaspoon chili garlic sauce (optional)
½ cup canola oil
4 cups broccoli florets
1 cup broccoli stems, trimmed and julienned
1 cup julienned carrots
1 cup drained water chestnuts, diced
1 tablespoon toasted sesame seeds

Equipment: Porcelain coated grid, Dutch Oven or a wok
Set the EGG for direct cooking with the porcelain coated grid.
Preheat the EGG to 500°F.

Combine the sesame oil, 1½ teaspoons of the garlic, and 1½ teaspoons of the ginger in a small bowl, add the chicken, and toss to coat. Let the chicken marinate for 30 minutes.

To make the sauce, mix the remaining 1½ teaspoons garlic, 1½ teaspoons ginger, rice wine, soy sauce, chicken stock, hoisin sauce, rice wine vinegar, sugar, cornstarch, and chili garlic sauce in a small bowl. Set aside.

Place the Dutch Oven on the grid and preheat for 10 minutes.

Place the canola oil and chicken in the Dutch Oven. Close the lid of the EGG and cook for 5 to 6 minutes, until seared on all sides. Add the broccoli florets and stems, carrots, and water chestnuts and cook for 2 to 3 minutes, stirring well. Add the sauce and continue to cook until the sauce has thickened. Remove the Dutch Oven from the EGG.

Transfer the stir-fry to a bowl and garnish with the sesame seeds. **Serves 6**

Smoked Turkey

Once you try this brined turkey, you'll agree that nothing does a better job of smoking meats than the EGG. The turkey has a subtle smoky flavor and is moist and succulent, but if you prefer a bolder smoky flavor, add more chips in increments during cooking. This turkey would be great for holidays, and you can use the leftovers to make wonderful sandwiches or Turkey & Wild Mushroom Pot Pie (page 111).

Ingredients

16 cups (1 gallon) water
½ cup firmly packed brown sugar
Rind of 1 navel orange
3 sprigs rosemary
1 cup kosher salt
3 yellow onions, quartered
2 heads garlic, halved
1 (12-pound) turkey
2 lemons, quartered
10 sprigs thyme
10 sprigs sage
1 cup chopped potatoes
¼ cup olive oil
Freshly ground black pepper
Garlic powder

> **Equipment: Plate Setter, hickory chips, V-Rack, 9 by 13-inch Drip Pan lined with aluminum foil, instant read thermometer**
> **Preheat the EGG to 350°F without the Plate Setter.**

Pour the water into a large bowl. Add the brown sugar, orange rind, rosemary, salt, two-thirds of the quartered onions, and 1 halved garlic head. Mix until the sugar and salt dissolve. Remove the giblets from inside the turkey and reserve for another use. Rinse the turkey well. Place the turkey in a 2½-gallon resealable plastic bag or any container that is large enough to hold the turkey and the liquid. Pour the brine over the turkey, making sure it's completely covered. Refrigerate for 12 hours, turning occasionally.

Soak 4 cups of hickory chips in water in a medium bowl for 1 hour.

Remove the turkey from the brine, rinse well to remove the brining liquid, and pat dry with paper towels. Discard the brining liquid and solids. Stuff the turkey with the lemon quarters, the remaining halved garlic head and onion, thyme, sage, and potatoes. Brush the turkey with olive oil and season with pepper and garlic powder.

Scatter 1 cup of the hickory chips over the hot coals and, using barbecue mitts, place the Plate Setter, legs up, in the EGG. Place the turkey on the V-Rack and put the V-Rack in the Drip Pan. Place the Drip Pan on the Plate Setter and close the lid of the EGG. Cook for 2½ hours, adding more chips every 30 minutes. If the turkey starts to brown too quickly, carefully tent the turkey with aluminum foil. Continue cooking until the instant read thermometer registers 165°F.

Remove the turkey from the EGG and let rest for 15 to 20 minutes. Carve and serve immediately. **Serves 8**

Turkey & Spinach Burgers with Sun-Dried Tomato Pesto

This might be one of the best turkey burgers you will ever eat! This is a bold statement, but if you usually eat beef burgers, this good-for-you burger just might change your mind. Though it might take a little more effort, be sure to make the Sun-Dried Tomato Pesto, as it adds a huge amount of flavor.

Ingredients

10 ounces spinach
1½ pounds white and dark ground turkey
1 tablespoon minced garlic
1½ teaspoons kosher salt
½ teaspoon freshly ground black pepper
½ cup mayonnaise
2 tablespoons whole-grain mustard
4 slices Swiss cheese
4 whole wheat hamburger buns
1 cup Sun-Dried Tomato Pesto (page 200)

Equipment: Cast Iron Grid
Set the EGG for direct cooking with the Cast Iron Grid.
Preheat the EGG to 500°F.

Rinse the spinach in a large bowl of water, then lift it from the water and place in a saucepan with some of the water still clinging to the leaves. Cook the spinach in the saucepan on the stovetop until wilted. Mix the turkey, spinach, garlic, salt, and pepper in a medium bowl. Form the turkey into 4 (6-ounce) patties and set aside. Blend the mayonnaise and mustard in a small bowl. Set aside.

Place the turkey burgers on the Grid and close the lid of the EGG. Grill for 5 minutes, turn the burgers over, close the lid, and cook for 4 minutes more. Add 1 slice of the cheese to each burger. Close the lid of the EGG and grill for 1 more minute, or until the cheese is melted.

Transfer the burgers to a platter and let them rest. Spread the cut sides of the buns with 1 tablespoon of pesto and place them on the Grid, pesto side down. Grill until the buns are toasted, about 20 seconds.

To assemble, brush 1½ teaspoons of pesto and 1 teaspoon of the mayonnaise mixture on the toasted sides of all the buns and place the burgers on the buns. Serve immediately, with the remaining pesto and mayonnaise mixture on the side. **Serves 4**

Turkey & Wild Mushroom Pot Pie

There is nothing better than a pot pie on a cold winter's night. Loaded with juicy, tender pieces of roasted turkey breast and wild mushrooms, this pie is the ultimate comfort food. You could also use meat from the smoked turkey recipe (page 108) to make this pie.

Ingredients

1½ cups mixed dried wild mushrooms
2 tablespoons unsalted butter
2 tablespoons olive oil
1 cup diced onions
1 cup diced carrots
1 cup diced celery
2 tablespoons minced garlic
⅓ cup all-purpose flour
¼ cup white wine
3 cups low-sodium chicken stock
1 cup diced potatoes
1 teaspoon minced fresh thyme
1 cup frozen green peas
2 cups chopped roasted turkey breast (page 112)
1 (9-inch) deep-dish pie shell and 1 pie dough
   disk (page 223)
1 large egg
1 tablespoon water

Equipment: Porcelain coated grid, Dutch Oven, Grill Gripper, Plate Setter, 9-inch pie plate
Set the EGG for direct cooking with the porcelain coated grid.
Preheat the EGG to 375°F.

Place the Dutch Oven on the grid to preheat for 10 minutes.

Cover the mushrooms with hot water and let rehydrate until needed. Heat the butter and olive oil in the Dutch Oven. Add the onions, carrots, and celery. Close the lid of the EGG and cook uncovered for 5 to 6 minutes, until the vegetables are light brown and softened. Add the garlic and stir for 1 minute, then add the flour and stir. Add the wine and cook for 3 minutes. Drain the mushrooms, reserving the liquid. Add the chicken stock and the reserved mushroom liquid to the Dutch Oven and stir well. Add the potatoes. Close the lid of the EGG and continue cooking, covered, for 10 minutes, or until the potatoes are cooked through. Add the reserved mushrooms, thyme, peas, and turkey, stir, and cook for 2 to 3 more minutes. Remove the Dutch Oven from the heat and let cool for 15 minutes.

Using the Grill Gripper and barbecue mitts, carefully remove the grid and add the Plate Setter, legs down. Replace the grid and preheat the EGG to 400°F.

Spoon the filling into the pie shell. Roll out the pie dough disk on a lightly floured surface until it is large enough to cover the top of the pie. Unroll the pie dough onto the pie. Press the top and bottom edges of the dough together and crimp. Using a knife, cut four small slits on the top of the crust. Beat the egg with the water and brush the top with the egg wash.

Place the pie on top of the grid and close the lid of the EGG. Cook for 30 to 40 minutes, until the dough is light brown and the filling is hot and bubbling. Let rest for 5 minutes before serving. **Serves 4 to 6**

Roasted Turkey Breast with White Wine, Soy Sauce & Mushrooms

Turkey breast is ideal for a small Thanksgiving gathering. This turkey is easy to prepare, and by adding the mushrooms to the Drip Pan, a rich, dark gravy is created as the turkey roasts. All you need is the Grilled Squash Casserole (page 163) and Chocolate Pecan Bourbon Pie (page 252), and you are set for Thanksgiving! You could also prepare this recipe using a whole turkey; just remember to baste the turkey often, as it helps make the meat juicier.

Ingredients

4 ounces mixed dried mushrooms
1 (8-pound) turkey breast
2 tablespoons extra-virgin olive oil
8 tablespoons plus 4 tablespoons unsalted butter
2 teaspoons sweet paprika
1 teaspoon garlic powder
1 teaspoon chopped fresh thyme
1 teaspoon kosher salt
1 teaspoon freshly ground black pepper
1 cup dry white wine
½ cup soy sauce
1 tablespoon minced fresh rosemary
4 cups water

Equipment: Plate Setter, V-Rack, 9 by 13-inch Drip Pan lined with aluminum foil, instant read thermometer
Set the EGG for indirect cooking with Plate Setter, legs up.
Preheat the EGG to 350°F.

In a small bowl, cover the mushrooms with hot water and let rehydrate until needed.

Coat the turkey breast with the olive oil. Carefully lift the skin of the breast and separate it from the meat. Thinly slice 8 tablespoons of the butter. Gently lift the skin and place the butter slices under the skin, making sure to place the butter evenly over the whole breast. Mix the paprika, garlic powder, thyme, salt, and pepper in a small bowl. Sprinkle the seasoning evenly over the turkey breast. Melt the remaining 4 tablespoons butter in a small sauce-pan on the stovetop over low heat. Add the wine, soy sauce, and rosemary and mix well.

Place the turkey breast on the V-Rack, put the V-Rack in the Drip Pan, and place the Drip Pan on the Plate Setter. Add the water, mushrooms, and mushroom liquid to the Drip Pan. Using a basting brush, coat the turkey with the butter mixture and close the lid of the EGG. Basting every 10 to 15 minutes, roast the turkey for 2½ to 3 hours, until the instant read thermometer registers 165°F. Remove the turkey from the EGG and transfer to a carving board. Reserve the pan gravy.

Let the turkey rest for 15 minutes. Reheat the pan gravy. Slice the turkey and serve immediately with the gravy.
Serves 8

eggsquisite!

seafood

recipes

Cedar-Planked Salmon with Honey Glaze

Grilling on a cedar plank infuses the salmon with a woodsy, smoky flavor while keeping the fish moist. The flavor is boosted by basting the fish with a honey glaze enlivened with citrus. Serve this right on the plank for a rustic presentation.

Ingredients

½ cup Dijon mustard
¼ cup honey
1 tablespoon balsamic vinegar
2 teaspoons grated orange zest
1 teaspoon minced fresh thyme plus extra for garnish
2 tablespoons extra-virgin olive oil
4 (7-ounce) salmon fillets, skin on
Kosher salt and freshly ground black pepper

**Equipment: Porcelain coated grid,
    2 cedar planks
Set the EGG for direct cooking with the
    porcelain coated grid.
Preheat the EGG to 400°F.**

Place the cedar planks in a pan, cover with water, and let soak for 1 hour.

Whisk the mustard, honey, balsamic vinegar, orange zest, and 1 teaspoon thyme together in a small bowl.

Place the cedar planks on the grid, close the lid of the EGG, and preheat for 3 minutes. Open the lid and turn the planks over, brush them with the olive oil, and place 2 salmon fillets on each plank. Season the salmon with salt and pepper and brush generously with the honey glaze. Close the lid of the EGG. Cook the salmon for 12 to 15 minutes for medium.

Remove from the heat, garnish with thyme, and serve immediately. **Serves 4**

Grilled Salmon on Toasted Croissant with Havarti & Avocado Relish

Grilled salmon sandwiches are perfect for breakfast, brunch, or lunch. Though it may seem that these have a lot of flavors going on, when combined they meld into one perfect, tasty sandwich!

Ingredients

1 large Hass avocado, halved, peeled, pitted, and chopped
½ cup diced Roma tomatoes
1 teaspoon chopped dill
1 tablespoon freshly squeezed lemon juice
Kosher salt and freshly ground black pepper
4 large croissants
6 tablespoons unsalted butter, melted
4 (3-ounce) salmon fillets
½ teaspoon Old Bay seasoning
4 large eggs
4 slices Havarti cheese

Equipment: Cast Iron Grid, Half Moon Griddle
Set the EGG for direct cooking with the Cast Iron Grid and the Half Moon Griddle.
Preheat the EGG to 400°F.

To make the avocado relish, use a fork to lightly mash the avocado in a small bowl. Add the tomatoes, dill, lemon juice, ¼ teaspoon salt, and ⅛ teaspoon pepper and toss. Set aside.

Cut the croissants in half lengthwise, brush with 2 tablespoons of the butter, and place, cut side down, on the Grid. Close the lid of the EGG and toast lightly. Transfer the croissants to a platter and set aside.

Brush the salmon fillets with 2 tablespoons of the butter. Season each fillet with Old Bay seasoning, salt, and pepper. Place the salmon on the exposed Grid. Add the remaining 2 tablespoons butter to the Griddle and crack the eggs into the butter. Close the lid of the EGG and grill the salmon and eggs for 3 minutes, turn both the salmon and eggs over, and continue cooking for 2 more minutes. The interior of the fish should be opaque. Transfer to a rimmed sheet pan.

To assemble, place a piece of salmon on the bottom half of a toasted croissant and top the salmon with an egg and a slice of cheese. Repeat this process for the remaining croissants. Return the croissants to the Grid, close the lid of the EGG, and let the cheese melt for 30 seconds. Spread 2 tablespoons of relish on top of each sandwich. Place the top of the croissant on the sandwich and serve immediately. **Serves 4**

Grilled Tuna with Salsa Verde

Grilled tuna, salsa verde, and pureed navy beans are combined in this wonderful rustic dish. Salsa verde, also known as green sauce, is a provincial Italian condiment made with green herbs—parsley, basil, and oregano—which give the sauce its bright green color. The dish is bumped up a notch by setting the tuna on a bed of navy bean puree. Navy beans are small white beans that are often used to make commercial baked beans. If you can't find navy beans, use Great Northern beans as a substitute.

Ingredients

Salsa Verde

2 cloves garlic
1 cup firmly packed fresh basil leaves
1 cup firmly packed fresh flat-leaf parsley leaves
¼ cup firmly packed fresh oregano leaves
2 tablespoons capers
1 tablespoon Dijon mustard
1 cup extra-virgin olive oil
Kosher salt and freshly ground black pepper

4 (8-ounce) tuna steaks
2 (15-ounce) cans navy beans, drained and rinsed
2 cloves garlic, minced
½ cup cream
4 tablespoons unsalted butter
Kosher salt and freshly ground white pepper

Equipment: Cast Iron Grid
Set the EGG for direct cooking with the Cast Iron Grid.
Preheat the EGG to 450°F.

To make the salsa, place the garlic, basil, parsley, oregano, capers, mustard, and olive oil in the bowl of a food processor fitted with the steel blade and pulse for 30 seconds. Season with salt and black pepper and set aside.

Place the tuna in a resealable plastic bag. Pour one-half of the salsa over the tuna, seal the bag, and marinate for 30 minutes. Reserve the remaining salsa. Place the beans, garlic, and cream in a small saucepan on the stovetop and simmer over low heat for 15 minutes. Pour the beans into the bowl of a food processor, add the butter, and pulse until the beans are pureed and smooth. Season with salt and white pepper and set aside.

Remove the tuna from the plastic bag and discard the marinade. Season the tuna with salt and white pepper and place on the Grid. Close the lid of the EGG and cook for 2 minutes per side for medium-rare. Using a long-handled spatula, transfer the tuna to a rimmed sheet pan.

Place a large spoonful of puree in the center of each plate, place a tuna steak on top, and serve with a drizzle of the reserved salsa. Pass the remaining salsa at the table. **Serves 4**

Smoked Halibut with Sake Sauce

Alder planks are used to give this halibut its unique smoky flavor. The fish is topped with a shiitake mushroom and sake sauce. Sake is a Japanese alcoholic beverage made from rice. Often referred to as rice wine, it is actually a beer, since it is made from grain rather than fruit. This recipe can also be prepared using grilled halibut rather than smoked. Just place the halibut right on the cooking grid to grill and, when done, serve with the sake sauce.

Ingredients

1 teaspoon toasted or cold-pressed sesame oil
¼ teaspoon white sesame seeds
¼ teaspoon black sesame seeds

Sake Sauce
3 cups thinly sliced shiitake mushrooms
2 cups chicken stock
1 cup sake
½ cup soy sauce
1 tablespoon minced fresh ginger
1 teaspoon minced garlic
1 jalapeño, seeded and chopped
2 tablespoons honey
1 tablespoon rice wine vinegar
1 tablespoon cornstarch
1 tablespoon water

¼ cup extra-virgin olive oil
4 (7-ounce) halibut fillets
Kosher salt and freshly ground black pepper
¼ cup thinly sliced scallions

**Equipment: Porcelain coated grid,
    2 alder planks
Set the EGG for direct cooking with the
    porcelain coated grid.
Preheat the EGG to 450°F.**

Place the alder planks in a pan, cover with water, and let soak for 1 hour.

Mix the sesame oil and white and black sesame seeds in a small bowl and set aside.

To make the sake sauce, mix the mushrooms, chicken stock, sake, soy sauce, ginger, garlic, and jalapeño in a small saucepan on the stovetop. Cover and simmer over low heat for 15 minutes, or until the sauce is hot and the flavors have combined. Add the honey and rice wine vinegar, stir, cover, and simmer over low heat for 15 minutes more. Place the cornstarch in a small bowl, add the water, and stir to dissolve. Using a whisk, add the cornstarch to the sauce, stirring constantly until the sauce has thickened. Remove the sauce from the heat and set aside.

Brush 1 side of the alder planks with olive oil and place 2 halibut fillets on the oiled side of each plank. Brush the halibut with olive oil and season with salt and pepper. Place the planks on the grid. Close the lid of the EGG and grill for 7 to 8 minutes, until the interior of the fish is opaque. Using a long-handled spatula, transfer the halibut to a plate.

Spoon the sake sauce over the halibut and sprinkle with the sesame seed mixture. Top with the scallions and serve immediately. **Serves 4**

Thai Sea Bass in Banana Leaves

Banana leaves are often used in Thai cooking to wrap around fish, much as Americans use aluminum foil. The leaves add subtle flavor to whatever food they surround. Banana leaves are not only useful for cooking; they also make a unique presentation. If you cannot find these leaves fresh in your local grocery or specialty food store, they are often sold frozen, or you can order them online. If you find yourself with extra leaves, just wrap them with plastic wrap, place them in a tightly sealed plastic freezer bag, and store them in the freezer.

Ingredients

1 (15-ounce) can coconut milk
1 teaspoon red curry paste
½ cup chicken stock
½ cup firmly packed chopped fresh basil
½ cup firmly packed chopped fresh mint
½ cup firmly packed chopped fresh cilantro
½ cup grated fresh ginger
¼ cup crushed garlic
1 thinly sliced red jalapeño or serrano pepper
4 banana leaves (about 12 inches square)
4 (6 to 7-ounce) sea bass fillets
1 lime, cut into 8 thin slices
2 tablespoons canola oil
Kosher salt and freshly ground black pepper

Equipment: Porcelain coated grid
Set the EGG for direct cooking with the porcelain coated grid.
Preheat the EGG to 350°F.

To make the sauce, combine the coconut milk, curry paste, and chicken stock in a small saucepan. Simmer on the stovetop over medium heat for 10 minutes, then keep warm.

Combine the basil, mint, cilantro, ginger, garlic, and jalapeño in a medium bowl and mix well. Lay the banana leaves out flat. Place 3 to 4 tablespoons of the herb mixture on the center of each leaf. Put a piece of fish on top of each mound of herbs, and top with 2 lime slices and ½ teaspoon of canola oil. Season with salt and pepper. For each packet, fold the sides of the leaf inward, fold the top and bottom over, tuck the ends under, and secure the leaf with butcher's twine.

Brush the leaves with the remaining canola oil and place on the grid. Close the lid of the EGG and grill for 7 to 8 minutes per side, until the interior of the fish is opaque (unwrap a package and insert a knife into the fish). Transfer the fish to individual plates, remove the twine, open the top, and spoon the sauce over the fish. Serve immediately. **Serves 4**

Whole Snapper with Lemon & Rosemary

Here is an uncomplicated recipe that is very healthful, looks beautiful, and tastes terrific. The fish you purchase should be fresh, as indicated by eyes that are crystal clear rather than milky. If your local fish market does not carry whole snapper, you can ask to order it. For extra flavor and an unusual presentation, after grilling the fish on the first side, turn the fish over and place thin slices of lemon over the entire body of the fish, much like scales, then place the whole fish on the grill pan and continue cooking.

Ingredients

1 (4 to 5-pound) whole snapper, cleaned and
   scales removed
10 cloves garlic, thinly sliced
1 lemon, thinly sliced
10 sprigs rosemary, leaves only
¼ cup plus ¼ cup extra-virgin olive oil
Kosher salt and freshly ground black pepper
¼ cup freshly squeezed lemon juice (from 1 to 2 lemons)
2 tablespoons water

Equipment: Porcelain coated grid, perforated grill pan
Set the EGG for direct cooking with the porcelain coated grid.
Preheat the EGG to 350°F.

Rinse the fish under cold water and pat dry with paper towels.

Make 3 to 4 slits vertically down to the bone on both sides of the fish. Place garlic slices, lemon slices, and a pinch of rosemary inside each slit. Drizzle the fish with ¼ cup of the olive oil and season with salt and pepper. Place any remaining garlic slices, lemon slices, and rosemary leaves inside the cavity of the fish.

Place the fish on the grid. Close the lid of the EGG and grill for 10 minutes per side. Transfer the fish to the grill pan. Close the lid and continue cooking for 30 minutes, or until the fish is opaque. Transfer the fish to a platter.

Using a whisk, mix the remaining ¼ cup olive oil, the lemon juice, and water in a small bowl. Pour the sauce over the grilled fish and serve immediately. **Serves 4**

Cioppino

Cioppino is an Italian-inspired fish stew usually made from leftover chopped fish. It was thought to have originated in San Francisco, where it was prepared on fishing boats by Italian immigrants. This very forgiving stew will work well with any fresh fish or seafood that you want to include.

Ingredients

¼ cup extra-virgin olive oil
8 ounces red snapper, cut into 2-inch cubes
6 ounces halibut, cut into 2-inch cubes
12 sea scallops
1 cup diced yellow onions
1 thinly sliced fennel bulb, fronds reserved
1 tablespoon minced garlic
2 cups white wine
1 cup water
1 cup Pernod
1 cup clam juice
1 (28-ounce) can crushed San Marzano tomatoes
1 pinch saffron
¼ cup firmly packed fresh tarragon leaves
12 clams, scrubbed
12 mussels, scrubbed and beards removed
12 large shrimp, peeled and deveined
4 ounces calamari, cut into rings
½ cup firmly packed torn fresh basil leaves
6 (1-inch-thick) slices ciabatta bread, grilled

Equipment: Porcelain coated grid, Dutch Oven
Set the EGG for direct cooking with the porcelain coated grid.
Preheat the EGG to 400°F.

Place the Dutch Oven on the grid to preheat for 10 minutes.

Pour the olive oil into the Dutch Oven. Add the snapper and halibut. Close the lid of the EGG and sear for 2 minutes. Turn the fish over, close the lid of the EGG, and sear for 2 more minutes. Transfer the fish to a plate and set aside. Add the scallops to the Dutch Oven and sear for 30 seconds. Turn the scallops over and cook for another 30 seconds. Transfer the scallops to the plate with the fish and cover with plastic wrap. Refrigerate until needed.

Add the onions, fennel, and garlic to the Dutch Oven and sauté for 1 minute. Carefully add the wine, water, Pernod, clam juice, tomatoes, saffron, and tarragon and mix well. Close the lid of the EGG and simmer uncovered for 20 minutes. Add the clams, close the lid of the EGG, and cook for 3 minutes. Add the mussels and shrimp, close the lid of the EGG, and cook for 3 minutes. Add the reserved fish and scallops and the calamari and basil. Close the lid of the EGG and cook for another 2 minutes. Place the bread slices on the Grid, around the Dutch Oven, and toast for 30 seconds per side. Remove the Dutch Oven and transfer the bread to a rimmed sheet pan.

To assemble, place a piece of the toasted bread in the bottom of each bowl, spoon the stew over the bread, sprinkle with the fennel fronds, and serve. **Serves 4**

Cedar-Wrapped Scallops with Orange Beurre Blanc

The slightly sweet and creamy sea scallop is the largest of all the scallops. These are wrapped in cedar grilling papers, then placed on the grid. The papers not only impart a woodsy taste but also make for a beautiful presentation. These scallops are served with an orange beurre blanc sauce, a classic white butter sauce infused with orange zest. They could be served as an appetizer or for a main course.

Ingredients

Orange Beurre Blanc
1 to 1½ teaspoons orange zest
⅓ cup sliced shallots
5 sprigs thyme
1 bay leaf
5 black peppercorns
1 cup white wine
½ cup heavy cream
8 tablespoons unsalted butter, cubed
1 teaspoon granulated sugar
Kosher salt and freshly ground black pepper

2 pounds jumbo sea scallops (about 20)
2 tablespoons plus 2 tablespoons extra-virgin olive oil
Kosher salt and freshly ground black pepper

Equipment: Porcelain coated grid, cedar grilling papers
Set the EGG for direct cooking with the porcelain coated grid.
Preheat the EGG to 400°F.

Place the cedar papers in a bowl, cover with water, and soak for 10 minutes.

To make the sauce, place the orange zest, shallots, thyme, bay leaf, peppercorns, and wine in a small saucepan on the stovetop over medium heat. Simmer for 10 minutes, or until most of the wine has evaporated. Add the cream and simmer for 5 to 7 minutes, until thickened. Remove the pan from the heat and whisk the butter into the sauce a little at a time. Add the sugar, season with salt and pepper, and mix well. Strain the sauce into a small bowl and keep in a warm place until ready to serve.

Brush the scallops with 2 tablespoons of the olive oil and season with salt and pepper on both sides. Place 3 scallops in the center of each cedar paper. Wrap the paper around the scallops and secure the paper in place using butcher's twine. Brush the outside of the cedar wraps with the remaining 2 tablespoons olive oil.

Place the scallop wraps on the grid. Close the lid of the EGG and grill for 3 minutes on each side, then open a wrap and slide a small knife into a scallop to check the interior.

Transfer the wraps to individual plates. Serve immediately with the sauce on the side. **Serves 4**

Glazed Lobster Salad
with Hearts of Palm & Grapefruit

This lobster salad makes a great luncheon salad. It can also be made using Grilled Whole Lobster (page 129) instead of just tails. For a complete meal, serve this with an Apple-Walnut Crostata (page 255) for dessert.

Ingredients

Pink Brandy Sauce

½ cup sour cream
¼ cup mayonnaise
3 tablespoons ketchup
1 teaspoon freshly squeezed lemon juice
1½ teaspoons brandy
½ teaspoon dry mustard
Kosher salt and freshly ground black pepper

Vinaigrette

½ cup freshly squeezed or bottled grapefruit juice
2 tablespoons champagne vinegar
1 teaspoon granulated sugar
½ cup canola oil
Kosher salt and freshly ground black pepper

1 (14-ounce) can hearts of palm
½ cup julienned red bell pepper
½ cup julienned orange bell pepper
½ cup julienned yellow bell pepper
1 cup julienned English cucumber
2 shallots, peeled and thinly sliced
2 ruby red grapefruit, peeled and segmented
4 (4-ounce) lobster tails
2 tablespoons extra-virgin olive oil
Old Bay seasoning
Kosher salt and freshly ground black pepper
1 tablespoon chopped fresh tarragon
4 butter lettuce leaves
1 tablespoon thinly sliced fresh chives

Equipment: Porcelain coated grid
Set the EGG for direct cooking with the porcelain coated grid.
Preheat the EGG to 500°F.

To make the sauce, mix the sour cream, mayonnaise, ketchup, lemon juice, brandy, and mustard in a small bowl and season with salt and pepper. Cover the bowl with plastic wrap and refrigerate until ready to serve.

To make the vinaigrette, combine the grapefruit juice, vinegar, sugar, and oil in a small bowl, mix well, and season with salt and pepper. Refrigerate until ready to serve.

Place the hearts of palm on the grid and grill, turning constantly, for 1 to 2 minutes. Using tongs, transfer them to a cutting board and slice diagonally. In a bowl, mix the hearts of palm, peppers, cucumber, shallots, and grapefruit.

Brush the lobster with the olive oil and season with Old Bay seasoning and salt and pepper. Place the lobster tails on the grid. Close the lid of the EGG and grill for about 4 minutes on each side.

Using kitchen scissors, cut along the underside of the tail from end to end, removing the underside of the shell but leaving the back of the shell and the bottom tail fan intact.

To assemble, whisk the tarragon into the vinaigrette, pour over the salad, and toss to coat. Place 2 tablespoons of the sauce in the center of each plate. Put a lettuce leaf on the sauce and ¾ cup of the salad inside the lettuce leaf. Top each salad with a lobster tail, garnish with chives, and serve. **Serves 4**

(See recipe photograph on page 114.)

Grilled Whole Lobster

Fresh lobster does not need a lot of ingredients to enhance its flavor. The meat is firm and sweet and is usually served with melted butter. Whole lobsters must be purchased live. It is difficult to find a more elegant dish than grilled lobster for a special-occasion luncheon or dinner.

Ingredients
1 cup unsalted butter
4 (1½-pound) live lobsters
Kosher salt and freshly ground black pepper
1 cup heavy cream
1 lemon, cut into 8 wedges

Equipment: Porcelain coated grid
Set the EGG for direct cooking with the
porcelain coated grid.
Preheat the EGG to 500°F.

To clarify the butter, melt it in a small saucepan on the stovetop over low heat. Skim the foam from the top with a spoon. Pour the melted butter into a glass measuring cup and refrigerate until it becomes solid. Poke a hole through the butter to the bottom of the cup with a knife; this will release the milk solids underneath. Pour the milk solids out and discard; the remaining butter is clarified. Melt the clarified butter.

Wearing heavy gloves, place one of the lobsters on a cutting board and hold the lobster firmly with the head toward you. Insert the tip of a sharp knife into the center of the head and quickly bring the knife down to the board. Split the front of the lobster in half, then split the tail of the lobster in half, lengthwise, leaving some of the shell unsplit in the center of the body. Repeat for the other lobsters.

Brush the inside of the lobsters with the clarified butter and season with salt and pepper. Place the lobster on the grid, meat side up, and pour ¼ cup of the cream into the cavities and over the meat. Close the lid of the EGG and cook for 8 to 10 minutes, brushing the lobster with the remaining cream every 2 minutes.

Transfer the lobsters to a platter and serve with the remaining clarified butter and lemon wedges. **Serves 4**

Greek Shrimp & Orzo Salad

Orzo is a type of pasta the size and shape of a grain of rice. It is used throughout the Middle East and the Mediterranean and is particularly popular in Greece. This orzo salad is loaded with other ingredients that are commonly used throughout Mediterranean countries—artichokes, garbanzo beans, mint, dill, and kalamata olives. Removing the pits from kalamata olives is easy. Just set the olive on a cutting board and hit it with the flat side of a large knife. The pit can then be easily separated. The salad will be most delicious if the shrimp are cooked just before needed: Chilling shrimp permanently hardens them.

Ingredients

1 pound large shrimp, peeled and deveined
1 tablespoon extra-virgin olive oil
Kosher salt and freshly ground black pepper
1½ cups whole wheat orzo, cooked according to
   package directions
1 cup peeled and diced English cucumber
1 cup halved grape tomatoes
1 cup drained canned garbanzo beans
1 cup drained, chopped canned artichoke hearts
1 cup pitted and chopped kalamata olives
1 cup crumbled feta cheese
½ cup thinly sliced red onion
2 tablespoons chopped fresh dill
2 tablespoons chopped fresh mint
¼ cup freshly squeezed lemon juice (from 1 to 2 lemons)
¼ cup red wine vinegar
1 teaspoon Dijon mustard
½ cup extra-virgin olive oil
1 tablespoon minced garlic

**Equipment: Porcelain coated grid,
   6 bamboo or metal skewers
Set the EGG for direct cooking with the
   porcelain coated grid.
Preheat the EGG to 500°F.**

If using bamboo skewers, place the skewers in a pan, cover with water, and let soak for 1 hour.

Place the shrimp on the skewers. Brush them with olive oil and season with salt and pepper. Place the skewers on the grid. Close the lid of the EGG and grill for 2 minutes on each side. Transfer the skewers to a rimmed sheet pan. Remove the shrimp from the skewers and place them in a large bowl. Add the orzo, cucumber, tomatoes, garbanzo beans, artichoke hearts, olives, cheese, onion, dill, and mint to the bowl and toss to blend.

Combine the lemon juice, vinegar, mustard, olive oil, and garlic in a small bowl and whisk to combine. Pour the dressing over the orzo salad and toss well. Season with salt and pepper and serve. **Serves 4**

"The Big Green Egg is the most versatile cooker I have ever used. In very little time you will be enjoying food prepared on it more than restaurant food." —Wess, Maryland

Grilled Oysters with Pink Peppercorn Mignonette

This is an easy and delicious way to cook oysters, but make sure that the oysters you purchase are fresh and still alive. To ensure freshness, tap the top of the shell with your fingers. If the oyster is still alive, it will shut its shell tightly; if it does not, discard it. Prior to grilling, keep the oysters in the refrigerator. Store them with the cupped-shell side down so that the liquid does not leak out, or they will become dry. After grilling, discard any unopened oysters, as this is an indication that the oyster is not safe to eat. This dish can be served as an appetizer or main course. Just remember that the cooking time will vary depending on the size of your oysters.

Ingredients

½ cup champagne vinegar
¼ cup minced shallots
1 tablespoon pink peppercorns, crushed
¼ cup minced fresh chervil or fresh flat-leaf parsley
48 fresh oysters

Equipment: Porcelain coated grid
Set the EGG for direct cooking with the
porcelain coated grid.
Preheat the EGG to 500°F.

To make the sauce, combine the vinegar, shallots, peppercorns, and chervil in a small bowl and refrigerate.

Place the oysters on the grid. Close the lid of the EGG and grill for 3 to 4 minutes, until the shells open and release steam. Transfer to a platter. If you have any oysters that do not open, try cooking for a minute or two longer. If they still do not open, discard, as they are not edible. For each oyster, remove the top lid of the shell and separate the oyster from the bottom shell, but do not remove it.

Spoon 1 teaspoon of the sauce over each oyster. Serve the oysters immediately in their shells. **Serves 4**

eggxotic!

vegetarian meals

recipes

Grilled Vegetable Lasagna

Layers of lasagna noodles are interspersed with grilled vegetables, cheese, and tomato sauce, then blanketed with Mornay sauce, for this vegetarian version of lasagna. Although lasagna noodles are used in this recipe, wonton skins, prepared according to package instructions, make a perfect and lighter substitute for traditional lasagna noodles. This dish can be made ahead of time and reheated for a quick weeknight dinner.

Ingredients

1 tablespoon plus ¼ cup extra-virgin olive oil
10 ounces fresh spinach leaves, washed and dried
2 zucchini, quartered lengthwise
2 yellow crookneck squash, quartered lengthwise
2 Japanese eggplants, quartered lengthwise
1½ cups portobello mushrooms, gills removed (6 ounces)
1½ teaspoons garlic powder
Kosher salt and freshly ground black pepper
2 roasted red bell peppers, chopped (page 170)
2 cups ricotta cheese (1 pound)
½ cup goat cheese (2 ounces), at room temperature
1 large egg
½ cup firmly packed fresh basil leaves, chopped
1 tablespoon fresh thyme leaves, chopped

Mornay Sauce
2 tablespoons unsalted butter
2 tablespoons all-purpose flour
1¼ cups whole milk
½ cup grated Parmigiano-Reggiano cheese (2 ounces)
¼ teaspoon ground nutmeg
¼ teaspoon freshly ground white pepper

5 cups Garden-Fresh Tomato Sauce (page 199)
1 pound lasagna noodles, cooked according to package directions
1 cup shredded mozzarella cheese (4 ounces)

> **Equipment: Porcelain coated grid, Grill Gripper, Plate Setter, 9 by 13-inch glass or ceramic baking dish**
> **Set the EGG for direct cooking with the porcelain coated grid.**
> **Preheat the EGG to 500°F.**

Heat 1 tablespoon of the olive oil in a large sauté pan on the stovetop over medium heat. Add the spinach and cook for 2 to 3 minutes, until wilted. Set aside.

Brush the zucchini, squash, eggplant, and mushrooms with the remaining ¼ cup olive oil and season with the garlic powder and salt and pepper. Place the vegetables on the grid. Close the lid of the EGG and grill for 2 minutes per side. Transfer the vegetables to a rimmed sheet pan and let cool slightly.

Using the Grill Gripper and barbecue mitts, carefully remove the grid and add the Plate Setter, legs down. Lower the temperature to 350°F.

(continued on page 138)

"The beauty of the Big Green Egg is that it holds heat so well, much better than a metal grill." —Paul, Michigan

Grilled Vegetable Lasagna *(continued)*

Dice the zucchini, squash, eggplant, and mushrooms into ½-inch cubes and place in a large bowl. Add the bell peppers and spinach and stir to incorporate. Combine the ricotta cheese, goat cheese, egg, basil, and thyme in a small bowl. Season with salt and pepper and mix well. Set aside.

To make the Mornay sauce, melt the butter in a small saucepan on the stovetop. Add the flour and cook on low heat for 3 minutes, or until the roux is bubbly and the flour is no longer raw. Using a whisk, add the milk. Simmer for 5 minutes, or until thick. Remove the pan from the heat and add the cheese, nutmeg, and pepper. Stir well to combine.

Reserve 2 cups of tomato sauce and keep warm in a small saucepan on the stovetop over low heat. To assemble the lasagna, spread 1 cup of the tomato sauce over the bottom of the baking dish. Add layers, starting with one-third of the noodles, then adding one-half of the grilled vegetables and 1 cup of the tomato sauce. Make 1 more layer and top the layer of tomato sauce with the remaining noodles.

Pour the Mornay sauce evenly over the lasagna ingredients and sprinkle with the mozzarella cheese. Place the baking dish on the Plate Setter and close the lid of the EGG. Bake for 45 minutes, or until the cheese is melted and the lasagna is thoroughly heated. Remove the baking dish and allow the lasagna to rest for 10 minutes.

Cut into 3 by 4-inch pieces and serve with the remaining heated tomato sauce. **Serves 8**

Spinach & Mushroom Quesadillas

This recipe takes a traditional quesadilla and adds sautéed spinach, wild mushrooms, and goat cheese to the mix. The filling is placed in a flour tortilla and grilled until the cheese is melted and yummy. Serve this with a side of homemade spicy tomato salsa.

Ingredients

Tomato Salsa (optional)
1 jalapeño, seeded and chopped
2 cups chopped tomatoes
3 cloves garlic
¼ cup chopped yellow onion
2 tablespoons freshly squeezed lime juice (1 to 2 limes)
½ cup firmly packed fresh cilantro leaves
Kosher salt and freshly ground black pepper

¼ cup extra-virgin olive oil plus extra for brushing
½ cup chopped red onion
4 cups mixed mushrooms (such as cremini, oyster, and shiitake), wild or cultivated
1 tablespoon minced garlic
1 pound fresh spinach leaves, washed and dried
4 (10-inch) flour tortillas
1 pound white American cheese, shredded
2 cups crumbled goat cheese (8 ounces)
Lime wedges

> **Equipment: Porcelain coated grid, Dutch Oven, Half Moon Griddle**
> **Set the EGG for direct cooking with the porcelain coated grid.**
> **Preheat the EGG to 400°F.**

Place the Dutch Oven on the grid and preheat for 10 minutes.

To make the salsa, place the pepper, tomatoes, and garlic in a small saucepan on the stovetop over medium heat. Simmer for 15 minutes, or until the peppers are tender and the skin begins to peel off the tomatoes. Strain the ingredients and remove the skins from the tomatoes. Place the tomato mixture, onion, lime juice, and cilantro in the bowl of a food processor fitted with the steel blade and pulse for 30 seconds. Season with salt and pepper.

Heat the ¼ cup of the olive oil in the Dutch Oven and add the onion and mushrooms. Close the lid of the EGG and cook slowly for 10 minutes, or until the onion is browned. Add the garlic and cook for 1 minute. Add the spinach and cook until it is wilted. Remove the Dutch Oven from the grid. Using a strainer, drain the mushroom mixture well and transfer it to a medium bowl to cool.

To assemble, spoon 1 cup of the American cheese in the center of each tortilla, place one-quarter of the mushroom mixture in each center, add the goat cheese, and fold the tortillas in half. Brush each outside surface with olive oil.

Place the Griddle on the grid to preheat for 10 minutes. Place two stuffed tortillas on the Griddle. Close the lid of the EGG and grill for 2 minutes per side, until the tortillas are golden brown and the cheese is melted. Transfer the quesadillas to a platter, and cook the other two tortillas.

Transfer the quesadillas to the same platter and cut each one into 4 wedges. Serve with salsa and lime wedges.
Serves 4

Caramelized Onion Tart

Caramelized onions are the star of this show. Though caramelizing onions takes time and patience, the result is well worth the wait. These sweet and creamy onions are added to a custard base, placed in a buttery tart shell, and baked in the EGG until golden brown. Add a mixed green salad and dinner is ready!

Ingredients

¼ cup extra-virgin olive oil
2 pounds thinly sliced Vidalia or other sweet onions
1 tablespoon granulated sugar
2 teaspoons minced garlic
1 (11-inch) tart shell (page 223)
1 cup shredded Gruyère cheese (4 ounces)
⅓ cup ricotta cheese
1 cup heavy cream
6 large egg yolks
¼ cup minced fresh chives
¼ teaspoon ground nutmeg
½ teaspoon kosher salt
¼ teaspoon freshly ground black pepper
½ cup grated Parmigiano-Reggiano cheese (2 ounces)

Equipment: Plate Setter, Baking Stone, 11-inch round tart pan
Set the EGG for indirect cooking with the Plate Setter, legs down, and the Baking Stone on top of the Plate Setter.
Preheat the EGG to 400°F.

Heat the olive oil in a large sauté pan on the stovetop over medium heat. Add the onions, sugar, and garlic and mix well using a wooden spoon. Turn the heat to low and cook for 2 hours, or until the onions are soft and caramel in color. Strain the onions, discarding any liquid. Transfer the caramelized onions to the tart shell and spread evenly.

Sprinkle the Gruyère cheese over the onions, and distribute the ricotta cheese over the onion mixture by teaspoonfuls. In a small bowl, mix the cream, egg yolks, chives, nutmeg, salt, and pepper. Pour the cream mixture over the tart. Place the tart on the Baking Stone and close the lid of the EGG. Bake for 10 minutes. Sprinkle the Parmigiano-Reggiano cheese over the tart and bake for an additional 10 minutes, or until the tart is set.

Remove the tart and place on a cooling rack. Let rest for 10 minutes before slicing. **Serves 6**

Grilled Polenta with Puttanesca Sauce

Polenta is a northern Italian dish made by boiling cornmeal in milk, cream, or chicken stock. Use high-quality, stone-ground yellow cornmeal for this polenta, which is first boiled and then baked. Serve this dish with the robust red sauce enhanced with capers and olives. Carefully follow the instructions for adding the eggs to the polenta to keep the eggs from curdling.

Ingredients

Puttanesca Sauce

1 tablespoon extra-virgin olive oil
1 tablespoon minced garlic
½ cup thinly sliced red onion
½ cup white wine
1 (12-ounce) can crushed tomatoes
1 roasted red bell pepper, chopped (page 170)
½ cup chopped assorted olives
2 tablespoons capers
¼ cup freshly squeezed lemon juice (1 to 2 lemons)
¼ cup firmly packed fresh basil leaves, rolled and
   thinly sliced
Kosher salt and freshly ground black pepper

Polenta

2 cups whole milk
2 cups chicken stock
1 cup polenta (not quick-cooking)
1 cup shredded fontina cheese (4 ounces)
½ cup grated Parmigiano-Reggiano cheese (2 ounces)
½ cup mascarpone cheese (4 ounces)
3 tablespoons extra-virgin olive oil
Kosher salt and freshly ground black pepper
4 large eggs, at room temperature
¼ cup shaved Parmigiano-Reggiano cheese (1 ounce)
¼ cup firmly packed fresh basil leaves, for garnish

Equipment: Plate Setter, oiled 8-inch square glass or ceramic baking dish
Set the EGG for indirect cooking with the Plate Setter, legs down.
Preheat the EGG to 350°F.

To make the sauce, place the olive oil, garlic, and onion in a medium saucepan on the stovetop and sauté over medium heat for 3 to 4 minutes. Add the wine, tomatoes, bell pepper, olives, and capers and simmer for 20 minutes, or until the sauce has thickened. Remove from the heat and stir in the lemon juice and basil. Season with salt and pepper and set aside.

To make the polenta, simmer the milk and chicken stock in a large saucepan on the stovetop over medium-low heat. Slowly add the polenta and cook, stirring, for 20 minutes, or until thick and creamy. Add the fontina, grated Parmigiano-Reggiano, and mascarpone cheeses and the olive oil to the pan. Season with salt and pepper and stir well. Using a whisk, beat the eggs in a small bowl and slowly add 1 cup of the polenta to the eggs, whisking constantly. Once incorporated, add the egg mixture back into the saucepan of polenta and stir until blended.

Pour the polenta into the prepared baking dish and spread evenly, using a spatula. Place the pan on the Plate Setter. Close the lid of the EGG and bake for 30 minutes, or until the polenta is firm. Remove the polenta and let cool for 10 minutes before serving.

To assemble, spoon ½ half cup polenta onto individual plates. Top with the sauce and shaved Parmigiano-Reggiano cheese, and garnish with basil leaves. **Serves 6**

Eggplant Rollatini

Rollatini is an Italian dish made of thin slices of eggplant that have been covered with cheese and then rolled and baked. For this dish, there is no need to salt the eggplant to reduce any bitterness. The EGG does a superb job of grilling eggplant—it turns out tender with a wonderful subtle smokiness. The peel of the eggplant is edible, so it is not necessary to peel it before cooking.

Ingredients

1 (2-pound) eggplant, cut lengthwise into ⅛-inch-thick slices (16 slices)

¼ cup extra-virgin olive oil

Kosher salt and freshly ground black pepper

1 large egg, beaten

2 cups shredded mozzarella cheese (8 ounces)

1 cup whole milk ricotta cheese (8 ounces)

¼ cup plus ¼ cup grated Romano cheese (2 ounces total)

½ cup firmly packed fresh basil leaves, rolled and thinly sliced

1½ cups Spicy San Marzano Tomato Sauce (page 200)

Equipment: Porcelain coated grid, Grill Gripper, Plate Setter, 9 by 13-inch glass or ceramic baking dish
Set the EGG for direct cooking with the porcelain coated grid.
Preheat the EGG to 500°F.

Brush the eggplant slices on both sides with the olive oil and season with salt and pepper. Place the eggplant on the grid. Close the lid of the EGG and grill for 2 minutes per side, or until tender. Transfer to a rimmed sheet pan and let cool.

Using the Grill Gripper and barbecue mitts, carefully remove the grid and add the Plate Setter, legs down. Raise the temperature to 600°F.

Mix the egg, mozzarella cheese, ricotta cheese, ¼ cup of the Romano cheese, and the basil in a small bowl. Season with salt and pepper and mix well. Place ½ cup of the Spicy San Marzano Tomato Sauce in the bottom of the baking dish. Place 2 tablespoons of the cheese mixture on one end of each slice of eggplant and roll the eggplant toward the other end. Repeat the process until all the eggplant is rolled. Place the eggplant, seam side down, in the pan, forming 2 rows. Ladle the remaining 1 cup tomato sauce over the top of the eggplant and sprinkle with the remaining ¼ cup of Romano cheese.

Place the baking dish on the Plate Setter. Close the lid of the EGG and bake for 15 minutes, or until the eggplant is thoroughly heated and the cheese is melted. Remove the baking dish and let the eggplant rest for 10 minutes before serving. Serve 4 rolls per person. **Serves 4**

Root Vegetable Pot Pie

Root vegetables are used to great effect in this rustic pot pie. Celery root, also known as celeriac, is combined in a creamy sauce with turnips, parsnips, and carrots, all of which impart a subtle sweet taste to an otherwise very savory pie. A glass of red wine and a roaring fire are all you will need to accompany this cool-weather dish.

Ingredients

¼ cup extra-virgin olive oil
1 cup diced red onions
1 cup diced celery
1 cup diced carrots
1 tablespoon minced garlic
¼ cup all-purpose flour
3 cups chicken stock
1 cup diced parsnips
1 cup diced turnips
1 cup diced celery root
1 cup diced russet potatoes
1 cup diced yams
⅓ cup heavy cream
2 tablespoons unsalted butter
¼ cup minced chives
Kosher salt and freshly ground black pepper
1 (9-inch) pie shell and 1 pie dough disk (page 223)
1 large egg
1 tablespoon water

> **Equipment: Porcelain coated grid, Dutch Oven, Grill Gripper, Plate Setter, 9-inch glass or ceramic deep-dish pie plate**
> **Set the EGG for direct cooking with the porcelain coated grid.**
> **Preheat the EGG to 400°F.**

Place the Dutch Oven on the grid and preheat for 10 minutes.

Heat the olive oil in the Dutch Oven. Add the onions, celery, and carrots. Close the lid of the EGG and sauté for 3 to 4 minutes, until the vegetables begin to brown. Add the garlic and continue to cook for 1 minute. Add the flour and stir until blended. Slowly add the chicken stock and simmer until the sauce has thickened. Add the parsnips, turnips, celery root, potatoes, and yams, cover the Dutch Oven, and close the lid of the EGG. Simmer, stirring occasionally, for 15 minutes, or until the vegetables can easily be pierced with a fork.

Remove the Dutch Oven from the heat and add the cream, butter, and chives, and season with salt and pepper. Let cool slightly.

Using the Grill Gripper and barbecue mitts, carefully remove the grid and add the Plate Setter, legs down.

Spoon the vegetables into the pie shell. Roll out the pie dough disk on a lightly floured surface until it is large enough to cover the top of the pie. Press the top and bottom edges of the dough together and crimp. Using a paring knife, add small vent holes to the top of the pie crust or prick with the tines of a fork. Mix the egg and water in a small bowl and brush the top of the crust with the egg wash.

Place the pie on the Plate Setter. Close the lid of the EGG and bake for 20 minutes, or until the crust is golden brown. Remove the pie and let rest for 15 minutes before serving. **Serves 4 to 6**

Veggie Noodle Stir-Fry

Use a vegetable peeler to slice the carrots, zucchini, and squash into wide, thin ribbons, then cut the ribbons lengthwise into thin julienned slices with a knife. You will have a medley of brightly colored vegetables all intertwined like long, thin, beautiful noodles. This is a dish that cooks in a matter of minutes and would go well as a side dish with roasted chicken or pork.

Ingredients

Sauce
½ cup freshly squeezed lemon juice (3 lemons)
½ cup freshly squeezed orange juice (1 orange)
½ cup rice wine vinegar
½ cup soy sauce
4 teaspoons red curry paste

½ cup peanut oil
1 cup sliced shallots
2 tablespoons minced fresh ginger
2 teaspoons minced garlic
2 cups julienned red bell pepper
2 cups snow peas
4 cups julienned napa cabbage
2 cups julienned carrots
2 cups julienned zucchini
2 cups julienned yellow crookneck squash
4 cups bean sprouts
18 to 20 scallions, green parts only,
   cut in half lengthwise
1 cup firmly packed fresh basil leaves
1 cup firmly packed fresh cilantro leaves
½ cup firmly packed fresh mint leaves
1 cup thinly sliced red radishes
1 cup chopped peanuts

Equipment: Porcelain coated grid, Dutch Oven
Set the EGG for direct cooking with the porcelain coated grid.
Preheat the EGG to 400°F.

Set the Dutch Oven on the grid and preheat for 10 minutes.

To make the sauce, use a whisk to stir the lemon juice, orange juice, vinegar, soy sauce, and red curry paste together in a small bowl.

Pour the peanut oil into the preheated Dutch Oven. Add the shallots, ginger, garlic, bell pepper, and snow peas. Close the lid of the EGG and sauté for 30 seconds. Add the cabbage, carrots, zucchini, squash, bean sprouts, and scallions and cook for 1 minute. Add the sauce and cook for 30 seconds. Remove the Dutch Oven from the heat, then add the basil, cilantro, and mint and stir.

Place the mixture in individual bowls and garnish with the radishes and peanuts. Serve immediately. **Serves 4 as a main course, or 8 as a side dish**

Dutch Oven Vegetable Fried Rice

The Dutch Oven is the ideal vessel to use when stir-frying in the EGG. Place it right on the grid to preheat it before adding the ingredients, and it's ready to go. A traditional wok with all-metal handles can also be used in lieu of the Dutch Oven. The fried rice is a great main course, but it also makes a great side dish to serve with Napa Cabbage Beef Wraps (page 73).

Ingredients
¼ cup peanut oil
1½ cups diced yellow onions
1½ cups diced carrots
1 tablespoon minced garlic
4 large eggs
1 tablespoon toasted sesame oil
2¾ cups uncooked long grain rice, cooked according to package directions and cooled
½ cup rice wine
⅓ cup soy sauce
1 cup English peas
½ cup thinly sliced scallions

Equipment: Porcelain coated grid, Dutch Oven or all-metal wok
Set the EGG for direct cooking with the porcelain coated grid.
Preheat the EGG to 500°F.

Preheat the Dutch Oven on the grid for 10 minutes.

Heat the peanut oil in the Dutch Oven and add the onions and carrots. Close the lid of the EGG and sauté for 3 to 4 minutes, until the carrots are tender. Add the garlic and cook for 1 minute, stirring occasionally. Using a wooden spoon, move the vegetables to the outer edges of the Dutch Oven, leaving the center exposed.

Using a whisk, beat the eggs and sesame oil in a small bowl. Pour the beaten eggs into the center of the Dutch Oven. Using a wooden spoon, stir until the eggs are scrambled.

Add the rice and rice wine. Close the lid of the EGG and and cook for 3 to 4 minutes, stirring often, until all the ingredients are combined. Add the soy sauce, peas, and scallions. Stir to combine and cook for 1 minute.

Transfer the rice to a bowl and serve immediately.
Serves 6 as a main course, or 8 as a side dish

Portobello Mushroom Burgers

Portobello mushrooms are large, meaty mushrooms that are substantial enough to substitute for meat in a burger. They are best marinated before grilling, so be sure to allow a little extra time for this process. These burgers are dressed with Muenster cheese, lettuce, and tomato, but you also could add Roasted Red Bell Peppers (page 170) and fresh spinach leaves.

Ingredients

1 tablespoon minced garlic
1 tablespoon minced fresh thyme
¼ cup soy sauce
¼ cup balsamic vinegar
¼ cup extra-virgin olive oil plus extra for brushing
4 large portobello mushrooms, gills and stems removed
½ cup mayonnaise
½ cup chopped fresh basil
1 tablespoon Dijon mustard
4 kaiser rolls
Kosher salt and freshly ground black pepper
4 thick slices red onion
4 slices Muenster cheese
1 beefsteak tomato, cut into 4 slices
4 green leaf lettuce leaves

Equipment: Cast Iron Grid
Set the EGG for direct cooking with the
    Cast Iron Grid.
Preheat the EGG to 400°F.

Whisk the garlic, thyme, soy sauce, vinegar, and olive oil in a small bowl. Place the mushrooms in a resealable plastic bag and pour the marinade over the mushrooms. Seal the bag and marinate for a minimum of 30 minutes or up to 1 hour.

Combine the mayonnaise, basil, and mustard in a small bowl. Set aside. Brush the insides of the rolls with olive oil and set aside. Remove the mushrooms from the marinade and season with salt and pepper. Place the mushrooms and onion slices on the Grid. Close the lid of the EGG and grill for 2 minutes on each side, until the mushrooms are tender. Place a slice of cheese on top of each mushroom and close the lid of the EGG for 1 minute. Open the lid and place the rolls on the Grid, cut sides down. Close the lid of the EGG and grill for 30 seconds, or until the rolls are lightly toasted. Transfer the mushrooms, onions, and rolls to a platter.

To assemble, spread the inside of the rolls with the basil mayonnaise. Place a mushroom on the bottom of each roll, top with a tomato slice, a lettuce leaf, and an onion slice. Serve immediately. **Serves 4**

Veggie Burgers

Packed with wholesome goodness, this is the perfect veggie burger! These burgers begin with brown rice and black beans and take off from there. The burger is finished with a hoisin glaze, placed on a toasted bun, and dressed like a traditional burger. Healthy never tasted so good! Do not be daunted by the ingredients list. It is mostly measure-and-stir!

Ingredients

½ cup brown rice, cooked and chilled

1 (15-ounce) can black beans, drained and rinsed

¼ cup Basic Barbecue Sauce (page 192)

¼ cup diced mixed mushrooms (such as white and cremini)

¼ cup quick-cooking oats

¼ cup plain dried bread crumbs, purchased or homemade

2 tablespoons minced roasted beets (page 175)

2 tablespoons finely chopped golden raisins

1 tablespoon grated yellow onion

1 tablespoon minced garlic

1 teaspoon chili powder

1 teaspoon kosher salt

¼ teaspoon ground cumin

¼ teaspoon freshly ground black pepper

2 tablespoons soy sauce

2 tablespoons hoisin sauce

1 tablespoon molasses

4 whole wheat buns

4 lettuce leaves

4 tomato slices

4 slices red onion

Equipment: Cast Iron Grid
Set the EGG for direct cooking with the Cast Iron Grid.
Preheat the EGG to 350°F.

Mix the brown rice, black beans, barbecue sauce, mushrooms, oats, bread crumbs, beets, raisins, onion, garlic, chili powder, salt, cumin, and pepper in a medium bowl. Let rest for 10 minutes. Using a whisk, combine the soy sauce, hoisin sauce, and molasses in a small bowl and set aside.

Divide the rice mixture into 4 equal parts and form patties. Place the burgers on the Grid. Close the lid of the EGG and cook for 3 minutes. Turn the burgers over and brush with the hoisin glaze. Close the lid of the EGG and continue cooking for 3 more minutes, or until heated through.

To assemble, place the cut sides of the buns on the Grid. Close the lid of the EGG and grill for 30 seconds, or until lightly toasted. Using a long-handled spatula, transfer the burgers to a rimmed sheet pan and brush each burger with more glaze. Transfer the toasted buns to a platter and place a burger on the bottom half of each bun. Top each burger with a lettuce leaf, a tomato slice, and an onion slice, and the top half of the bun. Serve immediately.
Serves 4

Vegetable Reuben Sandwich

You won't miss the corned beef in this vegetarian version of a classic Reuben sandwich. Marbled rye bread is the landing pad for sautéed mushrooms, peppers, spinach, and onions that are topped with Swiss cheese and sauerkraut, then grilled until warm and toasty.

Ingredients

Dressing
½ cup mayonnaise
¼ cup ketchup
¼ cup sweet relish
1 teaspoon prepared horseradish
½ teaspoon chili garlic sauce
½ teaspoon Worcestershire sauce

2 tablespoons extra-virgin olive oil
4 cups thinly sliced white mushrooms
1 cup sliced red onions
2 teaspoons minced garlic
½ roasted red bell pepper, chopped (page 170)
10 ounces fresh spinach leaves, washed and dried
Kosher salt and freshly ground black pepper
8 slices marbled rye bread
8 slices Swiss cheese
1 cup fresh sauerkraut
4 tablespoons unsalted butter

Equipment: Porcelain coated grid, Dutch Oven, Half Moon Griddle
Set the EGG for direct cooking with the porcelain coated grid.
Preheat the EGG to 400°F.

Place the Dutch Oven on the grid and preheat for 10 minutes.

To make the dressing, combine the mayonnaise, ketchup, relish, horseradish, chili garlic sauce, and Worcestershire sauce in a small bowl and mix well.

Place the olive oil in the Dutch Oven and add the mushrooms, onions, and garlic. Close the lid of the EGG and sauté for 3 to 4 minutes, until caramelized. Add the bell pepper and spinach, close the lid of the EGG, and cook for 2 to 3 minutes. Season with salt and pepper.

Remove the Dutch Oven and put the Griddle on the grid.

To assemble, spread 4 slices of bread on one side with 2 teaspoons of the dressing each. Place a slice of cheese on top of each slice of bread, followed by one-quarter of the spinach mixture and ¼ cup of the sauerkraut. Place another slice of cheese over the sauerkraut and top with a slice of bread.

Melt 2 tablespoons of butter on the Griddle. Place two sandwiches on the Griddle, close the lid of the EGG, and cook for 1 minute on each side. Transfer the sandwiches to a platter. Melt the remaining 2 tablespoons of butter on the Griddle and cook the other two sandwiches. Remove and serve immediately. **Serves 4**

eggstensive!

side dishes

recipes

Barbecued Baked Beans

Once you make homemade baked beans in the EGG, you will never again settle for just opening a can of beans off the shelf. Cannellini beans (Italian white beans) are blended with applewood-smoked bacon in a rich, smoky sauce that's near perfection. Serve these with Barbecued Beef Ribs (page 56) or Shredded Pork Sandwich with Fennel Slaw (page 90).

Equipment: Porcelain coated grid, Dutch Oven
Set the EGG for direct cooking with the porcelain coated grid.
Preheat the EGG to 400°F.

Ingredients

12 ounces applewood-smoked bacon
   (12 to 14 slices), diced
2 cups finely diced yellow onions
3 cups Basic Barbecue Sauce (page 192)
1 cup firmly packed light brown sugar
½ cup maple syrup
½ cup yellow mustard
4 (15-ounce) cans cannellini beans, drained and rinsed,
   1 cup bean liquid reserved
1 cup water
Kosher salt and freshly ground black pepper

Place the Dutch Oven on the grid and preheat for 10 minutes.

Add the bacon to the Dutch Oven. Close the lid of the EGG and cook until crisp. Transfer the bacon with a slotted spoon to a paper towel to drain and set aside, reserving the fat in the Dutch Oven. Add the onions to the bacon fat. Close the lid of the EGG and cook for 8 minutes, or until caramelized.

Add the reserved bacon, barbecue sauce, brown sugar, maple syrup, mustard, reserved cannellini bean liquid, and water to the Dutch Oven, and mix well. Add the cannellini beans and stir. Cover the Dutch Oven. Close the lid of the EGG and cook for 30 minutes, stirring occasionally. Remove the lid of the Dutch Oven, close the lid of the EGG, and simmer, continuing to stir, for 15 minutes, or until the sauce has thickened. Season with salt and pepper when the beans are nearly done. Let the beans rest for 10 minutes before serving. **Serves 8**

Twice-Baked Potatoes with Smoked Gouda & Grilled Scallions

Smoked Gouda is the secret ingredient in these twice-baked potatoes. Loaded with butter, heavy cream, and cheese, these might be the most decadent potatoes you have ever tasted. They would be perfect served with Standing Rib Roast (page 70) at a dinner party or with a simple grilled steak.

Ingredients

3 large russet potatoes (about 1 pound each)
¼ cup extra-virgin olive oil
Kosher salt and freshly ground black pepper
8 tablespoons unsalted butter
1 cup plus ½ cup grated smoked Gouda cheese
   (6 ounces total)
¾ cup heavy cream
1 tablespoon Basic Barbecue Rub (page 196)
¼ cup chopped scallions

> **Equipment: Porcelain coated grid,
>   9 by 13-inch glass or ceramic
>   baking dish**
> **Set the EGG for direct cooking with the
>   porcelain coated grid.**
> **Preheat the EGG to 400°F.**

Brush each potato with olive oil, pierce holes in it with the tines of a fork, and season with salt. Wrap each potato with aluminum foil and place on the grid. Close the lid of the EGG and cook for 30 minutes. Turn the potatoes over, close the lid of the EGG, and cook for 30 minutes more, or until the potatoes are soft and easily pierced with a fork. Transfer the potatoes to a rimmed sheet pan and let rest for 15 minutes.

Unwrap the potatoes, cut them in half lengthwise, and scoop out the flesh of each potato, leaving a little of the potato around the edges of the shells. Place the flesh in a large bowl. Add the butter and 1 cup of the cheese.

Heat the cream in a small saucepan on the stovetop over low heat for 1 to 2 minutes, then add the barbecue rub and the scallions. Add the cream to the potato-cheese mixture, and using an electric mixer, beat on medium speed until combined. Season with salt and pepper. Spoon the mixture into the shells and top with the remaining ½ cup of cheese.

Put the potatoes in a baking dish and place on the grid. Close the lid of the EGG and heat for 3 to 5 minutes, or until the cheese is melted. Serve immediately. **Serves 6**

Candied Sweet Potatoes

Sweet potatoes are an edible root and are a member of the morning glory family. They have dark orange skin with a rich, vivid orange interior; they are often confused with yams, which have pale yellow skin and a light yellow interior. These sweet potatoes are baked in the EGG, then peeled, sliced, and layered in a baking dish. Enhanced with orange juice, brown sugar, and corn syrup, they're topped with thin orange slices, then returned to the EGG and baked until wonderfully caramelized. They are sure to get rave reviews!

Ingredients

2 pounds sweet potatoes

1½ cups plus 2 tablespoons firmly packed light brown sugar

¼ cup freshly squeezed orange juice

1 cup plus 2 tablespoons light corn syrup

6 tablespoons unsalted butter, cut into cubes

1 navel orange, peeled and thinly sliced

Equipment: Plate Setter, 9 by 13-inch glass or ceramic baking dish
Set the EGG for indirect cooking with the Plate Setter, legs down.
Preheat the EGG to 400°F.

Place the sweet potatoes on the Plate Setter. Close the lid of the EGG and cook for 7 to 8 minutes. Turn the potatoes, close the lid of the EGG, and continue cooking for 7 to 8 minutes, until easily pierced with a fork. Remove the potatoes from the Plate Setter and let cool completely.

Peel the sweet potatoes and cut them into ¼-inch-thick rounds. Lay the potatoes in the baking dish. Sprinkle 1½ cups of the brown sugar evenly over the sweet potatoes. Drizzle with the orange juice and 1 cup of the corn syrup and dot with the butter. Place the orange slices on the sweet potatoes, drizzle the remaining 2 tablespoons corn syrup on the orange slices, and sprinkle with the remaining 2 tablespoons brown sugar. Place the baking dish on the Plate Setter. Close the lid of the EGG and bake for 1 hour, or until the sweet potatoes are tender. Serve immediately. **Serves 6**

Honey-Roasted Acorn Squash

Acorn squash is a dark green winter squash that has a vivid orange interior. The squash is cut in half and a healthy blend of oats, raisins, and nuts is added in the center before drizzling with honey and baking. Try this with Slow-Roasted Leg of Lamb (page 76) for a perfect dinner on a cold winter night!

Ingredients

1 large egg, beaten
¼ cup firmly packed light brown sugar
8 tablespoons unsalted butter, melted
1 cup all-purpose flour
½ teaspoon ground cinnamon
¼ teaspoon ground nutmeg
1 teaspoon kosher salt
¼ cup dark raisins
¼ cup golden raisins
¼ cup rolled quick-cooking oats
½ cup chopped pecans
2 acorn squashes
¼ cup extra-virgin olive oil
¼ cup honey

**Equipment: Plate Setter, 9 by 13-inch glass or ceramic baking dish lined with aluminum foil
Set the EGG for indirect cooking with the Plate Setter, legs down.
Preheat the EGG to 400°F.**

Combine the egg, sugar, butter, flour, cinnamon, nutmeg, and salt in a large bowl. Add the dark and golden raisins, the oats, and pecans and gently fold together.

Cut each squash in half crosswise. Using a tablespoon, remove the seeds from the center of each squash. With a sharp knife, cut a thin slice off the bottom of each squash half so that it will rest flat in the pan. Place the squash in the prepared baking dish and fill the center of each half with the oatmeal-raisin mixture. Combine the oil and honey in a small bowl and stir well. Drizzle the mixture over the squash.

Place the baking dish on the Plate Setter. Close the lid of the EGG and bake for 40 to 45 minutes, until the squash is easily pierced with a fork. Remove the baking dish from the EGG and allow to cool for 10 minutes before serving.
Serves 4

Grilled Squash Casserole

Yellow crookneck squash and zucchini are both referred to as summer squash. The yellow crookneck has a long, slender neck and a wider body and is mild and creamy when cooked. Zucchini is green, long, and slender and has a light-colored interior and a delicate flavor. When mixed in a casserole, they create a comforting dish that can be served on weeknights as well as with your Thanksgiving meal.

When purchasing squash, try to pick the smaller, younger ones; they will be more tender, and the skin will not be as tough.

Ingredients

1 pound yellow crookneck squash, quartered lengthwise
1 pound zucchini, sliced
2 (½-inch) slices yellow onion
¼ cup extra-virgin olive oil
Kosher salt and freshly ground black pepper
1 cup heavy cream
1 cup mayonnaise
3 large eggs, beaten
1 cup shredded sharp Cheddar cheese (4 ounces)
1 cup shredded Monterey Jack cheese (4 ounces)
½ cup grated Parmigiano-Reggiano cheese (2 ounces)
1 cup plus 1 cup Ritz cracker crumbs
1 cup thinly sliced scallions
2 teaspoons minced garlic
1 cup panko
4 tablespoons unsalted butter, melted

Equipment: Porcelain coated grid, Grill Gripper, Plate Setter, oiled 9 by 13-inch glass or ceramic baking dish
Set the EGG for direct cooking with the porcelain coated grid.
Preheat the EGG to 350°F.

Brush the squash, zucchini, and onion with olive oil and season with salt and pepper.

Place the squash, zucchini, and onion on the grid. Close the lid of the EGG and grill for 8 to 10 minutes, turning frequently until tender. Transfer the squash, zucchini, and onion to a rimmed sheet pan and allow to cool completely. Place the vegetables on a cutting board and chop into medium pieces.

Using the Grill Gripper and barbecue mitts, carefully remove the grid and add the Plate Setter, legs down.

Combine the cream, mayonnaise, eggs, cheeses, 1 cup of the cracker crumbs, scallions, and garlic in a large bowl. Add the grilled vegetables and, using a wooden spoon, stir until combined. Pour the mixture into the prepared baking dish and spread evenly, using a spatula. Toss the remaining 1 cup cracker crumbs and the panko with the melted butter. Sprinkle the crumbs evenly over the top of the squash.

Place the baking dish on the Plate Setter. Close the lid of the EGG and bake for 30 to 35 minutes, until set. Remove the baking dish from the EGG and let rest for 15 minutes before serving. **Serves 10**

"After many years of buying metal cookers that only lasted a few years here in cold, wet Michigan, I bought a Big Green Egg. The ability to cook year-round now is a major plus!" —Ron, Michigan

Mac & Cheese

The following version of this ultimate comfort food has a combination of five cheeses that come together to form a rich, creamy sauce that clings to the macaroni. Though macaroni and cheese is thought of as a typical American dish, it is believed to be of Italian origin. Elbow macaroni is generally used in this dish, but shells, twists, or ribbons will also work just fine.

Ingredients

4 tablespoons unsalted butter
4 tablespoons all-purpose flour
1 teaspoon dry mustard
2 teaspoons Worcestershire sauce
2 teaspoons Tabasco sauce
1 teaspoon kosher salt
½ teaspoon freshly ground black pepper
3 cups heavy cream
2 cups whole milk
2 cups shredded sharp Cheddar cheese (8 ounces)
1 cup shredded Gruyère cheese (4 ounces)
1 cup shredded fontina cheese (4 ounces)
1 cup shredded mozzarella cheese (4 ounces)
½ cup grated Parmigiano-Reggiano cheese (2 ounces)
1 pound medium pasta shells or macaroni, cooked
  al dente

Topping
2 cups panko
2 teaspoons paprika
4 tablespoons unsalted butter, melted

Equipment: Plate Setter, Dutch Oven
Set the EGG for indirect cooking with
   the Plate Setter, legs down.
Preheat the EGG to 350°F.

Melt the butter in a large pot on the stovetop. Add the flour and, using a whisk and stirring constantly, cook for 2 minutes. Continue stirring as you add the dry mustard, Worcestershire sauce, Tabasco sauce, salt, and pepper and cook for 2 to 3 minutes. Slowly add the cream and milk and continue cooking, stirring constantly, for 7 to 8 minutes, until the sauce bubbles slightly. Do not let the sauce boil.

Remove the pan from the heat and add the cheeses to the sauce. Using a wooden spoon, stir until the cheese is melted. Add the pasta and fold it into the sauce. Pour the pasta into the Dutch Oven.

To make the topping, use a fork to mix the panko, paprika, and butter in a small bowl, blending well. Sprinkle the mixture over the top of the pasta and place the uncovered Dutch Oven on the Plate Setter. Close the lid of the EGG and bake for 30 minutes, or until golden brown. Remove and let rest for 10 minutes before serving. **Serves 6**

Warm Southwestern Potato Salad

If ever there were a macho potato salad, this is it! Grilled cactus and chopped jicama add an unexpected twist to this warm, spicy red potato salad. To complete the Southwestern theme, these ingredients are tossed in a dressing of freshly squeezed lime juice and adobo sauce mixed with a heavy dose of chopped cilantro. Though the cactus adds a unique flavor to this salad, if it is not available at your local grocery store, it can be omitted.

Ingredients

2 pounds red potatoes, halved
¼ cup olive oil
1 tablespoon Red Chile Rub (page 197)
Kosher salt and freshly ground black pepper
1 large cactus leaf
1 medium red onion, thickly sliced
1 medium jicama, peeled and diced
1 teaspoon sliced pickled red jalapeño, seeded
   and chopped
¼ cup freshly squeezed lime juice (2 to 3 limes)
¼ cup extra-virgin olive oil
1 tablespoon adobo sauce (from a can of chipotles in
   adobo sauce)
½ cup chopped fresh cilantro

Equipment: Cast Iron Grid
Set the EGG for direct cooking with the
   Cast Iron Grid.
Preheat the EGG to 350°F.

Toss the potatoes with the olive oil in a medium bowl and add the rub. Season with salt and pepper and blend well. Place the potatoes on the Grid. Close the lid of the EGG and grill, turning occasionally, for 20 minutes, or until tender when pierced with a fork. Transfer the potatoes to a rimmed sheet pan.

Using a paring knife, remove the thorns from the cactus. Place the cactus leaf and the onion slices on the Grid. Close the lid of the EGG and grill for 2 minutes on each side. Transfer the cactus and onion to another rimmed sheet pan.

Cut the potatoes, cactus, and onion into bite-size pieces and place in a large bowl. Add the jicama and jalapeño and mix well.

To make the dressing, mix the lime juice, olive oil, and adobo sauce in a small bowl. Pour the dressing over the potato mixture and add the cilantro and ½ teaspoon salt. Toss to combine. Serve immediately, while the salad is still slightly warm. **Serves 6 to 8**

(See recipe photograph on page 154.)

Panzanella Salad

Panzanella is an Italian salad that contains tomatoes, onions, basil, and large chunks of bread. You can use any type of crusty bread, but you'll love the way ciabatta grills in the EGG. Ciabatta (Italian for "slipper") is a long, wide loaf that is soft on the inside, with a thin, crisp crust. Do not substitute a soft-crusted bread, because the bread is what this salad is all about.

Ingredients

2 tablespoons plus ⅓ cup extra-virgin olive oil
3 cups 1-inch cubes ciabatta bread
2 cups diced heirloom tomatoes
1 cup halved grape tomatoes
1 cup canned garbanzo beans, drained and rinsed
1 cup peeled and diced English cucumber
1 cup small fresh mozzarella *di bufala* balls (bocconcini)
½ cup chopped fresh basil leaves
1 teaspoon Dijon mustard
1 teaspoon minced garlic
¼ cup red wine vinegar
Kosher salt and freshly ground black pepper

Equipment: Cast Iron Grid, perforated grill pan
Set the EGG for direct cooking with the Cast Iron Grid and perforated grill pan. Preheat the EGG to 400°F.

In a medium bowl, mix 2 tablespoons of the olive oil and the bread cubes, turning to coat. Place the bread on the grill pan and grill, turning constantly, for 2 to 3 minutes, until toasted light brown. Transfer to a rimmed sheet pan.

Combine the heirloom tomatoes, grape tomatoes, garbanzo beans, cucumber, mozzarella balls, and basil in a large bowl and mix well. Add the toasted bread, toss, and set aside.

Whisk the remaining ⅓ cup olive oil, the mustard, garlic, and vinegar together in a small bowl. Season with salt and pepper. Drizzle the dressing over the tomato mixture and toss gently. Serve immediately. **Serves 4**

Roasted Red Bell Peppers

Bell peppers come in five vibrant colors—green, red, purple, yellow, and orange. They add not only flavor but also appealing color to many dishes. Of all the colors, the red pepper has the sweetest and most subtle flavor, which is why it is used throughout this book. This method for roasting peppers is easy and they can be used for cooking or in salads and sandwiches.

Ingredients
4 red bell peppers

> **Equipment: Cast Iron Grid**
> **Set the EGG for direct cooking with the Cast Iron Grid.**
> **Preheat the EGG to 500°F.**

Place the peppers on the Grid. Cook on all sides, turning constantly with long-handled tongs. Grill for 8 to 10 minutes, until blackened all over.

Transfer the peppers to a large resealable plastic bag. Seal tightly and allow the peppers to steam in the bag for about 10 minutes. Remove the peppers from the bag and peel away the skin. Slice the peppers open and remove the stem, seeds, and ribs. **Makes approximately 2 cups**

Grill-Roasted Tomatoes

Grilling or slow-roasting a tomato intensifies the tomato's flavor. Roma tomatoes are used in this recipe, but you can grill any variety of tomato in this manner—just adjust your grilling time according to the size of the tomato. Grilled tomatoes can be served as a side or used in sandwiches, sauces, or salads.

Ingredients
2 pounds Roma tomatoes
¼ cup extra-virgin olive oil
¼ teaspoon kosher salt
⅛ teaspoon freshly ground black pepper

> **Equipment: Cast Iron Grid**
> **Set the EGG for direct cooking with the Cast Iron Grid.**
> **Preheat the EGG to 400°F.**

Cut the tomatoes in half lengthwise, through the stem end. Place the tomatoes, olive oil, salt, and pepper in a medium bowl and toss to coat.

Using tongs, place the tomatoes on the Grid, cut side down. Close the lid of the EGG and cook for 2 minutes. Turn the tomatoes over, close the lid of the EGG, and continue cooking for 2 to 3 minutes, until the skin starts to peel away from the flesh of the tomato.

Remove the tomatoes from the EGG, transfer to a plate, and allow to cool. **Serves 6**

Grilled Caesar Salad

Lightly grilled romaine is used in a Caesar salad made with traditional dressing. This recipe is purported to have been created in Mexico by a chef named Caesar Cardini. Anchovies are included, though they are not thought to have been part of the original recipe. Even though this recipe is a departure from the original, there is no doubt Caesar would have loved this version!

Ingredients

Dressing
2 egg yolks
2 cloves garlic
3 anchovy fillets
1 tablespoon Dijon mustard
1 cup extra-virgin olive oil
½ cup grated Parmigiano-Reggiano cheese (2 ounces)
¼ cup freshly squeezed lemon juice (1 to 2 lemons)
½ teaspoon Worcestershire sauce
¼ teaspoon Tabasco sauce
Kosher salt and freshly ground black pepper

Croutons
4 tablespoons unsalted butter
4 cloves garlic, crushed
2 cups ½-inch cubes ciabatta bread
Kosher salt and freshly ground black pepper

2 heads romaine lettuce, cut in half lengthwise
1 tablespoon extra-virgin olive oil
¼ cup grated Parmigiano-Reggiano cheese (1 ounce)

Equipment: Cast Iron Grid, perforated grill pan
Set the EGG for direct cooking with the Cast Iron Grid and perforated grill pan.
Preheat the EGG to 400°F.

To make the dressing, place the egg yolks, garlic, anchovies, and mustard in the bowl of a food processor fitted with the steel blade. Pulse for 10 seconds. Slowly add the olive oil in a steady stream. Add the cheese, lemon juice, Worcestershire sauce, and Tabasco sauce. Season with salt and pepper and pulse until combined. Refrigerate.

To make the croutons, melt the butter in a small saucepan on the stovetop, add the garlic, and cook over low heat for 10 minutes, making sure not to let the butter brown. Strain the butter into a small bowl. Add the bread cubes, season with salt and pepper, and toss together. Place the bread on the perforated grill pan and grill for 2 to 3 minutes, turning constantly, until toasted light brown on all sides. Using barbecue mitts, remove the grill pan from the Grid and allow the croutons to cool.

Brush the inside of each lettuce half with olive oil. Place the lettuce on the Grid, cut side down. Close the lid of the EGG and grill for 1 minute, or until lightly browned. Remove and let cool.

To assemble, place a lettuce half on each plate, grilled side up. Pour the desired amount of dressing over the lettuce and top with croutons and cheese. Serve immediately. **Serves 4**

Prosciutto-Wrapped Haricots Verts

Haricot *is the French word for "bean," and* vert *is the word for "green." Haricots verts are smaller and thinner than most American green beans, and they also tend to be a little more tender. These delicate beans can be served at an elegant dinner, either as an appetizer or as a side. If you can't find haricots verts, American-size green beans are an acceptable substitute. Try this dish with Beef Wellington (page 287).*

Ingredients
8 ounces haricots verts, trimmed

2 tablespoons plus 1 tablespoon extra-virgin olive oil plus extra for drizzling

Kosher salt and freshly ground black pepper

2 ounces prosciutto, thinly sliced

2 tablespoons freshly squeezed lemon juice

1 teaspoon Dijon mustard

1 ounce Parmigiano-Reggiano cheese, shaved

Equipment: Porcelain coated grid, perforated grill pan

Set the EGG for direct cooking with the porcelain coated grid and perforated grill pan.

Preheat the EGG to 400°F.

In a medium bowl, toss the haricots verts with 2 tablespoons of the olive oil and season with salt and pepper. Place the haricots verts on the perforated grill pan, close the lid of the EGG, and grill for 2 to 3 minutes, until slightly soft. Using barbecue mitts, remove the grill pan from the grid and transfer the beans to a work surface.

Divide the cooked beans into 6 bundles and wrap each bundle with prosciutto slices.

Whisk together the lemon juice, the 1 tablespoon olive oil, and the mustard in a small bowl until emulsified.

Place the bundles of haricots verts directly on the grid. Close the lid of the EGG and cook for 1 minute. Transfer the bundles to a platter. Drizzle with a little olive oil and sprinkle with cheese. Serve immediately. **Serves 6**

Roasted Beets
with Goat Cheese & Truffle Oil

Beets have a wonderful, earthy flavor and can be found in deep red or gold. Pairing them with goat cheese and truffle oil turns them into an elegant side salad. If you are unable to find truffle oil, you can substitute a high-quality olive oil.

Ingredients

6 red or golden beets, or a combination, trimmed and washed
¼ cup extra-virgin olive oil
Kosher salt and freshly ground black pepper
8 ounces goat cheese, sliced into ¼-inch-thick rounds, chilled
White truffle oil or extra-virgin olive oil for drizzling
1 head frisée, washed and patted dry (optional)

Equipment: Plate Setter
Set the EGG for indirect cooking with the Plate Setter, legs down.
Preheat the EGG to 400°F.

Toss the beets with the olive oil and 1 tablespoon of salt in a medium bowl. Wrap each beet in aluminum foil and place on the Plate Setter. Close the lid of the EGG and cook for 45 minutes to 1 hour, until a fork easily pierces the beets. Transfer to a rimmed sheet pan and let cool. Using a paring knife, peel the beets and slice them into ¼-inch rounds.

To serve, alternate slices of beets with slices of cheese on individual plates. Drizzle the beets and cheese with truffle oil and season with salt and pepper. Garnish with frisée leaves, if desired, and serve. **Serves 4**

Cauliflower au Gratin

Here, cauliflower—a member of the lowly cabbage family—is given the royal treatment. First the cauliflower is grilled, then it is mixed with a creamy cheese sauce, topped with panko (Japanese bread crumbs), and baked in the EGG. This elegant dish can be served at any holiday meal or dinner party with Standing Rib Roast (page 70). Though this is a side dish, it can also serve as a main course for vegetarians if you double the recipe.

Ingredients

Mornay Sauce
2 tablespoons unsalted butter
2 tablespoons all-purpose flour
¼ teaspoon kosher salt
⅛ teaspoon freshly ground black pepper
1 cup heavy cream
1 cup whole milk
1 cup shredded white Cheddar cheese (4 ounces)

1 head cauliflower (about 1 pound), cored and
    cut into large pieces
¼ cup extra-virgin olive oil
Kosher salt and freshly ground black pepper
1 cup shredded white Cheddar cheese (4 ounces)
1 cup panko

**Equipment: Porcelain coated grid, Grill Gripper, Plate Setter, 7 by 11-inch glass or ceramic baking dish
Set the EGG for direct cooking with the porcelain coated grid.
Preheat the EGG to 400°F.**

To make the Mornay sauce, melt the butter in a heavy-bottomed medium saucepan on the stovetop over medium heat. Using a whisk, add the flour, salt, and pepper, stirring constantly for 2 minutes. Slowly add the cream to the flour mixture, stirring constantly to avoid lumps. Add the milk, stir well, and let simmer for 5 minutes, or until thickened. Remove the pan from the heat and add the cheese, stirring constantly, until it is completely melted. Keep the sauce warm over low heat.

Put the cauliflower in a medium bowl. Pour the olive oil over the cauliflower, add the salt and pepper, and toss. Place the cauliflower on the grid and close the lid of the EGG. Cook, turning occasionally, for 6 minutes, or until the cauliflower can easily be pierced with a fork. Place the cauliflower in the baking dish.

Using the Grill Gripper and barbecue mitts, carefully remove the Grid and add the Plate Setter, legs down. Preheat the EGG to 400°F.

Pour the sauce evenly over the cauliflower. Toss the cheese and panko together in a small bowl and sprinkle this mixture evenly over the cauliflower. Place the baking dish on the Plate Setter. Close the lid of the EGG and bake for 25 minutes, or until light golden brown. Remove the baking dish and let the cauliflower rest for 10 minutes before serving. **Serves 6**

Roasted Fennel
with Parmigiano-Reggiano

The bulb, fronds, and seeds of the anise-flavored fennel plant are used often in the culinary world. Grilled fennel bulbs can be used in soups, salads, and even risotto. Roast it, then toss with orange segments and braise in the EGG with chicken stock. The roasted fennel is delicious with Whole Snapper with Lemon & Rosemary (page 123).

Ingredients

3 fennel bulbs, trimmed and quartered, fronds reserved
2 teaspoons extra-virgin olive oil
Kosher salt and freshly ground black pepper
½ cup navel orange segments (from 1 orange)
¼ cup chicken stock
¼ cup freshly squeezed orange juice
2 tablespoons unsalted butter, cubed
½ cup plus 2 tablespoons grated Parmigiano-Reggiano cheese

Equipment: Porcelain coated grid, Grill Gripper, Plate Setter, 8-inch square glass or ceramic baking dish
Set the EGG for direct cooking with the porcelain coated grid.
Preheat the EGG to 500°F.

Using a basting brush, coat the fennel with the olive oil, then season with salt and pepper. Place the fennel on the grid. Close the lid of the EGG and grill, turning occasionally, for 5 minutes, or until the fennel is browned on all sides. Transfer the fennel to a medium bowl.

Using the Grill Gripper and barbecue mitts, carefully remove the Grid and add the Plate Setter, legs down. Lower the temperature to 400°F.

Add the orange segments to the fennel, and toss well. Place the fennel and oranges in the baking dish. Pour the chicken stock and the orange juice over the fennel, dot with the butter, and sprinkle with ½ cup of the cheese. Set aside.

Place the baking dish on the Plate Setter. Close the lid of the EGG and bake for 20 minutes, or until the cheese is melted and the fennel is tender. Remove the pan from the EGG.

Sprinkle with the remaining 2 tablespoons cheese. Chop 1 tablespoon of the reserved fennel fronds and sprinkle over the top. Serve immediately. **Serves 4**

Roasted Corn with Cotija Cheese & Chipotle Butter

Butter is laced with chipotle chiles—dried smoked jalapeño peppers—then used to baste this corn on the cob as it roasts right on the Grid. Peeling back the husks and tying them with butcher's twine makes for easy basting and a playful presentation.

Ingredients

4 ears corn
8 tablespoons unsalted butter, at room temperature
2 tablespoons chopped dried chipotle chiles
¼ teaspoon kosher salt
½ cup crumbled cotija cheese or feta cheese (2 ounces)
¼ cup finely chopped fresh cilantro
1 fresh lime, cut into quarters

Equipment: Cast Iron Grid
Set the EGG for direct cooking with the Cast Iron Grid.
Preheat the EGG to 400°F.

Place the corn into a large pan and cover with cold water. Let soak for 1 hour.

Pull the husks back from each ear of corn and tie them into a bundle with butcher's twine. Completely remove the silk from each ear. Combine the butter, chiles, and salt in a small bowl and mix well. Using a knife or small spatula, spread 1 tablespoon of the butter evenly over each ear.

Place the corn on the Grid with a piece of aluminum foil under each husk to prevent the husks from burning. Close the lid of the EGG and grill for 6 minutes, basting the corn with the chipotle butter and turning every 2 minutes. Continue grilling for 6 more minutes, or until the corn is tender.

Transfer the corn to a platter and coat with more chipotle butter. Sprinkle with the cheese and cilantro. Serve immediately with lime wedges. **Serves 4**

Creamed Corn

When mounds of fresh-from-the-field sweet corn appear in your local market, you can be sure that summer is in full swing. In this recipe, whole ears of corn packed with plump, sweet kernels are placed right on the grid to roast. The crisp kernels are then removed from the cob and blended with chicken stock and heavy cream to make this delicious side dish. Pair this with All-American Burgers (page 283) for a meal that's sure to be a winner with children and adults alike.

Ingredients

8 ears yellow corn, husks and silk removed

2 tablespoons plus 6 tablespoons unsalted butter

8 ounces applewood-smoked bacon (about 6 slices), chopped

1 cup minced onions

1 tablespoon minced garlic

2 cups chicken stock

1 sprig rosemary

1 cup heavy cream

¼ cup cornmeal

¼ cup granulated sugar

Kosher salt and freshly ground black pepper

Equipment: Porcelain coated grid, Dutch Oven
Set the EGG for direct cooking with the porcelain coated grid.
Preheat the EGG to 400°F.

Place the corn on the grid. Close the lid of the EGG and grill, turning often, for 10 minutes, or until the corn is tender. Let cool.

Using a sharp knife, remove the corn kernels from the cobs; you should have about 8 cups. Place half of the corn kernels in the bowl of a food processor fitted with the steel blade and pulse until the corn is pureed. Reserve the remaining corn kernels. Set aside.

Place the Dutch Oven on the grid and preheat for 10 minutes.

Add 2 tablespoons of the butter and the bacon to the Dutch Oven. Close the lid of the EGG and cook until the bacon is lightly crisp. Add the onions and garlic and continue cooking for 1 minute. Add the whole corn kernels and the pureed corn kernels, the chicken stock, rosemary sprig, and cream. Close the lid of the EGG and simmer for 30 minutes, or until the liquid has reduced. Add the cornmeal and continue cooking for 5 to 7 minutes more, stirring occasionally, until thickened. Remove the Dutch Oven from the heat. Add the sugar and the remaining 6 tablespoons butter. Season with salt and pepper. Remove the rosemary sprig and serve.
Serves 6

Dutch Oven Succotash

Succotash *translates from the Narragansett Indian word as "boiled whole kernels of corn." This traditional Southern dish is best made in the summer, when corn is fresh and sweet, tomatoes are reaching peak flavor, and fresh lima beans can be purchased from your local market. Succotash goes well with just about any grilled meat and adds a burst of color to any plate.*

Ingredients

2 tablespoons extra-virgin olive oil
1 cup chopped yellow onions
1 tablespoon minced garlic
8 cups yellow corn kernels (about 8 ears)
2 red bell peppers, seeded and diced
4 cups fresh or frozen lima beans, cooked
2 cups chicken stock
1 teaspoon chopped fresh rosemary
1 teaspoon chopped fresh thyme
1 cup chopped Roma tomatoes
4 tablespoons unsalted butter
¼ cup chopped fresh flat-leaf parsley
Kosher salt and freshly ground black pepper

Equipment: Porcelain coated grid, Dutch Oven
Set the EGG for direct cooking with the porcelain coated grid.
Preheat the EGG to 400°F.

Place the Dutch Oven on the grid and preheat for 10 minutes.

Heat the olive oil in the Dutch Oven. Add the onions and garlic. Close the lid of the EGG and sauté for 2 to 3 minutes, using a wooden spoon to stir, until the onions are translucent. Add the corn, bell peppers, lima beans, chicken stock, rosemary, and thyme and stir until combined. Place the lid on the Dutch Oven, close the lid of the EGG, and simmer for 5 minutes.

Open the EGG, remove the lid of the Dutch Oven, and add the tomatoes. Replace the lid of the Dutch Oven, close the lid of the EGG, and cook for 5 minutes, or until the vegetables are tender. Remove the Dutch Oven from the EGG, add the butter and parsley, season with salt and pepper, and stir. Serve immediately. **Serves 6 to 8**

Grilled Corn
with Roasted Garlic Butter

A summer barbecue isn't complete without grilled corn on the cob. Mix a dollop of creamy butter with fresh roasted garlic and add to the corn when it is hot off the grill. The only other thing you'll need is a napkin!

Ingredients
4 ears corn
8 tablespoons unsalted butter, at room temperature
12 cloves roasted garlic (page 202)
1 teaspoon kosher salt
½ teaspoon freshly ground black pepper

Equipment: Porcelain coated grid
Set the EGG for direct cooking with the porcelain coated grid.
Preheat the EGG to 400°F.

Place the corn in a large pan and cover with water. Let soak for 1 hour. Using a wooden spoon, combine the butter, garlic, salt, and pepper in a small bowl until thoroughly blended.

Remove the corn from the water and place on the grid. Close the lid of the EGG and grill, turning occasionally, for 45 minutes, or until the corn is tender. Transfer the corn to a rimmed sheet pan. Husk the corn and transfer to a platter. Serve with the roasted garlic butter. **Serves 4**

Roasted Corn with Blue Cheese & Ancho Chile

Gorgonzola, Roquefort, and Stilton are all varieties of cheese that have been treated with mold to form either blue or green veins. These cheeses tend to be sharp and pungent. Sprinkling a little blue cheese and ancho chile powder on top of roasted corn gives it a bit of zip and spice. Serve this with Beer-Brined Chicken (page 98).

Ingredients

4 ears corn
4 tablespoons unsalted butter, at room temperature
Kosher salt
1 teaspoon ancho chile powder
½ cup crumbled blue cheese (2 ounces)

Equipment: Porcelain coated grid
Set the EGG for direct cooking with the
**   porcelain coated grid.**
Preheat the EGG to 425°F.

Remove the husks and silks from each ear of corn, rinse well, and pat dry. Brush each ear of corn with butter and sprinkle with salt. Wrap each ear separately in aluminum foil, twisting the ends to seal tightly.

Place the ears on the grid. Close the lid of the EGG and grill, turning occasionally, for 45 minutes, or until the corn is tender.

Remove the corn from the grid and remove the foil. Sprinkle each ear with ¼ teaspoon ancho chile powder and 2 tablespoons cheese. Serve immediately. **Serves 4**

Brussels Sprouts & Pancetta Carbonara

Grilled brussels sprouts give this carbonara a rich, smoky flavor. If you don't have pancetta on hand, you can substitute high-quality bacon or, if you want a vegetarian dish, omit the meat altogether. This dish makes a great dinner on its own, but can also be served as a side with grilled chicken or fish.

Ingredients

1 pound brussels sprouts, halved
2 tablespoons extra-virgin olive oil
Kosher salt and freshly ground black pepper
10 ounces pancetta, sliced ¼ inch thick
4 large eggs
1 cup heavy cream
1 cup grated Parmigiano-Reggiano cheese (4 ounces)
1 pound spaghetti
Shaved Parmigiano-Reggiano cheese

Equipment: Cast Iron Grid
Set the EGG for direct cooking with the Cast Iron Grid.
Preheat the EGG to 400°F.

Toss the brussels sprouts and olive oil together in a small bowl and season with salt and pepper. Place the brussels sprouts on the Grid. Close the lid of the EGG and grill, turning occasionally, for 8 to 10 minutes, until tender. Set aside. Place the pancetta on the Grid. Close the lid of the EGG and grill for 3 to 4 minutes, until slightly crisp. Transfer the pancetta to a cutting board and dice, then move to a rimmed sheet pan and set aside. In a small bowl, whisk together the eggs, cream, and grated cheese.

Cook the spaghetti in a large pot of water on the stovetop until al dente. Drain over a bowl, reserving 1 cup of the cooking liquid. Return the pasta to the pot and set on the stovetop over low heat. Add the egg mixture, brussels sprouts, pancetta, and the reserved pasta liquid. Season with salt and pepper and mix well. Transfer to a dish and top with shaved Parmigiano-Reggiano cheese.
Serves 6

Braised Leeks

Leeks belong to the same family as garlic and onions and are often used to flavor soups and sauces. They are long and sleek with white stalks and tough, dark green tops. For this recipe, the dark green tops are removed and only the white stalks are used, which are here braised in chicken stock and heavy cream, making them tender, mild, and delicious. These go well with Whole Snapper with Lemon & Rosemary (page 123).

Ingredients
4 leeks
1 cup chicken stock
½ cup heavy cream
1 teaspoon cornstarch
1 teaspoon minced garlic
¼ teaspoon kosher salt
¼ teaspoon freshly ground black pepper
1 teaspoon chopped fresh flat-leaf parsley

Equipment: Plate Setter, 7 by 11-inch glass or ceramic baking dish
Set the EGG for indirect cooking with the Plate Setter, legs down.
Preheat the EGG to 400°F.

Remove the dark green tops and root end of the leeks. Using the white part only, cut the leeks in half lengthwise and rinse well. Place the leeks, cut side up, in the baking dish.

Using a whisk, combine the chicken stock, cream, cornstarch, garlic, salt, and pepper in a small bowl and mix well. Pour the liquid evenly over the leeks.

Place the baking dish on the Plate Setter. Close the lid of the EGG and bake for 30 minutes, or until the leeks are tender. Remove the baking dish from the EGG and let the leeks rest for 10 minutes. Garnish with parsley and serve.
Serves 4

Grilled Vegetable Ratatouille

Ratatouille comes from the French region of Provence. This dish is a medley of vegetables that can be either cooked separately and tossed together or cooked in one pot. The vegetables are grilled first and then tossed in Spicy San Marzano Tomato Sauce. This dish can be served either hot or cold.

Ingredients

⅓ cup plus 2 tablespoons olive oil
1 pound yellow crookneck squash, quartered lengthwise
1 pound zucchini, quartered lengthwise
1 pound eggplant, cut into ½-inch-thick rounds
Kosher salt and freshly ground black pepper
6 ounces portobello mushrooms, sliced ¼ inch thick
1 red onion, cut into 6 (¼-inch) slices
6 Roma tomatoes, halved lengthwise
6 cloves roasted garlic, crushed (page 202)
1 tablespoon red wine vinegar
½ cup Spicy San Marzano Tomato Sauce (page 200) or your favorite tomato sauce
1 cup firmly packed chopped fresh basil leaves

Equipment: Cast Iron Grid
Set the EGG for direct cooking with the Cast Iron Grid.
Preheat the EGG to 500°F.

Pour ⅓ cup of the olive oil into a large bowl, toss in the squash, zucchini, and eggplant, and season with salt and pepper. Brush the mushrooms and red onion with the remaining 2 tablespoons olive oil.

Place the squash, zucchini, eggplant, red onion, and tomatoes on the Grid. Close the lid of the EGG and cook for 4 to 5 minutes on each side, until light brown and tender. Transfer to a rimmed sheet pan. Place the mushrooms on the Grid. Close the lid of the EGG and cook for 2 minutes per side. Transfer to the rimmed sheet pan.

Remove the skin from the tomatoes and cut into bite-size pieces. Cut the red onions, zucchini, squash, eggplant, and mushrooms into bite-size pieces. Place all the vegetables into a large bowl and toss with the garlic, vinegar, tomato sauce, and basil. Serve immediately.
Serves 6

Cremini Mushroom & Cheese Turnovers

Because cremini mushrooms are a baby version of the portobello, they are often referred to as Baby Bellas. In this dish, mushrooms, spinach, and two kinds of cheese are blended into a filling that is encased in a triangle of puff pastry and baked until golden. Great for lunch, these can also be served as an appetizer or hors d'oeuvre.

Ingredients

3 tablespoons unsalted butter
3 tablespoons extra-virgin olive oil
2 tablespoons minced garlic
½ cup diced shallots
Kosher salt and freshly ground black pepper
4 cups quartered white mushrooms
4 cups quartered cremini mushrooms
10 ounces fresh spinach leaves, washed and dried
6 ounces cream cheese, at room temperature
1 cup shredded provolone cheese (4 ounces)
2 sheets puff pastry (1-pound box), thawed
1 egg white, beaten
1 tablespoon water

> **Equipment: Porcelain coated grid, Dutch Oven, Grill Gripper, Plate Setter, Baking Stone**
> **Set the EGG for direct cooking with the porcelain coated grid.**
> **Preheat the EGG to 400°F.**

Place the Dutch Oven on the grid and preheat for 10 minutes.

Heat the butter and olive oil in the Dutch Oven. Add the garlic and shallots. Close the lid of the EGG and sauté for 2 to 3 minutes. Season with salt and pepper. Add the white and cremini mushrooms and sauté for 2 to 3 minutes. Add the spinach and sauté for 5 to 6 minutes, until the spinach wilts. Remove the Dutch Oven from the EGG. Using a spoon, remove any excess liquid from the spinach mixture. Add the cream cheese and provolone cheese and stir until all the cheese is melted.

Using the Grill Gripper and barbecue mitts, carefully remove the grid and add the Plate Setter, legs down, and the Baking Stone on top of the Plate Setter.

Unroll the puff pastry onto a lightly floured surface. Cut each puff pastry sheet in half lengthwise and then cut in half crosswise, making four equal squares from each sheet. Place ¼ cup of the spinach mixture in the middle of each square, fold the pastry from corner to corner to form a triangle, and pinch the edges closed. Repeat this process until you have used all of the spinach mixture.

Lightly beat the egg white and water in a small bowl. Brush the top of the pastry with the egg wash. Place the pastry on the Baking Stone. Close the lid of the EGG and bake for 15 to 18 minutes, until golden brown. Using a long-handled spatula, transfer the turnovers to a platter and let rest for 10 minutes before serving. **Serves 4**

"The versatility of the Big Green Egg as a smoker, grill, and oven is unmatched. And just watch how it can start the conversation among family, friends, and neighbors!" —Ron, Michigan

eggspressive!

sauces & rubs

recipes

Basic Barbecue Sauce

Barbecue sauces vary from region to region, with every area claiming to have the best. This version is rich and thick and has just the right proportion of sweet and sour. A chipotle pepper is thrown in for a bit of heat; add a few more if you dare!

Ingredients

2 (15-ounce) cans tomato sauce
2 cups apple cider vinegar
½ cup Worcestershire sauce
1 cup firmly packed brown sugar
1 teaspoon kosher salt
1 teaspoon freshly ground black pepper
½ teaspoon celery seed
¼ teaspoon ground cinnamon
2 teaspoon smoked paprika
1 teaspoon ground cloves
1 teaspoon garlic powder
1 teaspoon onion powder
1 chipotle pepper in adobo

Place the tomato sauce, vinegar, Worcestershire sauce, and brown sugar in a medium saucepan and mix well.

Whisk the salt, pepper, celery seed, cinnamon, paprika, cloves, garlic powder, onion powder, and chipotle together in a small bowl until completely blended. Add to the saucepan and mix well. On the stovetop, simmer the sauce over low heat for 15 minutes, stirring occasionally, or until the sauce has thickened. Remove the chipotle with a slotted spoon and serve. You may refrigerate the sauce in a sealed container for up to 2 weeks.
Makes 8 cups

KC Barbecue Sauce

Kansas City barbecue sauce is traditionally a sweet, tomato-based sauce with molasses added. The version given here is thick, rich, and finger-licking good! You'll love using it on Spatchcocked Chicken (page 274), but you will find many creative ways to use this delectable sauce.

Ingredients

2 cups ketchup
½ cup apple cider vinegar
¼ cup molasses
½ cup honey
½ cup firmly packed light brown sugar
¼ cup yellow mustard
2 tablespoons Basic Barbecue Rub (page 196)
1 teaspoon kosher salt
½ teaspoon freshly ground black pepper

Combine all the ingredients in a medium saucepan and, using a wooden spoon, stir until blended. Simmer on the stovetop over low heat, stirring occasionally, for 10 minutes, or until the sauce is hot and the ingredients are combined. Refrigerate in an airtight container for up to 2 weeks. **Makes 3½ cups**

Note: To keep a portion of the sauce for more than one use when you intend to brush it on raw meat, be sure to transfer what you need to another container so you don't risk contaminating your entire supply.

Asian Barbecue Sauce

Hoisin sauce, a Chinese dipping sauce that is traditionally made from soybeans, is the primary component in this Asian barbecue sauce. Fresh ginger and chili garlic sauce are added to give this blend a bit of a kick. In this cookbook, the sauce is paired with Asian Pork Ribs (page 89), but it would be equally appealing on chicken wings.

Ingredients
1 cup hoisin sauce
½ cup rice wine vinegar
2 tablespoons grated fresh ginger
2 tablespoons minced garlic
2 teaspoons chili garlic sauce

Combine all the ingredients in a small saucepan and, using a whisk, mix well. Simmer on the stovetop over medium heat for 20 minutes, until the flavors are combined and the sauce is hot. Let cool. Store in an airtight container and refrigerate until ready to use. **Makes 2 cups**

Note: To keep a portion of the sauce for more than one use when you intend to brush it on raw meat, be sure to transfer what you need to another container so you don't risk contaminating your entire supply.

Asian Mop

Chinese five-spice powder is touted to be the perfect balance of sweet, sour, bitter, savory, and salty. Every recipe for five-spice powder consists of a different combination of cinnamon, anise, cloves, fennel, and ginger. This fragrant spice blend is used in the mop that helps make Asian Pork Ribs (page 89) so flavorful.

Ingredients
1 cup rice wine vinegar
2 teaspoons kosher salt
2 teaspoons five-spice powder
1 teaspoon freshly ground black pepper

Using a whisk, combine all the ingredients in a small bowl. If not using immediately, store in an airtight container in the refrigerator. **Makes 1 cup**

Note: To keep a portion of the mop for more than one use when you intend to brush it on raw meat, be sure to transfer what you need to another container so you don't risk contaminating your entire supply.

Beer Mop

You can really get creative with this mop recipe. Lager (light beer) is used here, but for a more pronounced flavor try using a more robust beer. You can also change the flavor by substituting a more exotic, flavored vinegar for the white vinegar. This mop does great things for Chutney-Glazed Beef Brisket (page 284).

Ingredients
1 cup white vinegar
1 cup beer
½ cup sliced red onion
2 cloves garlic, minced
1 tablespoon kosher salt

Using a whisk, combine all the ingredients in a small bowl. If not using immediately, store in an airtight container in the refrigerator for up to 1 week. **Makes 2 cups**

Note: To keep a portion of the mop for more than one use when you intend to brush it on raw meat, be sure to transfer what you need to another container so you don't risk contaminating your entire supply.

Basic Barbecue Rub

Bursting with flavor, Basic Barbecue Rub can be used on everything from Spatchcocked Chicken (page 274) to Barbecued Beef Ribs (page 56). It even adds a spicy kick to Barbecue Chicken Soup (page 53). When you are not sure what spice to use on your meat, this is it! If you would like to add a little more heat, increase the amount of cayenne pepper.

Ingredients
3 tablespoons sweet paprika
1½ teaspoons celery seed
2 teaspoons garlic powder
2 teaspoons cayenne pepper
¼ teaspoon ground cloves
2 tablespoons kosher salt
1 tablespoon freshly ground black pepper
¼ cup firmly packed light brown sugar

Combine all the ingredients in a small bowl and mix well. Store in an airtight container for up to 3 months. **Makes ¾ cup**

Red Chile Rub

Ancho chiles are the dried version of the poblano pepper. They are also the sweetest of the dried chiles. Here ground ancho chile is mixed with toasted spices to produce a favorite rub. It has even found its way into Red Chile & Lime Shortbread Cookies (page 261).

Ingredients
1 tablespoon cumin seed
1 tablespoon coriander seed
1 tablespoon red chile flakes
1 tablespoon ancho chile powder
1 tablespoon kosher salt
1 teaspoon sweet paprika
1 teaspoon garlic powder

Toast the cumin seed, coriander seed, and chile flakes in a small skillet on the stovetop for about 5 minutes, or until fragrant. Remove from the heat and allow to cool.

Transfer the toasted spices to a spice grinder along with the chile powder, salt, paprika, and garlic powder. Grind for 15 to 20 seconds, until the spices are completely ground. Transfer to an airtight container until ready to use. **Makes ½ cup**

Tricolor Pepper Rub

Peppercorns come from berries that grow in clusters on vines. The berries are dried and sold either whole or ground. The most common and recognized peppercorns are black; however, tricolored peppercorns, which can be found in the spice section of most grocery stores, are used in this rub. If these are not available, substitute black peppercorns.

Ingredients
2 tablespoons freshly ground tricolored peppercorns (black, white, and pink)
2 tablespoons sweet paprika
2 tablespoons garlic powder
2 tablespoons onion powder
2 tablespoons kosher salt
2 tablespoons dried oregano
1 tablespoon chili powder
1 teaspoon celery seed
2 tablespoons light brown sugar

Place all the ingredients in a small bowl. Using a wooden spoon, stir to blend well. Store in an airtight container. **Makes ¾ cup**

Note: To keep a portion of the rub for more than one use when you intend to brush it on raw meat, be sure to transfer what you need to another container so you don't risk contaminating your entire supply.

Garden-Fresh Tomato Sauce

Grilling tomatoes before adding them to this sauce gives the tomato flavor a big boost. This sauce can be used for topping Quail Egg Pizza with Prosciutto & Arugula (page 49), but it's also delicious on pastas or grilled meats. Since the sauce freezes well, you can make it in large quantities and freeze it in small batches for later use.

Ingredients

2 pounds Roma tomatoes, roasted and cooled (page 170)
¼ cup extra-virgin olive oil
1 tablespoon minced garlic
¼ cup dry white wine
½ teaspoon granulated sugar
1 teaspoon kosher salt
1 cup firmly packed fresh basil leaves
¼ teaspoon freshly ground black pepper

Peel the tomatoes. Place a mesh strainer over a small bowl and gently squeeze each tomato half over the strainer to remove any seeds. Reserve the liquid from the tomatoes and discard any seeds or pulp that remain in the strainer. Coarsely chop the tomatoes and place them in a small bowl.

Heat the oil in a medium saucepan on the stovetop over medium-low heat. Add the garlic and sauté for 1 minute, or until the garlic is golden in color. Add the tomatoes along with the remaining liquid, and the wine, sugar, and salt, stirring to blend. Gently simmer the sauce for 15 to 18 minutes, until the sauce has reduced and thickened.

Remove the tomato mixture from the heat and allow to cool completely in the pan. Add the basil and pepper and mix well. Place the sauce in the bowl of a blender or food processor and pulse for 1 to 2 minutes, until the sauce is smooth. **Makes 2½ cups**

Spicy San Marzano Tomato Sauce

The San Marzano tomato gets its name from a small town in Italy just outside Naples in the Campania region. The San Marzano is a plum tomato that is sweeter, has thinner skin, and has fewer seeds than the Roma tomato, making it ideal for this spicy sauce. If you want a hotter sauce, increase the amount of red chile flakes.

Ingredients
¼ cup extra-virgin olive oil
½ cup chopped yellow onion
2 tablespoons minced garlic
1 (28-ounce) can whole San Marzano tomatoes, chopped
½ to 1 teaspoon red chile flakes
1 teaspoon dried oregano
1 cup firmly packed fresh basil leaves
½ teaspoon kosher salt
¼ teaspoon freshly ground black pepper

Heat the olive oil in a 3-quart saucepan on the stovetop. Add the onion and sauté for 3 to 4 minutes, uncovered, until translucent. Add the garlic and cook for 1 minute, then add the tomatoes and chile flakes and simmer for 15 to 18 minutes, until the flavors are combined.

Remove the sauce from the heat and add the oregano, basil, salt, and pepper. Carefully spoon the sauce into the bowl of a food processor fitted with the steel blade or into a blender, or use an immersion blender. Puree the sauce until it is completely smooth.

Refrigerate for up to 1 week or freeze for up to 1 month in an airtight container or a resealable plastic bag.
Makes 3 cups

Sun-Dried Tomato Pesto

Sun-dried tomatoes are made by cutting tomatoes in half, removing the seeds, and letting them dry in the sun for several days. A much quicker method is to place the tomatoes on a tray, drizzle them with a little olive oil, and let them bake on very low heat for several hours. Drying the tomatoes intensifies their taste. You will find many uses for this pesto, from sandwich spreads to pizza toppings. You can readily find sun-dried tomatoes packed in oil at your local grocery store.

Ingredients
1¼ cups oil-packed sun-dried tomatoes (10 ounces)
1 tablespoon minced garlic
¼ cup pine nuts
¼ cup grated Parmigiano-Reggiano cheese (1 ounce)
¼ cup extra-virgin olive oil

Drain the tomatoes, reserving ¼ cup of the oil. Add the tomatoes to the bowl of a food processor fitted with the steel blade and pulse for 1½ minutes, or until finely chopped. Add the garlic, pine nuts, cheese, olive oil, and the reserved tomato oil. Turn the food processor on high and blend for 2 minutes, or until the pesto is completely smooth. **Makes 1½ cups**

Fresh Basil Pesto

Pesto is traditionally made by using a mortar and pestle to crush basil, garlic, and pine nuts, then adding olive oil to create a thin paste. This pesto is made in the food processor, but a blender will work, too. Although pesto is traditionally made using basil, today pestos are also made with such ingredients as sun-dried tomatoes, mint, and cilantro. Pesto can be refrigerated for up to 1 month or frozen in ice trays so the cubes can be removed one at a time and added to a variety of recipes.

Ingredients

2 cups firmly packed fresh basil leaves
½ cup fresh flat-leaf parsley
1 tablespoon minced garlic
⅓ cup pine nuts
⅓ cup grated Parmigiano-Reggiano cheese
   (1 to 2 ounces)
½ cup extra-virgin olive oil
¼ teaspoon kosher salt
¼ teaspoon freshly ground black pepper

Place the basil, parsley, garlic, pine nuts, and cheese in the bowl of a food processor fitted with the steel blade. Puree the ingredients for 2 to 3 minutes, until almost smooth. With the machine running, drizzle the olive oil through the feed tube and continue mixing until all the ingredients combine to form a thin paste. Season with the salt and pepper and blend for another 30 seconds.

Using a spatula, transfer the pesto to an airtight container and refrigerate for up to 1 month or in the freezer until ready to use. **Makes 1 cup**

Romesco Sauce

This version of the classic sauce, which originated in the Catalonia region of Spain, uses roasted garlic (page 202) and smoked almonds (page 204). Try it as a dipping sauce for Eggplant Fries (page 30).

Ingredients

2 cups boiling water
2 ancho chiles
1½ cups Roma tomatoes, skins removed
1 roasted red bell pepper (page 170)
5 cloves roasted garlic (page 202)
¼ cup smoked almonds (page 204)
¼ cup red wine vinegar
¼ cup extra-virgin olive oil
1 tablespoon honey
1 teaspoon kosher salt
¼ teaspoon freshly ground black pepper

Pour the water over the chiles in a small bowl. Cover the bowl with plastic and let the chiles soak for 15 minutes. Drain the chiles and remove the stems and seeds.

Place the ancho chiles, tomatoes, bell pepper, garlic, almonds, vinegar, olive oil, honey, salt, and pepper in the bowl of a food processor fitted with the steel blade. Blend for 1 minute. Refrigerate in an airtight container for up to 2 weeks. **Makes 1½ cups**

Roasted Garlic & Garlic Butter

Fresh garlic is a member of the onion family. It has a strong and pungent taste, but when roasted, it turns mild and sweet and has a creamy consistency. Mixed with butter, it can be used as a spread on bread or for cooking meats and vegetables.

Ingredients
2 heads garlic
2 tablespoons extra-virgin olive oil
Kosher salt and freshly ground black pepper
8 tablespoons unsalted butter, at room temperature

Equipment: Cast Iron Grid
Set the EGG for direct cooking with the Cast Iron Grid.
Preheat the EGG to 400°F.

To roast the garlic, use a paring knife to remove the top one-third of the garlic heads. Place each garlic head in the center of a small piece of aluminum foil. Add 1 tablespoon olive oil to each garlic head, sprinkle with salt and pepper, and wrap the garlic tightly in the foil. Place the garlic on the Grid and close the lid of the EGG. Grill for 30 to 35 minutes, turning occasionally, until the garlic cloves are soft. Using tongs, remove the garlic from the heat and allow to cool.

To make the garlic butter, place the butter in a small bowl. Separate the cloves from the garlic heads and squeeze each clove into the butter. Using a fork, mash the garlic into the butter, add salt and pepper, and mix well. Store the butter in an airtight container for up to 1 week or freeze for up to 1 month. **Makes ½ cup**

Note: To keep a portion of the butter for more than one use when you intend to brush it on raw meat or seafood, be sure to transfer what you need to another container so you don't risk contaminating your entire supply.

Smoked Almonds & Almond Butter

Almonds make a healthful snack and can also be used in cooking. Mesquite wood chips impart a wonderful, smoky flavor to these almonds, making them unbelievably flavorful. Since they freeze well, you can double or triple the recipe so you will always have a supply on hand. For variety, try using alder chips or Jack Daniels wood-smoking chips in place of the mesquite chips. You can use this same method to smoke pecans or walnuts.

Ingredients
½ cup whole almonds
1 cup unsalted butter, at room temperature
½ teaspoon kosher salt

Equipment: Plate Setter, mesquite chips
Preheat the EGG to 375°F without the Plate Setter.

To smoke the almonds, soak 2 cups of mesquite chips in water for 1 hour. Scatter the chips over the coals to smoke and, using barbecue mitts, place the Plate Setter, legs down, in the EGG. Once the chips begin to smoke, place the almonds in a small roasting pan on top of the Plate Setter and close the lid of the EGG. Let the almonds smoke for 8 minutes, or until they have a smoky flavor. Remove the pan from heat and let cool.

To make the smoked almond butter, place the almonds in the bowl of a food processor fitted with the steel blade. Pulse for 1 minute, add the butter and salt, and blend for 1 minute, or until the butter is almost smooth. Using a spatula, transfer the butter to an airtight container. Refrigerate for up to 1 week or freeze for up to 1 month.
Makes 1½ cups

Peach-Amaretto Butter

Amaretto is an almond-flavored liqueur that originated in Italy. Here, it's combined with cream cheese and peach preserves to produce a yummy spread for hot Buttermilk Biscuits (page 220).

Ingredients

8 tablespoons unsalted butter, at room temperature
1 (8-ounce) package cream cheese, at room temperature
¾ cup (6-ounce jar) peach preserves
⅓ cup confectioners' sugar
2 tablespoons amaretto

Combine all the ingredients in the bowl of a food processor fitted with the steel blade and pulse for 30 seconds, or until blended. Scrape the sides of the bowl with a rubber spatula and pulse for another 5 seconds. Put the butter in a small bowl and serve immediately or refrigerate in an airtight container for up to 3 weeks. **Makes 2 cups**

Coriander Butter

A tangy green herb with a pungent flavor, coriander is widely used in Asian and Mexican cooking. To make this savory butter, use coriander seeds along with lemon and orange zest. The butter enhances Apricot Bread with Rosemary & Coriander Butter (page 208), and it is also great on grilled vegetables. For an elegant appetizer, simply spread it on hot Naan Bread (page 217) or Pita Bread (215).

Ingredients

8 tablespoons unsalted butter, at room temperature
¼ cup all-purpose flour
2 tablespoons granulated sugar
1 tablespoon orange zest
1 teaspoon lemon zest
2 teaspoons ground coriander
1 teaspoon ground ginger
¼ teaspoon ground nutmeg
¼ teaspoon kosher salt

Combine all the ingredients in the bowl of a food processor fitted with the steel blade. Turn the processor on and let it run until all the ingredients are completely combined. Carefully remove the blade. Using a spatula, scrape the butter into a small bowl and refrigerate until ready to use, or freeze for up to 1 month. **Makes ⅔ cup**

eggcellent!

baked goods

recipes

Apricot Bread with Rosemary & Coriander Butter

This recipe produces two loaves of bread made with a hint of condensed milk, giving the dough a slightly sweet taste. After the dough is rolled out, it is dotted with coriander butter and topped with dried fruits and pistachios. Then the dough is rolled up, creating a pinwheel of flavors and colors. This bread is perfect for breakfast, or as an accompaniment to a dinner of Slow-Roasted Leg of Lamb (page 76) or Tandoori Chicken (page 100).

Ingredients

½ cup plus 2 cups evaporated milk
6 tablespoons condensed milk
2½ teaspoons active dry yeast
5½ cups bread flour plus extra as needed
6 tablespoons unsalted butter, melted
1 tablespoon salt
Olive oil for brushing
1 cup chopped pistachios
1 cup chopped dried apricots
¾ cup chopped dried dates
½ cup golden raisins
2 tablespoons chopped crystallized ginger
2 teaspoons finely chopped fresh rosemary
8 tablespoons Coriander Butter (page 205) or unsalted butter, cut into small pieces
1 large egg
2 tablespoons water

Equipment: Plate Setter, Baking Stone
Set the EGG for indirect cooking with the Plate Setter, legs down, and the Baking Stone on top of the Plate Setter. Preheat the EGG to 400°F.

Place ½ cup of the evaporated milk in a small saucepan on the stovetop and heat until warm. Pour the milk into a small bowl, then add the condensed milk and yeast. Set aside and allow the yeast to proof for 5 minutes, or until frothy.

Combine the flour, the remaining 2 cups evaporated milk, the butter, salt, and proofed yeast in the bowl of an electric mixer fitted with the dough hook. Mix the ingredients on low speed until the dough forms a ball. If the dough is still sticky, add more flour a little at a time, until the dough is smooth and elastic. Place the dough in a well-oiled bowl and turn to coat. Cover the bowl with plastic wrap and set aside in a warm place. Let the dough rise for 2½ hours, or until doubled in size.

Once the dough has doubled, push it down with the heel of your palms and place it on a lightly floured work surface. Knead briefly until the dough is smooth and elastic, then divide it in half and dust with flour. Using a rolling pin, roll each half into a 12 by 15-inch loaf, dusting with flour as necessary, to prevent the dough from sticking to the rolling pin. Brush each loaf with olive oil.

(continued on page 210)

Apricot Bread with Rosemary & Coriander Butter *(continued)*

Mix the pistachios, apricots, dates, raisins, ginger, and rosemary in a small bowl. Sprinkle half the mixture over each loaf, leaving one end exposed. Dot each loaf with half of the Coriander Butter. Starting with the filled short end of a loaf, carefully roll up the dough into a log, then stretch the ends of the dough and fold under, pressing to create a seal. Turn the dough seam side down. Repeat with the other loaf. Allow the loaves to rise for 45 minutes, or until doubled in size.

Cover 1 loaf with plastic wrap and set aside. Mix the egg with the water to make an egg wash. Brush the remaining loaf with the egg wash and place on the Baking Stone. Close the lid of the EGG and bake for 45 minutes, or until golden brown. With a large spatula, transfer the bread to a rimmed sheet pan. Let rest for 10 minutes before slicing. Repeat for the second loaf. **Serves 6**

Prosciutto, Fontina & Arugula Stromboli with Spicy San Marzano Tomato Sauce

. . . .

Stromboli consists of dough that is filled with meats and cheeses and then rolled into a loaf. Vary this recipe by changing the type of filling and cheese. No matter which ingredients you decide to try, the stromboli is even better served with Spicy San Marzano Tomato Sauce on the side.

Ingredients

¼ cup warm water (105° to 115°F)
2 teaspoons honey
1½ teaspoons active dry yeast
2 cups all-purpose flour plus extra as needed
1 cup whole wheat flour
1 tablespoon plus 3 tablespoons extra-virgin olive oil
1 large egg, beaten
1 tablespoon water
6 ounces prosciutto, thinly sliced
2 cups shredded mozzarella cheese (8 ounces)
1½ cups shredded fontina cheese (6 ounces)
½ pound Roma tomatoes, thinly sliced
½ cup firmly packed baby arugula leaves
¼ teaspoon kosher salt
¼ teaspoon freshly ground black pepper
2 cups Spicy San Marzano Tomato Sauce (page 200)

> **Equipment: Plate Setter, Baking Stone,**
> **9 by 13-inch glass or ceramic baking dish**
> **Set the EGG for indirect cooking with the**
> **Plate Setter, legs down, and the Baking**
> **Stone on top of the Plate Setter.**
> **Preheat the EGG to 400°F.**

Pour the water into a liquid measuring cup, add the honey, and gently stir until the honey is dissolved. Sprinkle the yeast over the water and set aside for 5 to 10 minutes, until the liquid becomes frothy.

Place the all-purpose flour and whole wheat flour in the bowl of an electric mixer fitted with the dough hook. With the mixer on the lowest speed, add the yeast mixture and 1 tablespoon of the olive oil and continue mixing until the liquid is completely incorporated. Increase the speed to medium and continue kneading the dough for 5 minutes, or until smooth and elastic.

Place the dough on a lightly floured surface and knead by hand for 2 minutes. Form the dough into a ball, place in a lightly oiled bowl, and turn to coat lightly. Cover the bowl with plastic wrap and set aside in a warm place for 1½ hours, or until doubled in size.

Mix the egg and water in a small bowl to create an egg wash. Set aside.

Turn the dough onto a lightly floured surface and, using a lightly floured rolling pin, roll it into a 15-inch square about ¼ inch thick. Brush three-quarters of the square with the remaining 3 tablespoons olive oil and arrange the prosciutto over the oiled portion. Layer the mozzarella cheese, fontina cheese, Roma tomatoes, and arugula on top of the prosciutto, leaving the last quarter of the dough exposed. Sprinkle with the salt and pepper.

Starting with the filled end of the dough, carefully roll the dough into a log, then stretch the ends of the dough and fold under, pressing to create a seal. Place the dough in the baking dish seam side down. Using a sharp knife, cut about six slits across the top of the stromboli and brush with the egg wash.

Place the stromboli on the preheated Baking Stone, seam side down, close the lid of the EGG, and bake for 45 minutes, or until golden brown. Transfer to a platter and allow to rest for 10 minutes. Slice and serve with the sauce.
Serves 6

Mediterranean Bread

This slightly sweet bread dough is filled with the flavors of the Mediterranean: black olive tapenade, Parmigiano-Reggiano cheese, and freshly roasted peppers all rolled into one. You will be glad that this recipe makes two loaves—one to eat straight off the grill and the other to share with your friends!

Ingredients

½ cup plus 2 cups evaporated milk

6 tablespoons condensed milk

2½ teaspoons active dry yeast

6 cups bread flour plus extra as needed

6 tablespoons unsalted butter, melted

1 tablespoon table salt

1 large egg

2 tablespoons water

Olive oil for brushing

¼ cup plus ¼ cup black olive tapenade

4 roasted red bell peppers, chopped (page 170)

2 cups grated Parmigiano-Reggiano cheese (8 ounces)

Equipment: Plate Setter, Baking Stone
Set the EGG for indirect cooking with the Plate Setter, legs down, and the Baking Stone on top of the Plate Setter.
Preheat the EGG to 400°F.

Place ½ cup of the evaporated milk in a small saucepan on the stovetop and cook over low heat until just warm. Pour the milk into a small bowl and add the condensed milk and active dry yeast. Allow the yeast to proof for 5 minutes, or until frothy.

Combine the flour, the remaining 2 cups of evaporated milk, the butter, salt, and proofed yeast to the bowl of an electric mixer fitted with the dough hook. Mix the ingredients on low speed until the dough forms a ball. If the dough is still sticky, add more flour a little at a time.

Place the dough in a well-oiled bowl and turn to coat. Cover the bowl with plastic wrap and set aside in a warm place for 2½ hours, or until doubled in size.

Mix the egg and water in a small bowl to create an egg wash. Set aside.

Once the dough has doubled, push down the dough with the heels of your palms and turn onto a lightly floured work surface. Knead briefly until the dough is smooth and elastic. Divide the dough in half. Using a lightly floured rolling pin, roll one-half of the dough into a 12 by 15-inch rectangle, dusting with flour as necessary to prevent sticking. Brush with olive oil.

Starting from the short end of the dough, spread ¼ cup tapenade over the rectangle, leaving about 4 to 5 inches of one end exposed. Add ½ cup peppers and sprinkle with 1 cup cheese. Starting with the filled short end of the dough, carefully roll up the dough into a log. Stretch the ends of the dough and fold under, pressing to create a seal. Turn the dough seam side down and allow it to rise for 45 minutes, or until doubled in size.

Brush the loaf with the egg wash and place it on the Baking Stone. Close the lid of the EGG and bake for 45 minutes, or until golden brown. Transfer the bread to a rimmed sheet pan. Let rest for 10 minutes before slicing. While the first loaf is baking, repeat the process for the second loaf. **Serves 6**

Lavash with Sea Salt & Toasted Sesame Seeds

Lavash is a crisp flatbread of Middle Eastern origin. It will go with just about any cheese or dip. To change its flavor, you can use other toppings, such as poppy seeds, cumin seeds, or freshly cracked black pepper. Try it with Smoked Trout Dip with Spinach & Artichokes (page 38).

Ingredients

1 cup plus 1½ cups all-purpose flour plus extra as needed
1 cup plus ½ cup whole wheat flour
2 teaspoons active dry yeast
1 tablespoon kosher salt
1 cup hot water (120° to 125°F)
1 cup dry white wine, at room temperature
¼ cup whole milk
⅓ cup black sesame seeds
⅓ cup white sesame seeds
Sea salt

> **Equipment: Plate Setter, oiled 10 by 15-inch cookie sheet**
> **Set the EGG for indirect cooking with the Plate Setter, legs down.**
> **Preheat the EGG to 400°F.**

Add 1 cup of the all-purpose flour and 1 cup of the whole wheat flour to the bowl of an electric mixer fitted with the dough hook. On the lowest speed, add the yeast, kosher salt, water, and wine. Mix the ingredients on low speed for 2 minutes. Slowly add the remaining ½ cup whole wheat flour and continue to knead the dough for 5 to 7 minutes, until smooth and elastic. Add the remaining 1½ cups all-purpose flour, ¼ cup at a time. If the dough is still sticky, add a little more all-purpose flour until the dough forms a ball.

Place the dough on a lightly floured surface and, using your hands, form the dough into a ball. Place the dough in a lightly oiled bowl and turn to coat. Cover the bowl with plastic wrap and set aside in a warm place to rise for 1 hour, or until doubled in size.

Press the dough down with the heels of your palms, cover the bowl with plastic wrap, and let the dough rise for 30 minutes, or until about one-third larger.

Place the dough on a lightly floured surface and form into a log. Cut the log into 8 equal pieces and form each piece into a rectangle about 8 by 10 inches. Dust the dough with flour and use a rolling pin to roll it about 1/16 inch thick.

Place 1 piece of dough on the cookie sheet. Using your hands, stretch the dough until it is as thin as possible without breaking. Brush the dough with milk and sprinkle with the black and white sesame seeds and sea salt.

Place the cookie sheet on the Plate Setter, close the lid of the EGG, and bake for 10 minutes, or until the cracker is light brown around the edges. Transfer the cracker from the pan onto a rack and allow to cool. Repeat the process with the remaining dough. Store in an airtight container.
Serves 6

Pita Bread

Pita bread, also known as pocket bread, is eaten throughout the Middle East and Mediterranean countries. Stuff it with grilled meat or roasted vegetables for a satisfying sandwich or cut it into small pieces and serve it with your favorite dip.

Ingredients

1½ cups warm water (105° to 115°F)
2 teaspoons honey
1½ teaspoons active dry yeast
2 tablespoons extra-virgin olive oil
2 teaspoons kosher salt
1½ cups whole wheat flour
2 cups plus ½ cup all-purpose flour plus extra as needed

Equipment: Plate Setter, Baking Stone
Set the EGG for indirect cooking with the Plate Setter, legs down, and the Baking Stone on top of the Plate Setter.
Preheat the EGG to 500°F.

Pour the water into a liquid measuring cup, add the honey, and gently stir until the honey is dissolved. Sprinkle the yeast over the water and set aside for 5 to 10 minutes, until the mixture becomes frothy.

Add the olive oil, salt, whole wheat flour, and 2 cups of the all-purpose flour to the bowl of an electric mixer fitted with the dough hook. With the mixer on low, add the yeast mixture and combine the ingredients for 2 to 3 minutes, until the dough forms a ball. Slowly add the remaining ½ cup all-purpose flour until the dough is no longer sticky. Continue kneading on medium speed for 7 to 8 minutes, until smooth and elastic, adding a little all-purpose flour at a time as necessary so the dough will not stick to the rolling pin.

Place the dough on a lightly floured surface and form it into a ball. Put the dough in a lightly oiled bowl and turn to coat lightly. Cover the bowl with plastic wrap and set it in a warm place to let the dough rise for 1 hour, or until doubled in size.

Turn the dough onto a lightly floured surface and form it into an 18-inch log. Using a sharp knife, cut the dough into 12 equal pieces. Form each piece into a ball and set the balls on a rimmed sheet pan. Cover with plastic wrap and set aside for 10 to 12 minutes.

Place 1 ball at a time on the lightly floured surface and, using a lightly floured rolling pin, roll the ball into a 5 to 6-inch disk. Place the dough disk on the preheated Baking Stone and close the lid of the EGG. Bake for 4 minutes, then turn the bread over. Close the lid of the EGG and bake for another 2 minutes, or until the pita has puffed up and is golden brown. Repeat this process until all the dough has been baked. Serve immediately. **Serves 6**

Pizza Dough

If you have never cooked a pizza over the coals, you are missing a real treat! The EGG produces the same results as cooking pizza in a brick oven. This particular dough recipe cooks thin and crisp and is the perfect base for your favorite toppings. You will get the best results if the EGG and the Baking Stone are very hot before you begin cooking.

Ingredients

1 cup warm water (105° to 115°F)
1 teaspoon granulated sugar
1 teaspoon active dry yeast
3 cups all-purpose flour plus extra as needed
1 teaspoon table salt
1 teaspoon olive oil
Cornmeal for dusting

Equipment: Plate Setter, Baking Stone, pizza peel or flat baking sheet
Set the EGG for indirect cooking with the Plate Setter, legs down, and the Baking Stone on top of the Plate Setter.
Preheat the EGG to 600°F.

Pour the water into a liquid measuring cup, add the sugar, sprinkle the yeast over the warm water, and let sit for 5 to 10 minutes, or until the liquid becomes frothy.

Pour the flour and salt into the bowl of an electric mixer fitted with the dough hook, add the yeast mixture, and mix on low speed until combined. Add the olive oil and continue to mix on low. Once blended, knead the dough on low speed for 5 to 6 minutes, until the dough becomes smooth and elastic.

Turn the dough onto a lightly floured surface and form into a ball. Place the dough in a well-oiled bowl and turn to coat with oil. Cover the bowl with plastic wrap and let sit for 1½ hours, or until doubled in size.

Turn the dough onto a lightly floured surface and knead briefly. Form the dough into a ball and, using a sharp knife, cut the dough into 4 equal parts. Shape each part into a disk and dust with flour.

To roll and bake, using a rolling pin, roll a dough disk into a 10 to 12-inch circle. Lightly dust the pizza peel with cornmeal. Place the rolled-out dough onto the pizza peel, top with the desired toppings, and gently slide the dough directly onto the preheated Baking Stone. Cook for 5 minutes or until the dough is lightly brown and crisp. Repeat for the remaining dough disks. **Makes 4 pizzas**

Naan Bread

Naan bread is Asian in origin and resembles pita bread, but it is much softer in texture. The EGG's ability to reach high temperatures makes it the perfect environment in which to make this bread.

Ingredients

3 cups bread flour
1 teaspoon active dry yeast
1 teaspoon table salt
2 tablespoons sunflower oil
1 teaspoon honey
¾ cup warm water (105° to 115°F)
4 tablespoons plain low-fat yogurt

**Equipment: Plate Setter, Baking Stone
Set the EGG for indirect cooking with the Plate Setter, legs down, and the Baking Stone on top of the Plate Setter.
Preheat the EGG to 425°F.**

Place the flour, yeast, and salt in a medium bowl. Using a wooden spoon, blend well, until combined. Add the sunflower oil, honey, water, and yogurt, stirring gently until a dough forms. Turn the dough onto a lightly floured surface and, using your hands, form the dough into a ball. Place the dough in a lightly oiled bowl and turn to coat. Cover the dough with plastic wrap and let it rise for 2 hours, or until doubled in size.

Turn the dough onto a lightly floured surface and cut into 8 equal pieces. Using your hands, roll each piece of dough into a ball. Using a lightly floured rolling pin, roll each ball into a ½-inch-thick disk.

Place the disks on the preheated Baking Stone and close the lid of the EGG. Bake for 4 minutes per side, or until golden brown. Serve immediately. **Serves 4**

Southwestern Cornbread

Jalapeño chiles add a little heat to this cornbread, making it ideal to serve as a side dish or to turn into a spicy stuffing. It also can be used for Stuffed Pork Chops with Poblano Cream Sauce (page 95).

Ingredients

2 cups cornmeal
1 cup all-purpose flour
2 teaspoons baking powder
2 teaspoons table salt
2 cups buttermilk
2 large eggs, beaten
½ cup sour cream
4 tablespoons unsalted butter, melted
1 cup roasted yellow corn kernels (about 1 ear; page 180)
¾ cup diced red bell pepper
2 jalapeños, seeded and chopped

**Equipment: Plate Setter, 9 by 13-inch glass or ceramic baking dish
Set the EGG for indirect cooking with the Plate Setter, legs down.
Preheat the EGG to 425°F.**

In a medium bowl, combine the cornmeal, flour, baking powder, and salt. Add the buttermilk, eggs, sour cream, butter, corn, bell pepper, and jalapeños. Using a large spatula, stir all the ingredients until combined.

Pour the batter into the baking dish and, using a spatula, spread evenly. Place the dish on the Plate Setter and close the lid of the EGG. Bake for 25 minutes, or until an inserted toothpick comes out clean. Remove from the grill and let rest for 10 minutes. Cut into 3-inch squares and serve immediately. **Serves 12**

Skillet Cornbread with Fresh Roasted Corn

Take the old-fashioned Southern route by baking this cornbread in a well-seasoned iron skillet. You can also use a baking dish or muffin pan (without paper liners); just be sure to adjust the cooking time. This recipe includes fresh roasted yellow corn and heavy cream producing a very rich and moist cornbread. Though it could be served with any of the grilled meats, it's the consummate accompaniment for Barbecue Chicken Soup (page 53) or EGGfest Chili (page 286).

Ingredients

2 cups all-purpose flour
1 tablespoon baking powder
1 teaspoon kosher salt
1 cup stone-ground yellow cornmeal
½ cup granulated sugar
3 large eggs, beaten
8 tablespoons unsalted butter, melted
2 cups heavy cream
1¼ cups roasted yellow corn kernels (about 2 ears; page 180)

Equipment: Plate Setter, 9 by 13-inch glass or ceramic baking dish
Set the EGG for indirect cooking with the Plate Setter, legs down.
Preheat the EGG to 425°F.

Sift the flour, baking powder, and salt together in a medium bowl. Using a wooden spoon, mix the cornmeal, sugar, and eggs in another medium bowl and stir well. Add the flour mixture to the cornmeal and continue stirring until completely blended. Add the butter, cream, and corn kernels and continue to mix until smooth.

Pour the batter into the skillet and, using a spatula, spread the batter evenly in the dish. Place on the Plate Setter and close the lid of the EGG. Bake for 35 minutes, or until golden brown and an inserted toothpick comes out clean. Remove the pan from the EGG and let cool for 10 minutes before cutting into 3-inch squares. **Serves 12**

Buttermilk Biscuits

You will find many uses for these light and flaky biscuits. Serve with a dollop of Peach-Amaretto Butter (page 205) or split them and fill with thin slices of juicy beef tenderloin and a bit of horse-radish cream (page 230) for a heartier breakfast.

Ingredients

1½ cups cake flour
1 cup all-purpose flour plus extra as needed
4 teaspoons baking powder
½ teaspoon baking soda
1 tablespoon granulated sugar
1 teaspoon table salt
8 tablespoons unsalted butter, cubed
½ cup solid vegetable shortening, cold
1¼ cups buttermilk, cold

**Equipment: Plate Setter, 9 by 13-inch glass or ceramic baking dish
Set the EGG for indirect cooking with the Plate Setter, legs down.
Preheat the EGG to 450°F.**

Sift the cake flour, all-purpose flour, baking powder, baking soda, sugar, and salt together in a large bowl. Add the butter and shortening. Using a pastry cutter or fork, work the butter and shortening into the flour until the butter is pea size. Using a fork, slowly stir the buttermilk into the flour until the dough forms a ball. Do not overwork the dough. The ingredients should be just incorporated, because overmixing will produce a tougher biscuit.

Turn the dough onto a lightly floured surface. Using a lightly floured rolling pin, roll the dough into a 1-inch-thick rectangle, dusting with flour as needed to prevent sticking. Fold the dough into thirds, then roll it again into a 1-inch-thick rectangle. Using a 3-inch diameter cookie cutter, cut the dough into 10 biscuits. Place the biscuits side by side in the baking dish. Place the dish on the Plate Setter, close the lid of the EGG, and bake for 20 to 22 minutes, until the biscuits are light golden brown.
Serves 4 to 6

Pie Dough

The combination of butter and vegetable shortening makes a crust light without sacrificing the buttery flavor. If you are making a pie that requires a top and bottom crust, double this recipe.

Ingredients

2 cups all-purpose flour plus extra as needed
½ teaspoon table salt
8 tablespoons unsalted butter, cubed
3 tablespoons vegetable shortening
4 to 5 tablespoons cold water

To make the dough by hand, put the flour and salt in a medium bowl and stir to blend. Add the butter and shortening and, using a pastry cutter or fork, work the butter into the flour until the pieces of butter are pea size. Add the water 1 tablespoon at a time and mix just until you can form a ball. Do not overwork the dough. Turn the dough onto a lightly floured surface and form the dough into a ball.

To make the dough with a food processor, put the flour and salt in the work bowl fitted with the steel blade. Add the butter and shortening. Pulse the machine to work the butter and shortening into the flour until the mixture resembles cornmeal. With the machine running, add the water, 1 tablespoon at a time, until the dough forms a ball. Do not overwork the dough.

Using the palm of your hand, flatten the ball into a disk, wrap with plastic wrap, and refrigerate for at least 30 minutes. Remove from the refrigerator about 15 minutes before rolling the dough.

If you need a pie shell or a tart shell for your recipe, use a rolling pin to roll the dough into a circle to fit your pan, allowing for the sides of the pan plus some overhang. Roll the dough on a lightly floured surface, using a lightly floured rolling pin. Roll the dough straight out and once or twice to the sides. Put the rolling pin down, pick up the dough with both hands, give the dough a quarter turn, then roll again. Repeat until the pie dough is the size you need. This technique helps keep the dough in an even circle.

To line the pie plate or tart pan, fold the dough in half, fold in half again, place in the pie plate or tart pan, then unfold. Alternatively, roll up the dough on a rolling pin and unroll it into the pan. Lightly press the dough into the bottom edge of the pie plate or tart pan. If you're making a pie, trim the edge of the dough to a ½-inch overhang and fold the dough under so it's even with the edge of the pie plate. If you're making a single-crust pie, you can crimp the edge. If you're making a tart, roll the rolling pin across the top of the tart pan to cut off any excess. Refrigerate the pie shell or tart shell until ready to use. **Makes 1 (8 to 12-inch) pie shell or 1 pie dough disk**

breakfasts

Italian Frittata with Prosciutto & Buffalo Mozzarella

Buffalo mozzarella (mozzarella di bufala) is made from a combination of whole cow's milk and the milk of the water buffalo. It is so highly regarded in Italy that it enjoys protected geographic status. This means that the producers, under Italian law, are responsible for protecting the quality and marketing of this cheese. Here, creamy buffalo mozzarella combines with fresh basil, fresh tomatoes, and prosciutto to make this version of frittata. If you have trouble finding buffalo mozzarella, use a good-quality mozzarella made solely from whole cow's milk in its place.

Ingredients

10 large eggs, beaten
½ cup heavy cream
½ teaspoon kosher salt
¼ teaspoon freshly ground black pepper
3 ounces thinly sliced prosciutto, cut into small pieces
½ cup chopped fresh basil
1 cup chopped grilled Roma tomatoes (page 170)
1½ cups diced mozzarella *di bufala* (6 ounces)
16 cloves roasted garlic (page 202)

**Equipment: Plate Setter, oiled 8-inch square glass or ceramic baking pan
Set the EGG for indirect cooking with the Plate Setter, legs down.
Preheat the EGG to 400°F.**

Place the eggs, cream, salt, and pepper in a large bowl and mix well. Pour the egg mixture into the oiled baking dish. Add layers of prosciutto, basil, and tomatoes. Top with the cheese and roasted garlic, distributing them evenly over the egg mixture.

Place the baking dish on the Plate Setter. Close the lid of the EGG and bake for 40 to 45 minutes, until the eggs are set.

Let the frittata rest for 5 minutes. Cut it into 6 equal wedges and serve immediately. **Serves 6**

Grilled Salmon Frittata
with Cream Cheese, Capers & Dill

Perfect for a brunch or luncheon, grilled salmon, tomato, and onion are combined with heavy cream, cream cheese, capers, and dill, giving this dish an elegant air. Fresh salmon should be available at most supermarkets all year long.

Ingredients

1 large red onion, sliced ½ inch thick
1 Roma tomato, cored and halved lengthwise
1 tablespoon plus 1 tablespoon canola oil
Kosher salt and freshly ground black pepper
2 (8-ounce) salmon fillets
½ teaspoon Old Bay seasoning
1 large lemon, halved
10 large eggs, beaten
½ cup heavy cream
2 tablespoons unsalted butter, melted
4 ounces cream cheese, cut into small pieces
1 tablespoon capers
1 teaspoon chopped fresh dill

> **Equipment: Porcelain coated grid, Grill Gripper, Plate Setter, oiled 8-inch square glass or ceramic baking dish**
> **Set the EGG for direct cooking with the porcelain coated grid.**
> **Preheat the EGG to 650°F.**

Brush the onion and tomato slices with 1 tablespoon of the canola oil, season with salt and pepper, and set aside. Rinse the salmon in cold water and pat dry. Brush each salmon fillet with the remaining 1 tablespoon canola oil. Season with the Old Bay and salt and pepper.

Place the onion, tomato, and salmon on the grid. Close the lid of the EGG and grill for 3 minutes, or until browned on one side. Using a long-handled metal spatula, turn the onion, tomato, and salmon over. Close the lid of the EGG and grill for 3 more minutes, or until the salmon is browned on the exterior and opaque in the center. Using the spatula, transfer the onion, tomato, and salmon to a rimmed sheet pan. Squeeze a lemon half on each salmon fillet. Let cool.

Using the Grill Gripper and barbecue mitts, carefully remove the grid and add the Plate Setter, legs down. Reduce the temperature of the EGG to 400°F.

Using a fork, break the salmon into bite-size pieces and put in a small bowl. Chop the onion and tomato and add to the small bowl. Set aside. Mix the eggs, cream, butter, ½ teaspoon kosher salt, and ¼ teaspoon pepper in a medium bowl until completely combined.

Pour the egg mixture into the oiled baking dish. Add the ingredients, one at a time, to the egg mixture, beginning with the salmon mixture and continuing with the cheese and capers. Sprinkle with the dill and place on the Plate Setter. Close the lid of the EGG and bake for 35 minutes, or until the eggs have set. Remove the pan and let rest for 10 minutes before serving. **Serves 6**

Spicy Spanish Frittata with Chorizo

This spicy frittata is all about bold flavors. Smoky Spanish chorizo sausage is combined with manchego cheese, a sheep's milk cheese that comes from La Mancha, Spain. The chorizo and cheese are blended with eggs, grilled scallions, peas, and cream. The frittata is then baked to intensify the smoky flavors.

Ingredients

10 large eggs, beaten
½ cup heavy cream
½ teaspoon kosher salt
¼ teaspoon freshly ground black pepper
1 cup diced, grilled Spanish chorizo
¼ cup chopped grilled scallions
¾ cup shredded manchego cheese (3 ounces)
¼ cup chopped pimientos
¼ cup fresh green peas
¼ teaspoon smoked Spanish paprika

Equipment: Plate Setter, oiled 8-inch square glass or ceramic baking dish
Set the EGG for indirect cooking with the Plate Setter, legs down.
Preheat the EGG to 400°F.

Mix the eggs, cream, salt, and pepper in a medium bowl. Pour the egg mixture into the oiled baking dish. Add the following ingredients, one at a time, to the egg mixture: chorizo, scallions, cheese, pimientos, and peas. Sprinkle with the paprika.

Place the dish on the Plate Setter. Close the lid of the EGG and bake for 35 minutes, or until the eggs are set. Remove the pan from the grill.

Let the frittata rest for 10 minutes before serving. **Serves 6**

Beef Tenderloin Sandwich with Horseradish Cream

It doesn't get any better than this succulent steak-and-egg combo! It is the ultimate breakfast sandwich and is sure to become an EGGhead favorite. Don't try to eat this one on the run, though, because you're apt to need several napkins.

Ingredients

Horseradish Cream
¼ cup sour cream
1 tablespoon prepared horseradish
1 tablespoon minced fresh chives
¼ teaspoon kosher salt
¼ teaspoon freshly ground black pepper

4 tablespoons plus 2 tablespoons unsalted butter
4 English muffins, cut in half
4 slices beefsteak tomato, ¼ inch thick
4 (4-ounce) beef tenderloin steaks
Kosher salt and freshly ground black pepper
4 large eggs
4 slices white Cheddar cheese

Equipment: Cast Iron Grid, Half Moon Griddle
Set the EGG for direct cooking with the Cast Iron Grid and the Half Moon Griddle, set flat side up on one-half of the Cast Iron Grid.
Preheat the EGG to 400°F.

To make the horseradish cream, whisk the sour cream, horseradish, chives, salt, and pepper in a small bowl until blended. Set aside.

Melt 4 tablespoons of the butter in a small saucepan on the stovetop over low heat. Using a pastry brush, spread the muffin halves with butter. Place the muffin halves on the Griddle, cut side down, until toasted and lightly browned. Using a long-handled spatula, transfer the muffins to a platter. Spread each of 4 muffin halves with 2 teaspoons of the horseradish cream. Set aside.

Brush all the tomato slices first and then the steaks with butter, and season with salt and pepper. Place the steaks on the Grid and, while they are cooking, melt the remaining 2 tablespoons butter on the Griddle. Crack the eggs onto the hot Griddle. Close the lid of the EGG and cook for 3 minutes, or until the whites of the eggs are set. Using a long-handled spatula, turn the steaks and eggs over and top each egg with a slice of cheese. Close the lid of the EGG and continue to cook for 2 minutes, or until the cheese is melted. Using a long-handled spatula, remove each steak and place it on the bottom half of an English muffin. Top each steak with 1 egg, a slice of tomato, and the top of the English muffin. Place the assembled sandwiches on the Grid. Close the lid of the EGG and heat for 1 minute, until the sandwiches are hot.

Transfer the sandwiches to a platter and serve immediately. **Serves 4**

Applewood-Smoked Bacon & Grilled Vegetable Strata

You can make a strata and bake it immediately. Or you can let it sit uncooked in the refrigerator overnight and bake it the next morning. Because it can be prepared in advance, it is a great dish to serve when you have houseguests.

Ingredients

10 large eggs, beaten
½ cup plus ½ cup heavy cream
½ teaspoon kosher salt
¼ teaspoon freshly ground black pepper
1 red bell pepper
1 green bell pepper
1 pound red potatoes, sliced ¼ inch thick
1 small red onion, sliced ½ inch thick
8 scallions
1 pound applewood-smoked bacon
5 to 6 medium croissants (12 ounces)
2 cups plus 2 cups shredded sharp Cheddar cheese
  (1 pound total)
1 tablespoon minced fresh chives

> **Equipment: Porcelain coated grid, Half Moon Griddle, Grill Gripper, Plate Setter, oiled 9 by 13-inch glass or ceramic baking dish**
> **Set the EGG for direct cooking with the porcelain coated grid.**
> **Preheat the EGG to 450°F.**

Using a whisk, mix the eggs, ½ cup of the cream, kosher salt, and pepper in a large bowl. Refrigerate.

Place the bell peppers on the grid. Close the lid of the EGG and grill, turning often, for 10 minutes, or until tender.

Transfer the peppers to a sealable plastic bag. Seal the bag and let the peppers steam for 5 minutes. Remove the peppers from the bag and, using your hands, peel off the skin. Cut the ends off the peppers and remove and discard the seeds. Place them on a rimmed sheet pan and set aside. Place the potatoes and red onion on the grid. Close the lid of the EGG and grill for 3 to 4 minutes per side, until the potatoes and red onions are tender. Add the scallions and grill for 30 seconds on each side, until just wilted. Using a long-handled spatula, transfer the potatoes, red onions, and scallions to the rimmed sheet pan. Set aside.

Place the Griddle, smooth side up, on the grid to preheat for 5 minutes. Place the bacon on the Griddle. Close the lid of the EGG and cook for 5 to 6 minutes, turning occasionally, until crisp. Using tongs, transfer the bacon to the rimmed sheet pan.

Using the Grill Gripper and barbecue mitts, carefully remove the Griddle and the grid and add the Plate Setter, legs down. Reduce the heat of the EGG to 400°F.

Transfer the bell peppers, potatoes, red onion, scallions, and bacon to a cutting board. Using a knife, coarsely chop the vegetables and bacon into bite-size pieces. Cut the croissants into 1-inch cubes. Add the vegetables, bacon, and croissant cubes to the egg mixture. Stir well. Pour one-half of the mixture into the oiled baking dish and sprinkle with 2 cups of the shredded cheese. Pour the rest of the egg mixture into the dish and sprinkle with the remaining 2 cups cheese. Drizzle with the remaining ½ cup cream and sprinkle with the minced chives.

Place the baking dish on the Plate Setter. Close the lid of the EGG and bake for 40 minutes, or until the eggs are set. Remove the pan and let the strata rest for 10 minutes before serving. **Serves 6**

Stone-Ground Grits
& Sausage Casserole

Long associated with the Southern part of the United States, grits are no longer confined to the South. They can be found throughout the country served in a variety of ways—as a side dish, a pudding, a soufflé, or most commonly as breakfast food. This casserole is great for breakfast or brunch, especially because it can be prepared the night before, refrigerated, and baked the next morning.

Ingredients

5 cups water
2½ cups white stone-ground grits
1 cup heavy cream
2 cups plus 2 cups shredded white Cheddar cheese
   (1 pound)
8 tablespoons unsalted butter, cubed
1 pound pork sausage links, grilled and chopped
½ cup sliced fresh chives
2 teaspoons kosher salt
½ teaspoon freshly ground black pepper
1 cup panko (Japanese bread crumbs)

Equipment: Plate Setter, oiled 9 by 13-inch glass or ceramic baking dish
Set the EGG for indirect cooking with the Plate Setter, legs down.
Preheat the EGG to 400°F.

Bring the water to a boil in a large stock pot. Slowly add the grits and simmer on low for 30 to 35 minutes, stirring occasionally with a wooden spoon to prevent sticking, until the water has been absorbed. Remove the grits from the heat, whisk in the cream, and add 2 cups of the cheese, the butter, sausage, chives, salt, and pepper. Continue mixing until the cheese is melted. Pour the grits into the oiled baking dish and, using a spatula, spread evenly. Top with the remaining 2 cups cheese. Sprinkle the panko on top of the cheese.

Place the dish on the Plate Setter. Close the lid of the EGG and bake for 30 minutes, or until firm. Remove the pan and let the casserole rest for 10 minutes before serving. **Serves 6**

Apple Pancake

Apple pancake can be served with maple syrup or crème fraîche, but this recipe is so yummy that all it really needs is a dusting of confectioners' sugar, a knife, and a fork! This can be served as a sweet accompaniment to a savory breakfast, or as a dessert with your favorite ice cream or homemade caramel sauce (page 255).

Ingredients

½ cup all-purpose flour
2 tablespoons granulated sugar
¼ teaspoon table salt
2 large eggs, beaten
1 cup heavy cream
½ teaspoon vanilla extract
2 Granny Smith apples, peeled, cored, and sliced
½ teaspoon ground cinnamon
¼ teaspoon ground nutmeg
1 tablespoon lemon zest (1 to 2 lemons)
¼ teaspoon kosher salt
4 tablespoons unsalted butter
2 tablespoons freshly squeezed lemon juice
½ cup firmly packed brown sugar
Confectioners' sugar for dusting

**Equipment: Plate Setter, Baking Stone, 8-inch glass or ceramic pie plate
Set the EGG for indirect cooking with the Plate Setter, legs down.
Preheat the EGG to 500°F.**

Place the pie plate on the Plate Setter to preheat for 30 minutes. Combine the flour, sugar, table salt, eggs, cream, and vanilla in a medium bowl and mix well. Set aside. Place the apple slices in a medium bowl. Add the cinnamon, nutmeg, lemon zest, and kosher salt. Toss to combine. Place the butter in the hot pie plate and let the butter melt. Pour the apple mixture into the butter and sauté for 8 to 10 minutes, until the apples are tender. Add the lemon juice and sprinkle with the brown sugar. Pour the batter evenly over the top of the apple mixture.

Carefully remove the pie plate from the heat and place the Baking Stone on top of the Plate Setter. Place the pie plate on top of the Baking Stone. Close the lid of the EGG and bake for 12 minutes, or until the batter is set and firm.

Transfer to a baking dish and allow the pancake to cool slightly. Carefully invert the pancake onto a large platter. Dust with confectioners' sugar and serve immediately.
Serves 4

Baked French Toast
with Pears & Cherries

Challah bread is used for this French toast, but you can make the recipe your own. Try substituting brioche or French bread, and add your favorite nuts, fruits, or flavoring.

Ingredients

4 Bartlett pears, peeled, cored, and diced
¾ cup dried cherries
½ cup chopped walnuts
¼ cup butter, melted
½ teaspoon plus ½ teaspoon ground cinnamon
¼ teaspoon ground nutmeg
¼ teaspoon plus ½ teaspoon table salt
½ cup firmly packed light brown sugar
6 large eggs, beaten
¼ cup heavy cream
1 teaspoon vanilla extract
3 tablespoons granulated sugar
½ (8-ounce) loaf challah bread or brioche,
    sliced ¾ inch thick
Confectioners' sugar (optional)
Warm maple syrup (optional)

Equipment: Plate Setter, buttered 7 by 11-inch glass or ceramic baking dish
Set the EGG for indirect cooking with the Plate Setter, legs down.
Preheat the EGG to 400°F.

Combine the pears, cherries, walnuts, butter, ½ teaspoon of the cinnamon, the nutmeg, and ¼ teaspoon of the salt in a medium bowl until well blended. Pour the fruit mixture into the buttered baking dish, sprinkle with the brown sugar, and spread evenly in the bottom of the dish. Combine the eggs, cream, vanilla, the remaining ½ teaspoon cinnamon, sugar, and the remaining ½ teaspoon salt in a large bowl and mix well. Dredge each bread slice in the egg mixture, and layer the bread, one slice slightly overlapping the other, until the fruit mixture is completely covered. Pour the remaining egg mixture over the bread and cover the dish with aluminum foil.

Place the dish on the Plate Setter. Close the lid of the EGG and bake for 15 minutes. Remove the foil, close the lid of the EGG, and continue baking for 10 minutes, or until the eggs are completely cooked. Remove the dish and let rest for 5 minutes.

Run a knife along the edges of the dish and carefully invert the French toast onto a platter. Dust with confectioners' sugar and serve with maple syrup. **Serves 6**

Tropical Breakfast Muffins

Laced with fresh pineapple, white chocolate, and macadamia nuts, these muffins are so good that you could even top them with your favorite cream cheese frosting and serve them for dessert. Do not line the muffin pan cups with paper liners when baking in the EGG, because the papers will burn. Just butter and flour the cups, and then add the batter. Once the muffins are baked and cooled, they should come out of the cups easily.

Ingredients
2 cups all-purpose flour
1 teaspoon baking powder
1 teaspoon baking soda
½ teaspoon table salt
½ cup granulated sugar
8 tablespoons unsalted butter, melted
½ cup half-and-half
3 large eggs
1 tablespoon coconut extract
2 cups diced fresh pineapple
1½ cups shredded, sweetened coconut (4 ounces)
1 cup crushed macadamia nuts
8 ounces white chocolate chunks

Equipment: Plate Setter, buttered and floured muffin pans (do not use paper liners)
Set the EGG for indirect cooking with the Plate Setter, legs down.
Preheat the EGG to 400°F.

Using a wooden spoon, stir the flour, baking powder, baking soda, salt, and sugar in a small bowl and mix well. Add the butter, half-and-half, eggs, and coconut extract. Continue stirring until completely combined. Using a spatula, fold the pineapple, coconut, macadamia nuts, and white chocolate into the batter. This batter will be very thick. Using a spoon, fill the prepared muffin pan cups three-quarters full. Do not overfill. Place the muffin pans on the Plate Setter. Close the lid of the EGG and bake for 20 minutes, or until a toothpick inserted into a muffin comes out clean. Remove from the EGG and let the muffins cool in the pans.

Remove the muffins from the pan and serve.
Makes 18 muffins

Lemon & Lavender Scones

Lavender is a member of the mint family, and its flowers are widely used in the culinary world. Dried lavender buds are steeped in milk and cream to give these scones their slightly sweet floral flavor. If you cannot find lavender in your local supermarket or specialty food market, it can be ordered from a specialty spice company. If you are unable to find lavender, substitute 1 cup of dried cranberries or cherries for a distinctive flavor.

Ingredients

½ cup whole milk
¼ cup heavy cream
1 tablespoon dried lavender
2½ cups all-purpose flour
1 cup cake flour
½ cup granulated sugar
1 tablespoon baking powder
½ teaspoon table salt
5 tablespoons unsalted butter, cubed
1 tablespoon lemon zest (1 to 2 lemons)
2 large eggs, beaten

Glaze

1 cup confectioners' sugar
2 tablespoons freshly squeezed lemon juice
2 tablespoons unsalted butter, melted

Equipment: Plate Setter, Baking Stone
Set the EGG for indirect cooking with the Plate Setter, legs down, and the Baking Stone on top of the Plate Setter.
Preheat the EGG to 450°F.

In a small saucepan on the stovetop over medium-low heat, combine the milk, cream, and lavender. Let the milk steep for 3 to 4 minutes, until the lavender flavor has blended into the liquids. Do not boil. Remove the pan from the heat and strain the milk mixture into a small bowl, discarding the lavender. Set aside and let the milk cool completely.

Combine the all-purpose flour, cake flour, sugar, baking powder, and salt in a large bowl. Mix until well blended. Using a pastry cutter or fork, work the butter into the flour until the butter is pea size. Add the lemon zest and mix well. Add the beaten eggs to the milk mixture and stir well. Using a fork, slowly add the milk mixture to the dry ingredients, stirring until a dough forms.

Turn the dough onto a lightly floured surface. Form the dough into a ball and, using a sharp knife, divide the dough into 3 equal parts. Using a rolling pin, flatten each section into a 5-inch circle. Cut each circle into 4 equal wedges.

Place the scones on the Baking Stone. Close the lid of the EGG and bake for 18 minutes, or until an inserted toothpick comes out clean. Using a spatula, transfer the scones to a platter. Let cool for 10 minutes.

To make the glaze, whisk the confectioners' sugar, lemon juice, and butter in a small bowl until smooth. Drizzle 1 tablespoon of the glaze over each scone. Serve immediately. **Makes 12 scones; serves 6**

eggxhilarating!

desserts

recipes

Grilled Pineapple Upside-Down Cake

For this delicious cake, fresh pineapple rings are grilled and then placed on the bottom of the cake pan before the cake batter is added. Once the cake is baked and inverted onto a plate, the caramelized pineapple rings will be sitting on top of the cake like a crown. This would be a great dessert to serve after grilled Beef Kabobs with Chimichurri (page 59).

Ingredients

½ cup plus ½ cup firmly packed light brown sugar
1 (14-ounce can) sweetened condensed milk
7 fresh pineapple slices, ¼ inch thick
1½ cups all-purpose flour
1½ teaspoons baking powder
¼ teaspoon table salt
1 cup unsalted butter
3 large eggs
5 large egg yolks
1½ teaspoons vanilla extract
1 cup granulated sugar
7 maraschino cherries

> **Equipment: Porcelain coated grid, Grill Gripper, Plate Setter, oiled 9-inch round cake pan**
> **Set the EGG for direct cooking with the porcelain coated grid.**
> **Preheat the EGG to 325°F.**

Mix ½ cup brown sugar and the condensed milk in a small bowl, blending well. Cut a hole, the same diameter as the cherries, in the center of each pineapple slice. Dredge the pineapple slices in the milk mixture and place them on the grid. Close the lid of the EGG and cook for 2 minutes on each side. Transfer the pineapple to a plate and let cool.

Using the Grill Gripper and barbecue mitts, carefully remove the grid and add the Plate Setter, legs down.

Sift the flour, baking powder, and salt together in a medium bowl. Set aside. Melt the butter in a saucepan on the stovetop and let cool. Set aside. In a large bowl, whisk the eggs and egg yolks together. Add the vanilla, remaining ½ cup brown sugar, and granulated sugar and stir until all the ingredients are incorporated. Slowly add the flour mixture to the egg mixture. Add the melted butter and mix well.

Arrange the pineapple slices on the bottom of the cake pan. Place a cherry in the center of each pineapple ring, then pour the batter over the top of the pineapple. Use a spatula to smooth the batter until it is evenly distributed.

Place the cake pan on the Plate Setter. Close the lid of the EGG and bake for 30 to 35 minutes, until an inserted toothpick comes out clean. Remove the pan and let cool for 10 minutes.

Gently run a knife around the outside edge of the pan. Cover the top of the cake pan with a platter and, holding the cake pan and the platter firmly together, gently turn the platter right side up with the pan upside down. Remove the pan and serve. **Serves 6**

(See recipe photograph on page 242.)

Bananas Foster

This classic banana dessert, first prepared by Paul Belange at Brennan's Restaurant in New Orleans, is traditionally served over vanilla ice cream. It is usually prepared at the tableside. At the end of the preparation, the banana liqueur and rum are ignited, making for a dramatic presentation.

Ingredients

8 tablespoons unsalted butter
½ cup firmly packed brown sugar
½ cup granulated sugar
½ teaspoon ground cinnamon
4 bananas, peeled and sliced lengthwise
¼ cup banana liqueur
½ cup dark rum
1 pint vanilla ice cream

Equipment: Porcelain coated grid, Dutch Oven
Set the EGG for direct cooking with the porcelain coated grid.
Preheat the EGG to 400°F.

Place the Dutch Oven on the grid.

Stir the butter, brown sugar, granulated sugar, and cinnamon together in the Dutch Oven. Close the lid of the EGG and cook for 3 to 4 minutes, whisking constantly until smooth. Add the bananas, cut side down. Close the lid of the EGG and cook for 2 to 3 minutes, until the bananas are completely coated in the sugar mixture. Add the banana liqueur and the rum. Using a long match, carefully light the liqueur and rum, and cook until the flame burns off. Remove the Dutch Oven from the grid.

Portion the ice cream into bowls, spoon the bananas and sauce over the top, and serve immediately. **Serves 4**

Pound Cake with Strawberries & Berry Coulis

Strawberries mean summer has arrived! This is the perfect dessert to make when strawberries and raspberries are fresh and plentiful. This pound cake is particularly moist because of the addition of yogurt to the recipe. The coulis is a thick strained fruit sauce and joins the macerated berries on top of the cake. The coulis is also delightful served over ice cream with fresh berries.

Ingredients

Pound Cake
1 cup unsalted butter, at room temperature
3 cups granulated sugar
6 large eggs
3 cups cake flour
¼ teaspoon table salt
¼ teaspoon baking soda
1 cup plain yogurt
2 teaspoons vanilla extract

Strawberry-Raspberry Coulis
1 pound fresh strawberries, hulled and quartered
1 cup raspberries, fresh or frozen
1 cup granulated sugar
2 tablespoons freshly squeezed lemon juice

Whipped Cream
1 cup heavy cream
½ cup confectioners' sugar
½ teaspoon vanilla extract

Equipment: Plate Setter, oiled and floured loaf pan
Set the EGG for indirect cooking with the Plate Setter, legs down.
Preheat the EGG to 325°F.

To make the pound cake, in a large bowl using an electric mixer, cream the butter and sugar for 3 to 5 minutes. Add the eggs, 1 at a time, with the mixer on low. Blend until the eggs are completely incorporated. Mix the flour, salt, and baking soda in a separate bowl. With the mixer on low, add the yogurt and the flour mixture, alternately, until both are completely incorporated. Add the vanilla and continue mixing for 15 seconds.

Pour the batter into the prepared loaf pan and place the pan on the Plate Setter. Close the lid of the EGG and bake for 1 hour, or until an inserted toothpick comes out clean.

To make the coulis, using a small paring knife, quarter the strawberries and place them in a small bowl with the raspberries. Add the sugar and lemon juice. Using a spoon, toss the strawberries and raspberries in the sugar. Place half of the strawberries and raspberries in the bowl of a blender or food processor fitted with the steel blade and refrigerate the other half. Puree the berries in the blender for 3 minutes on high. Strain the coulis into a small bowl.

To make the whipped cream, using a whisk or electric mixer, beat the cream, confectioners' sugar, and vanilla for 5 minutes, or until light and fluffy.

To assemble, place a slice of cake on each plate. Top with the macerated strawberries and raspberries, spoon the coulis over the berries, and top with the whipped cream.
Serves 6 to 8

Black & White Cupcakes

Serving cupcakes at a barbecue is very traditional, but you probably wouldn't think of baking the cupcakes on the barbecue grill. For these cupcakes, chocolate cake is married with a Cointreau-laced icing. Cointreau is an orange-flavored liqueur produced in France using a combination of sweet and bitter oranges. Buy the best-quality chocolate to make these exceptionally rich cupcakes. When baking these in the EGG, do not use paper liners inside the muffin pans, as the papers will burn.

Ingredients

1½ cups cake flour
½ cup all-purpose flour
1½ cups granulated sugar
1 teaspoon baking soda
¼ teaspoon baking powder
½ teaspoon table salt
1 cup warm water
1 tablespoon instant coffee
½ cup unsweetened cocoa powder
2 large eggs
½ cup canola oil
1 teaspoon orange extract
2 cups semisweet chocolate chips

Icing

10 tablespoons unsalted butter, at room temperature
2¼ cups confectioners' sugar
2 tablespoons freshly squeezed orange juice
3 tablespoons Cointreau
1 teaspoon orange zest

Equipment: Plate Setter, oiled and floured 12-cup muffin pan (do not use paper liners)
Set the EGG for indirect cooking with the Plate Setter, legs down.
Preheat the EGG to 350°F.

Combine the cake flour, all-purpose flour, sugar, baking soda, baking powder, and salt in a medium bowl. Stir until blended. Pour the water into another medium bowl. Add the instant coffee and cocoa powder. Using a whisk, stir until the coffee and cocoa are completely dissolved. Add the eggs, canola oil, and orange extract to the bowl and mix until completely combined. Add the flour mixture to the liquid, a little at a time, stirring constantly. Fold the chocolate chips into the batter. Pour the batter into a 4-cup liquid measuring cup. Pour ⅓ cup of the batter into each muffin cup.

Place the pan on the Plate Setter. Close the lid of the EGG and bake for 25 minutes, or until an inserted toothpick comes out clean. Remove the pan. Allow the cupcakes to cool completely before removing them from the cups.

To make the icing, in a large bowl using an electric mixer, beat the butter until it is light and creamy. Add the confectioners' sugar and continue beating until the sugar is completely incorporated. Slowly add the orange juice, Cointreau, and orange zest and beat until the icing is light and fluffy. Spread the icing on top of the cupcakes and serve. **Makes 12 cupcakes**

Kahlúa Coffee Brownies

Three types of chocolate are blended in these rich, fudgelike brownies, resulting in the most decadent brownies you will ever taste. Once baked, top them with a cream cheese frosting flavored with Kahlúa, a coffee liqueur from Mexico. If you love coffee and chocolate, these are a real treat!

Ingredients

1 cup unsalted butter
1 tablespoon instant coffee
4 ounces unsweetened chocolate
4 large eggs
2 cups granulated sugar
1½ cups all-purpose flour
⅛ teaspoon table salt
1 cup bittersweet chocolate chips
1 cup white chocolate chips

Kahlúa Icing
1 (8-ounce) package cream cheese, at room temperature
4 tablespoons unsalted butter
2 tablespoons Kahlúa
2½ cups confectioners' sugar

**Equipment: Plate Setter, oiled 9 by 13-inch glass or ceramic baking dish
Set the EGG for indirect cooking with the Plate Setter, legs down.
Preheat the EGG to 350°F.**

Melt the butter in a medium saucepan on the stovetop over low heat. Add the coffee and stir until dissolved. Remove the saucepan from the heat, add the unsweetened chocolate, and stir until smooth. Add the eggs, 1 at a time, and continue mixing. Add the sugar and mix well. Add the flour and salt and gently combine. Using a spatula, fold the bittersweet chocolate and white chocolate chips into the batter. Spread the batter evenly into the prepared baking dish.

Place the baking dish on the Plate Setter. Close the lid of the EGG and bake for 20 minutes, or until an inserted toothpick comes out clean. Remove and let the brownies cool before icing them.

To make the icing, in a large bowl using an electric mixer, beat the cheese and butter for 3 to 4 minutes, until creamy. Add the Kahlúa and confectioners' sugar and mix for 1 to 2 minutes, until completely blended. Using a spatula, spread the icing on the brownies.

Cut the brownies into 3-inch squares and serve.
Makes 12 brownies

Chocolate Pecan Bourbon Pie

Pecan pie is a typical Southern dish made from corn syrup, brown sugar, and pecans and is often served on holidays. This traditional pie filling has a touch of bourbon and combines with dark chocolate morsels. It is perfect for a fall dinner or winter holiday dessert and would be especially good served after a smoked turkey dinner (page 108).

Ingredients

1 cup dark corn syrup
3 large eggs, beaten
5 tablespoons unsalted butter, melted
1 cup firmly packed light brown sugar
¼ cup bourbon
2 tablespoons all-purpose flour
1 cup semisweet chocolate chips
1 cup chopped pecans
1 (9-inch) pie shell (page 223)

Whipped Cream

1 cup heavy cream
½ cup confectioners' sugar
½ teaspoon vanilla extract

Equipment: Plate Setter
Set the EGG for indirect cooking with the Plate Setter, legs down.
Preheat the EGG to 400°F.

Using a wooden spoon, mix the corn syrup, eggs, butter, brown sugar, bourbon, and flour in a medium bowl until combined. Add the chocolate and pecans and blend well. Pour the filling into the pie shell.

Place the pie plate on the Plate Setter. Close the lid of the EGG and bake for 45 minutes, or until the filling is set and the pie is golden brown. Remove the pie and let cool completely, then refrigerate.

To make the whipped cream, using a whisk or an electric mixer, beat the cream, confectioners' sugar, and vanilla for 5 minutes, or until light and fluffy. Serve slices of pie garnished with the whipped cream or pass separately.
Serves 6 to 8

Apple-Walnut Crostata with Caramel Sauce

A crostata is nothing more than a fruit tart that is meant to be rustic, so do not be too concerned if this is your first time working with pie dough. Three different types of apple are used in this crostata: the tart, green Granny Smith; the sweet, crisp, red Fuji; and the very sweet Golden Delicious. By blending these three different varieties, the flavor of the crostata becomes more complex and balanced. Fresh berries, pears, or peaches work equally well.

Ingredients

1 pie dough disk (page 223)
¼ cup firmly packed light brown sugar
1 teaspoon freshly squeezed orange juice
1 teaspoon ground cinnamon
¼ teaspoon ground nutmeg
3 cups apple slices, ⅛ inch thick (1 cup each
   Granny Smith, Fuji, and Golden Delicious)
½ cup chopped walnuts
4 tablespoons unsalted butter, cubed
1 large egg white, beaten
1 tablespoon water
1 tablespoon granulated sugar

Caramel Sauce

1 cup granulated sugar
¼ cup water
1 cup heavy cream
4 tablespoons unsalted butter

> **Equipment: Plate Setter, Baking Stone, pizza peel**
> **Set the EGG for indirect cooking with the Plate Setter, legs down, and the Baking Stone on top of the Plate Setter.**
> **Preheat the EGG to 400°F.**

Dust the pizza peel with flour. Roll the pie dough into a 12-inch circle on a lightly floured surface and place the dough on the peel.

Mix the brown sugar, orange juice, cinnamon, and nutmeg in a large bowl. Add the apples and walnuts and toss until well coated with the brown sugar mixture. Spread the apple mixture in the center of the pastry, leaving a 2-inch border of dough exposed. Fold over the pastry edge toward the center, leaving the edges and folds of the dough very rustic. Dot the exposed apples with the butter. Mix the egg white and water in a small bowl and brush the outside of the dough with the egg wash. Sprinkle the top of the crostata with the granulated sugar.

Carefully transfer the crostata to the Baking Stone. Close the lid of the EGG and bake for 40 minutes, or until golden brown. Using the pizza peel, transfer the crostata to a platter.

To make the sauce, using a whisk, stir the sugar and water together in a small, heavy-bottomed saucepan on the stovetop. Cook over medium heat for 15 minutes, occasionally brushing the sides of the pan with a wet brush. Do not stir. When the sugar is amber in color, slowly add the cream, whisking constantly for 3 to 5 minutes, until the sugar is dissolved. Remove the pan from the heat and whisk the butter into the caramel, 1 tablespoon at a time, until smooth and creamy. Let the caramel sauce cool for 10 to 15 minutes. Pour into a bowl and serve with the crostata. **Serves 6**

Apple Crumble

Slightly tart Granny Smith apples, which originated in Australia, are ideal for baking. They are crisp, hold their color longer than most apples, and do not break down as quickly as most apples when cooked. The tart flavor of this apple is a nice contrast with the sweet topping. Though wonderful on its own, try serving the crumble with whipped cream or a scoop of your favorite ice cream.

Ingredients

1½ cups sour cream
2 large eggs, beaten
½ cup all-purpose flour
¾ cup granulated sugar
¼ teaspoon table salt
2 teaspoons vanilla extract
3 tablespoons Grand Marnier
4 pounds Granny Smith apples

Topping

⅔ cup all-purpose flour
½ cup firmly packed brown sugar
½ cup granulated sugar
3½ teaspoons ground cinnamon
½ teaspoon ground nutmeg
8 tablespoons unsalted butter, cut into cubes
1¼ cups walnut pieces

Equipment: Plate Setter, 9 by 13-inch glass or ceramic baking dish
Set the EGG for indirect heat with the Plate Setter, legs down.
Preheat the EGG to 350°F.

Using a whisk, mix the sour cream and eggs in a large bowl. Add the flour, sugar, salt, vanilla, and Grand Marnier. Stir until completely combined. Core and peel the apples, cut them in half lengthwise, and cut each half into thin slices. The apples may also be sliced in the bowl of a food processor fitted with the slicing blade. Add the sliced apples to the sour cream mixture and blend gently until the apples are completely coated. Pour the apple mixture into the pan and, using a rubber spatula, spread evenly.

Place the baking dish on the Plate Setter. Close the lid of the EGG and bake for 45 minutes, or until the custard is set. Remove the pan from the EGG and let cool for 5 minutes.

To make the topping, place the flour, brown sugar, granulated sugar, cinnamon, and nutmeg in the bowl of a food processor fitted with the steel blade. Pulse until the ingredients are thoroughly blended. Add the butter and walnuts and pulse briefly until the butter is roughly pea size. Sprinkle the topping evenly over the apples.

Place the pan on the Plate Setter. Close the lid of the EGG and bake another 15 minutes, or until golden brown. Serve hot or cold. **Serves 6**

Blackberry, Peach & Amaretto Cobbler

There's something magical about the way the batter reacts in this very Southern dish. It's poured into the pan before anything else is added and then topped with the fruit filling. While baking in the EGG, the batter slowly rises to the top, creating a beautiful golden crust. Underneath lies a luscious combination of blackberries and peaches in a thick amaretto syrup. If you can't find fresh blackberries or peaches, use any fresh berry that is available at your local market or substitute thawed frozen fruit.

Ingredients

½ cup plus 1 cup granulated sugar
½ teaspoon ground cinnamon
2 teaspoons lemon zest
2 tablespoons freshly squeezed lemon juice
¼ cup amaretto
1 tablespoon cornstarch
½ teaspoon plus ¼ teaspoon table salt
5 cups peach slices, ½ inch thick
2½ cups fresh blackberries
10 tablespoons unsalted butter
1 cup all-purpose flour
1 tablespoon baking powder
¾ cup whole milk
½ teaspoon vanilla extract
Vanilla ice cream, whipped cream, or powdered
   confectioners' sugar (optional)

Equipment: Plate Setter, 9 by 13-inch baking dish
Set the EGG for indirect cooking with the Plate Setter, legs down.
Preheat the EGG to 400°F.

Mix ½ cup sugar, cinnamon, lemon zest, lemon juice, amaretto, cornstarch, and ½ teaspoon of the salt in a large bowl. Add the peaches and blackberries. Toss to coat. Set aside.

Melt the butter in a small saucepan on the stovetop over low heat and pour into the baking dish. Whisk the flour, remaining 1 cup granulated sugar, baking powder, milk, vanilla, and ¼ teaspoon salt together in a small bowl. Pour the batter into the baking dish over the melted butter. Top with the fruit mixture.

Place the dish on the Plate Setter. Close the lid of the EGG and bake for 45 minutes, or until the crust is light golden brown. Remove and let cool for 15 minutes.

Serve with vanilla ice cream, whipped cream, or confectioners' sugar, if desired. **Serves 6**

Roasted Peaches
with Pecan Praline Stuffing

Peaches are a member of the rose family. There are
many varieties, and they are usually classified by
their pit or stone. In a clingstone peach, the flesh
clings most tightly to the pit. These are the sweetest
and juiciest of the peaches. However, the freestone
is the peach usually found in your local grocery. The
pit of the freestone is easily removed, making it
ideal for eating or baking. For this simple dessert,
use ripe and juicy freestone peaches, fill them with
pecan praline stuffing, and bake in the EGG. Dessert
doesn't get any better or easier than this!

Ingredients

4 ripe peaches, unpeeled
1 tablespoon freshly squeezed lemon juice
¾ cup firmly packed light brown sugar
¼ cup all-purpose flour
½ teaspoon ground cinnamon
½ teaspoon table salt
¼ teaspoon ground ginger
¼ teaspoon ground nutmeg
3 tablespoons plus 3 tablespoons unsalted butter, cubed
¼ cup chopped pecans

**Equipment: Porcelain coated grid, 9 by
13-inch glass or ceramic baking dish
Set the EGG for direct cooking with the
porcelain coated grid.
Preheat the EGG to 400°F.**

Cut the peaches in half and remove the pits. Using a
teaspoon, core the red centers from each of the peach
halves. Dip the cut side of each peach into the lemon
juice. Place the peaches in the baking dish, cut side up.

In a medium bowl, stir the brown sugar, flour, cinnamon,
salt, ginger, and nutmeg until completely blended.
Add 3 tablespoons of the butter to the flour mixture.
Using a fork or pastry cutter, cut the butter into the dry
ingredients until the pieces of butter are pea size. Using
a spatula, fold the chopped pecans into the flour mixture
until the pecans and the flour mixture are completely
combined. Place 2 tablespoons of the filling into the
center of each peach half. Put the peaches inside the
baking dish and put the remaining 3 tablespoons butter
in the pan.

Place the baking dish on the grid. Close the lid of the
EGG and bake for 20 minutes, or until the stuffing has
set and the peaches begin to soften. Remove the dish
and let the peaches rest for 10 minutes before serving.
Serves 8

EGGstraordinary Doughnuts

These doughnuts take a bit of time to make, but they are melt-in-your-mouth delicious and well worth the effort. After cooking, they are tossed in cinnamon and granulated sugar, but any topping can be used, from confectioners' sugar or melted chocolate to a lemon glaze. Doughnuts are fun to make for a crowd—just be aware that they will disappear fast, so you might want to double the recipe.

Ingredients
½ cup warm water (105° to 110°F)
1 tablespoon active dry yeast
¼ cup whole milk
¼ cup buttermilk
3 tablespoons vegetable shortening, melted
¼ cup plus 1 cup granulated sugar
1½ cups plus ½ cup all-purpose flour
1 tablespoon baking powder
1 teaspoon table salt
2 teaspoons ground cinnamon
4 cups peanut oil

> **Equipment: Porcelain coated grid,
>   Dutch Oven**
> **Set the EGG for direct cooking with the
>   porcelain coated grid.**
> **Preheat the EGG to 400°F.**

Pour the warm water into a medium bowl, add the yeast, and let sit for 5 minutes, or until frothy. Add the milk, buttermilk, shortening, ¼ cup of the sugar, 1½ cups of the flour, the baking powder, and salt. Mix well. Continue to add the remaining ½ cup flour until a soft dough forms.

Turn the dough onto a lightly floured surface. Knead briefly, about 5 times. Using a rolling pin, roll the dough ½ inch thick. Use a 2½-inch round biscuit cutter or a small drinking glass to cut the dough into rounds. Place the dough onto a lightly floured cookie sheet and cover with plastic wrap. Let the dough rise for 1 hour, or until doubled in size.

Mix the cinnamon and the remaining 1 cup sugar in a small bowl until blended. Set aside.

Fill the Dutch Oven with 2 inches of peanut oil. Place the Dutch Oven on the grid and heat the oil to 375°F. Carefully place 3 or 4 of the doughnuts into the hot oil. Close the lid of the EGG and cook for 1 to 2 minutes, until a light golden brown. Using tongs, turn each doughnut over. Close the lid of the EGG and cook for another 1 to 2 minutes. Transfer the doughnuts to a plate lined with paper towels to drain. Repeat the process until you have fried all the dough.

Toss the cooked doughnuts, a few at a time, in the cinnamon-sugar mixture until coated. Serve. **Makes 12 doughnuts**

Red Chile & Lime Shortbread Cookies

This traditional butter shortbread has a bit of Red Chile Rub added, giving these cookies a subtle hint of heat. Scoring the dough into wedges before it is baked makes it very easy to break into individual cookies. Once cooled, gently break the cookies along the lines. This dough may also be rolled out and cut with a cookie cutter, if you prefer.

Ingredients

8 tablespoons unsalted butter
¼ cup granulated sugar
½ teaspoon table salt
2 teaspoons lime zest (1 to 2 limes)
1 teaspoon Red Chile Rub (page 197)
1 cup plus 2 tablespoons all-purpose flour

Equipment: Plate Setter, 9-inch round cake pan
Set the EGG for indirect cooking with the Plate Setter, legs down.
Preheat the EGG to 300°F.

In a large bowl using an electric mixer, beat the butter, sugar, salt, lime zest, and Red Chile Rub on low speed until the butter is creamed but not completely smooth. Scrape the butter off the sides of the bowl. With the mixer on low, gradually add the flour until the dough forms a ball.

Transfer the dough to a lightly floured surface. Using a rolling pin, roll the dough ¼ inch thick. Place the dough in the cake pan. Spread the dough evenly with your fingers, pressing the dough into the edges of the pan. Using a paring knife, score the dough into 8 to 12 equal wedges. Do not cut all the way through the dough.

Place the cake pan on the Plate Setter. Close the lid of the EGG and bake for 7 to 8 minutes, or until light brown. Let the shortbread cool.

Break the shortbread into wedges and serve. **Makes 8 to 12 cookies**

egghead recipes

recipes

Caribbean Stuffed Peppers

Jerk seasoning, which comes from Jamaica, is often used to impart flavor to grilled meats. The ingredients in jerk seasoning vary but generally include chiles, thyme, garlic, and onions, and so-called sweet spices, such as cinnamon, ginger, allspice, and cloves. In this version, the blend of chiles and spices is added directly to the ground meat, and the highly spiced meat is used to stuff bell peppers.

Ingredients

6 bell peppers (red, yellow, green, or a combination)
2 tablespoons olive oil
1 pound ground chuck or ground round
1 cup diced red onion
2 tablespoons minced garlic
3 tablespoons jerk seasoning
1 cup white rice
2 cups chicken stock
1 (28-ounce) can diced tomatoes, drained
1 Scotch bonnet chile pepper
4 sprigs thyme
2 bay leaves
1 (1½-inch) piece peeled fresh ginger
1 (15-ounce) can black beans, drained and rinsed
½ cup firmly packed chopped fresh cilantro
½ cup thinly sliced scallions
2 tablespoons freshly squeezed lime juice (1 to 2 limes)
½ cup crumbled cotija cheese (2 ounces)

Equipment: Porcelain coated grid, Dutch Oven, perforated grill pan
Set the EGG for direct cooking with the porcelain coated grid.
Preheat the EGG to 350°F.

Place the Dutch Oven on the grid and preheat for 10 minutes.

Cut off the tops of the bell peppers and remove the seeds and ribs. If the peppers will not sit upright, cut a thin slice of flesh off the base to level the bottom. Set aside.

Pour the olive oil into the Dutch Oven to heat briefly. Add the ground chuck, onion, and garlic. Close the lid of the EGG and cook for 3 to 4 minutes, until the meat is browned. Add the jerk seasoning and stir. Close the lid of the EGG and continue to cook for 3 to 4 minutes, until the ground beef is completely cooked. Add the rice, chicken stock, tomatoes, chile pepper, thyme sprigs, bay leaves, and ginger to the Dutch Oven and stir gently. Place the lid on the Dutch Oven and close the lid of the EGG. Simmer for 15 minutes, or until the rice is cooked and the liquid is absorbed.

Remove the Dutch Oven from the heat and let it sit, covered, for 10 minutes. Remove the lid and, using a fork, gently fluff the rice mixture. Remove and discard the chile pepper and thyme sprigs. Gently stir in the black beans, cilantro, scallion, and lime juice. Fill each of the bell peppers with 1 to 1½ cups of the filling.

Place the peppers on the perforated grill pan and place the pan on the grid. Close the lid of the EGG and cook for 30 minutes, or until the ingredients are thoroughly cooked. Transfer the peppers from the EGG to a platter and sprinkle each pepper with cheese. Serve immediately.
Serves 6

ABTs

You will find ABTs wherever EGGheads gather. This classic EGG dish is taken to the next level by adding Red Chile Rub, a red pepper glaze, and applewood-smoked bacon. These are great for a big gathering, especially on game day.

Ingredients

12 whole jalapeño peppers or red Fresno peppers
½ cup red pepper jelly
2 tablespoons water
24 Little Smokies sausages
8 ounces cream cheese, cubed, at room temperature
½ cup firmly packed fresh cilantro leaves
12 ounces applewood-smoked bacon (12 to 14 slices), cut in half
2 tablespoons Red Chile Rub (page 197)

**Equipment: Plate Setter, porcelain coated grid, perforated grill pan
Set the EGG for indirect cooking with the Plate Setter, legs up, and the porcelain coated grid on top of the Plate Setter.
Preheat the EGG to 350°F.**

Remove the stems from the peppers, cut in half lengthwise, and remove the seeds and membranes. Set aside.

To make the glaze, heat the red pepper jelly and water in a small saucepan on the stovetop, stirring occasionally with a wooden spoon. Set aside.

Place the Little Smokies in the bowl of a food processor fitted with the steel blade. Pulse briefly, until coarsely chopped. Add the cheese and cilantro and continue pulsing until combined. Place 1 tablespoon of the cheese mixture into the cavity of each pepper half. Wrap each half with a half-slice of the applewood-smoked bacon, and secure the bacon with a toothpick. Sprinkle each pepper with the Red Chile Rub. Place the peppers on the perforated grill pan and place the pan on the grid. Close the lid of the EGG. Cook, brushing often with a generous portion of the red pepper glaze, for 30 minutes, or until the bacon is crisp.

Transfer the ABTs to a platter and serve immediately.
Serves 6

Tomatoes with Cornbread Stuffing

Nothing tastes better than the first plump, ripe, juicy tomatoes of the season. Whether they are homegrown or from a roadside market, they signal that summer is near. For this dish, you can use any type of fresh tomatoes that are available, as long as they are round tomatoes rather than Roma. Only the round ones will sit upright on the grid once they are stuffed.

Ingredients

2 cups crumbled Southwestern Cornbread (page 217)

1 cup julienned prosciutto

½ cup diced mozzarella cheese (2 ounces)

½ cup plus ¼ cup grated Parmigiano-Reggiano cheese (3 ounces total)

¼ cup chopped oil-packed sun-dried tomatoes

¼ cup chopped fresh basil

2 tablespoons plus ¼ cup extra-virgin olive oil

Kosher salt and freshly ground black pepper

8 vine-ripened tomatoes, tops removed and cored

Equipment: Porcelain coated grid, perforated grill pan
Set the EGG for direct cooking with the porcelain coated grid.
Preheat the EGG to 350°F.

Using a wooden spoon, combine the cornbread, prosciutto, mozzarella cheese, ½ cup of the Parmigiano-Reggiano cheese, the sun-dried tomatoes, basil, and 2 tablespoons of the olive oil in a medium bowl. Season the stuffing with salt and pepper and mix well. Cut the tops off the tomatoes and, using a teaspoon or melon baller, remove some of the flesh from inside the tomatoes and discard it. Using a spoon, fill each tomato with some of the cornbread mixture, drizzle the tomatoes with the remaining ¼ cup olive oil, and sprinkle the tops of the tomatoes with the remaining ¼ cup Parmigiano-Reggiano cheese. Place the tomatoes on the perforated grill pan.

Place the grill pan with the tomatoes on the grid. Close the lid of the EGG and cook for 20 minutes, or until browned and heated thoroughly. Using a long-handled spatula, transfer the tomatoes to a platter. Let the tomatoes rest for 5 minutes before serving. **Serves 4**

Tomato Pie

This is the perfect savory pie to make when tomatoes are at their peak, using beefsteak, Roma, or other vine-ripened tomatoes. It is perfect for lunch with Grilled Caesar Salad (page 171) or can be served as a side dish with Slow-Roasted Leg of Lamb (page 76) or Spatchcocked Chicken (page 274).

Ingredients

3 or 4 tomatoes
¼ cup olive oil
Kosher salt and freshly ground black pepper
1 (9-inch) pie shell (page 223)
½ cup grated Parmigiano-Reggiano cheese (2 ounces)
1 cup grated white Cheddar cheese (4 ounces)
1 cup mayonnaise
1 cup cooked and crumbled applewood-smoked bacon (about 6 slices)
½ cup chopped scallions
½ cup julienned fresh basil leaves

Equipment: Porcelain coated grid, Grill Gripper, Plate Setter
Set the EGG for direct cooking with the porcelain coated grid.
Preheat the EGG to 400°F.

Cut the tomatoes in half and place them in a small bowl, toss with the olive oil, and season with salt and pepper. Place the tomatoes on the grid and close the lid of the EGG. Cook for 2 minutes per side, or until the tomatoes are roasted and the skin pulls away from the tomato. Using a long-handled spatula, transfer the tomatoes from the grid to a platter and let cool completely. Peel and slice thinly.

Using the Grill Gripper and barbecue mitts, carefully remove the grid and add the Plate Setter, legs down.

To blind bake the pie shell, cover with aluminum foil and place pie weights on top of the foil. Place the pie plate on the Plate Setter, close the lid of the EGG, and bake for about 12 minutes. Set aside and let cool.

Using a wooden spoon, mix the Parmigiano-Reggiano cheese, Cheddar cheese, and mayonnaise in a medium bowl and stir well. Cover the bottom of the pie shell with the bacon, and layer with the scallions, basil, and sliced tomatoes. Season the tomatoes with pepper. Spread the cheese mixture evenly in the pie shell.

Place the pie plate on the Plate Setter again and close the lid of the EGG. Bake for 20 minutes, or until the top is lightly browned. Remove the pie plate and let stand for 10 minutes before slicing. Serve immediately. **Serves 6**

Crab-Stuffed Portobello Mushrooms

Portobello mushrooms are large, meaty brown mushrooms. When the mushrooms are ready to stuff, be sure to handle the crabmeat gently so that it does not break into small pieces. Served with a piquant rémoulade sauce, this dish can be served as an appetizer or main course.

Ingredients

Rémoulade
½ cup mayonnaise
¼ cup chopped dill gherkin pickles
1 tablespoon chopped pimientos
1 tablespoon capers
½ teaspoon Worcestershire sauce
¼ teaspoon Tabasco sauce
1 tablespoon freshly squeezed lemon juice
1 tablespoon chopped fresh dill

2 tablespoons plus 4 tablespoons unsalted butter, melted
2 tablespoons minced shallot
1 tablespoon minced garlic
2 tablespoons all-purpose flour
1 cup whole milk
1 teaspoon Old Bay seasoning
¼ cup grated Parmigiano-Reggiano cheese (1 ounce)
1 tablespoon Dijon mustard
1 teaspoon Worcestershire sauce
½ teaspoon Tabasco sauce
1 pound lump crabmeat
¼ cup chopped fresh chives
Kosher salt and freshly ground black pepper
4 to 6 large portobello mushrooms, stems and gills removed
¼ cup panko (Japanese bread crumbs)
1 teaspoon sweet paprika

Equipment: Plate Setter, 9 by 13-inch glass or ceramic baking dish
Set the EGG for indirect cooking with the Plate Setter, legs down.
Preheat the EGG to 400°F.

To make the rémoulade, place all the ingredients into the bowl of a food processor fitted with the steel blade. Turn the food processor on and let it run for 30 seconds only. Refrigerate until ready to serve.

Melt 2 tablespoons of the butter in a small saucepan on the stovetop over medium heat. Add the shallot and garlic and cook for 2 to 3 minutes, until the shallot is translucent. Add the flour and cook for 1 minute, until the flour is incorporated. Using a whisk, add the milk and Old Bay seasoning. Stir for 5 minutes, or until the sauce thickens. Remove the pan from the heat and add the cheese, mustard, Worcestershire sauce, and Tabasco sauce. Stir until completely blended. Let cool completely.

Place the crabmeat in a medium bowl. Add the chives and season with salt and pepper. Using a rubber spatula, mix gently. Pour the sauce over the crab and gently fold the mixture together until combined.

Melt the remaining 4 tablespoons butter in a small saucepan on the stovetop. Brush some butter on both sides of the portobello mushrooms, and place the mushrooms in the baking dish. Spoon the crab filling into the prepared mushrooms. Brush the filling with the remaining melted butter, top with panko, and sprinkle with paprika.

Place the baking dish on the Plate Setter and close the lid of the EGG. Bake for 20 to 25 minutes, or until golden brown. Place the mushrooms on a platter or plates, and serve with the rémoulade. **Serves 4 to 6**

Baked Brie

This is a great party dish, and it's easy to make. Just be sure that you seal the puff pastry tightly around the edges so that the Brie cheese does not escape during baking. Feel free to experiment with other jellies, fruits, and nuts.

Ingredients

2 sheets puff pastry (1-pound box), thawed
1 (2-pound) wheel Brie cheese
½ cup raspberry preserves
½ cup dried cherries
½ cup golden raisins
½ cup smoked pecans (page 204)
1 large egg, beaten
1 tablespoon water

Equipment: Plate Setter, Baking Stone
Set the EGG for indirect cooking with the Plate Setter, legs down.
Preheat the EGG to 400°F.

Unroll a sheet of puff pastry. Using a sharp knife, remove the rind from the top of the cheese. Discard the rind and place the whole cheese in the center of the unrolled sheet of puff pastry. Spread the top of the exposed cheese with the raspberry preserves and set aside.

Place the cherries, raisins, and pecans in the bowl of a food processor fitted with the steel blade. Pulse on and off, until the fruit is coarsely chopped into small pieces.

Spread the fruit mixture evenly over the top of the preserves. Unroll the remaining sheet of puff pastry and place it on top of the cheese. Tuck the edges of the puff pastry under and press to seal, trimming any excess.

Mix the egg and water in a small bowl. Use a pastry brush to brush the egg wash over the top and sides of the puff pastry. Transfer the cheese, wrapped in its puff pastry, to a cold Baking Stone. Using barbecue mitts, place the Baking Stone on the Plate Setter and close the lid of the EGG. Bake for 25 minutes, or until golden brown.

Using a large spatula, transfer the baked Brie to a platter and let cool for 5 minutes before serving. **Serves 8**

Moussaka

Although this eggplant and meat dish is served throughout the Middle East, it is the Greek version that is most familiar.

Ingredients

2 pounds eggplant, unpeeled, sliced ¼ inch thick
½ cup extra-virgin olive oil
Freshly ground black pepper

Filling

2 tablespoons unsalted butter
1 pound ground beef or lamb
1 cup chopped yellow onions
1 tablespoon minced garlic
1 tablespoon dried oregano
1 teaspoon ground cinnamon
1 teaspoon granulated sugar
¼ teaspoon ground nutmeg
2 tablespoons tomato paste
½ cup tomato sauce
¼ cup red wine
1 tablespoon white wine vinegar
½ teaspoon kosher salt
¼ teaspoon freshly ground black pepper

Mornay Sauce

4 tablespoons unsalted butter
⅓ cup all-purpose flour
2 cups whole milk
1 cup heavy cream
½ cup grated Parmigiano-Reggiano cheese (2 ounces)
½ cup shredded Gruyère cheese (2 ounces)
¼ teaspoon ground nutmeg
Kosher salt and freshly ground white pepper

½ cup grated Parmigiano-Reggiano cheese (2 ounces)
½ cup shredded Gruyère cheese (2 ounces)

Equipment: Plate Setter, Baking Stone, oiled 9 by 13-inch glass or ceramic baking dish
Set the EGG for indirect cooking with the Plate Setter, legs down.
Preheat the EGG to 375°F.

To prepare the eggplant, brush the eggplant with olive oil and season lightly with pepper. Place the eggplant slices on the Plate Setter and close the lid of the EGG. Cook for 2 minutes on each side, or until softened and brown. Transfer the eggplant onto a rimmed sheet pan. Set aside.

To make the filling, melt the butter in a large sauté pan on the stovetop and cook the meat, onions, garlic, oregano, cinnamon, sugar, and nutmeg over medium heat, until the meat is thoroughly cooked. Add the tomato paste, tomato sauce, wine, vinegar, salt, and pepper. Stir well and cook for 1 minute. Set aside.

To make the Mornay sauce, melt the butter in a medium saucepan on the stovetop over medium heat, add the flour, and cook for 1 minute. Add the milk and cream. Simmer on medium heat for 5 minutes, or until thickened. Remove the pan from the heat and add the Parmigiano-Reggiano cheese, the Gruyère cheese, and the nutmeg. Season the sauce with salt and white pepper. Set aside.

To assemble, arrange half of the eggplant over the bottom of the oiled baking dish. Spread the meat mixture evenly over the eggplant, pour the sauce evenly over the top, and sprinkle with the remaining cheeses.

Place the Baking Stone on top of the Plate Setter and set the baking dish on top of the Baking Stone. Close the lid of the EGG and bake for 35 minutes, or until light golden brown in color. Remove the baking dish and let the moussaka rest for 10 minutes before serving. **Serves 6**

Sausage & Mushroom Quiche

Quiche is a classic French custard-based tart made from eggs and cream. There are many different types of quiche, with the bacon-laden quiche Lorraine being the most popular. This version is heartier, with the addition of sausage, mushrooms, and three kinds of cheese that bake to perfection in the EGG. This dish freezes well, so make an extra quiche or two for later use.

Ingredients

1 tablespoon unsalted butter
8 ounces sausage, crumbled
4 cups sliced white mushrooms (8 ounces)
1 teaspoon freshly ground black pepper
1/3 cup cream cheese, at room temperature
    (2 to 3 ounces)
1 cup ricotta cheese (8 ounces)
1/2 cup all-purpose flour
1 tablespoon baking powder
1/2 teaspoon kosher salt
7 large eggs, beaten
2 cups shredded Monterey Jack cheese (8 ounces)
1 cup shredded extra-sharp Cheddar cheese (4 ounces)
1/2 cup grated Parmigiano-Reggiano cheese (2 ounces)
1/2 cup heavy cream
1 cup thinly sliced scallions (about 6)
1 (9-inch) pie shell (page 223)

Equipment: Plate Setter
Set the EGG for indirect cooking with
**   the Plate Setter, legs down.**
Preheat the EGG to 350°F.

Melt the butter in a large skillet on the stovetop over medium heat, add the sausage, and sauté for 4 to 6 minutes, until the sausage is browned. Add the mushrooms and sauté for 3 to 4 minutes, until the mushrooms are tender. Season with the black pepper and stir well. Remove the pan from the heat to cool.

In a large bowl, using an electric mixer, combine the cream cheese, ricotta cheese, flour, baking powder, and salt on low speed. Add the eggs, 1 at a time, and continue mixing until they are completely incorporated. Using a wooden spoon or spatula, stir in the sausage mixture, Monterey Jack cheese, Cheddar cheese, Parmigiano-Reggiano cheese, cream, and scallions. Pour the mixture into the pie shell.

Set the pie plate on the Plate Setter and close the lid of the EGG. Bake for 35 minutes, or until golden brown. Remove the quiche from the EGG and let rest for 10 minutes before serving. **Serves 6**

Spatchcocked Chicken

This is an easy method and a great way to prepare a whole chicken without cutting it into pieces. To spatchcock a chicken, remove the backbone. The chicken then opens like a book, so that it lies perfectly flat when grilled. This recipe would be terrific served with Barbecued Baked Beans (page 156) and grilled corn on the cob (page 182).

Ingredients

1 (4 to 5-pound) chicken
6 cups water
½ cup kosher salt
½ cup granulated sugar
5 cloves garlic, crushed
10 whole cloves
3 tablespoons canola oil
¼ cup Basic Barbecue Rub (page 196)
½ cup KC Barbecue Sauce (page 192)

Equipment: Cast Iron Grid, hickory chips, instant read thermometer
Preheat the EGG to 300°F without the Grid.

Cut the chicken, from the neck down, along both sides of the backbone. Then remove the backbone, so that the chicken lies flat. Combine the water, salt, sugar, garlic, and cloves in a large bowl. Whisk until the salt and sugar are dissolved. Place the chicken in a large resealable plastic bag and pour the brine over the chicken. Place the bag inside a bowl or pan and refrigerate overnight.

Remove the chicken from the brine and discard the brine. Rinse well and pat dry. Brush the chicken with the canola oil and season with the barbecue rub.

Place 1 cup of hickory chips in a large bowl. Cover with water and soak for 1 hour. Scatter the hickory chips over the preheated charcoal and let the chips smoke for a few minutes. Spray the Grid with cooking spray and, using barbecue mitts, place it on the EGG.

Place the chicken, skin side down, on the Grid. Close the lid of the EGG and cook for 20 minutes, checking occasionally. Turn the chicken over and brush it liberally with one-third of the barbecue sauce. Close the lid of the EGG and cook for another 10 minutes. Turn the chicken over and brush it with the barbecue sauce. Close the lid of the EGG and cook for another 20 minutes. Then continue basting every 5 minutes, until the instant read thermometer registers 165°F.

Transfer the chicken to a platter, baste with barbecue sauce, and let the chicken rest for 10 minutes. Carve and serve. **Serves 4**

Seafood Paella

There are many variations of this Spanish saffron rice dish, some including pork, chicken, or chorizo. This version is made exclusively with seafood, but this is a great dish to experiment with, as the combinations of meat and shellfish are endless. You can also try adding artichokes or diced tomatoes. There are special pans for making paella, but the Dutch Oven does an amazing job.

Ingredients

¼ cup extra-virgin olive oil

½ pound large sea scallops

1 cup diced yellow onions

½ cup diced red bell pepper

1 tablespoon minced garlic

2 cups Arborio rice

1 cup white wine

1 cup clam juice

3½ cups chicken stock

1 teaspoon saffron

1 teaspoon sweet paprika

1 pound littleneck clams, scrubbed

1 pound mussels, scrubbed and beards removed

1 pound large shrimp, peeled, deveined, tails left on

1 cup fresh or frozen peas

1 tablespoon chopped fresh flat-leaf parsley

2 tablespoons freshly squeezed lemon juice

Kosher salt and freshly ground black pepper

2 lemons, cut into wedges

Equipment: Porcelain coated grid, Dutch Oven
Set the EGG for direct cooking with the porcelain coated grid.
Preheat the EGG to 500°F.

Place the Dutch Oven on the grid and preheat for 10 minutes.

Pour the oil into the Dutch Oven, add the scallops, and sauté for 1 minute. Using a slotted spoon, transfer the scallops to a small bowl and set aside. Add the onions, bell pepper, and garlic to the Dutch Oven and close the lid of the EGG. Sauté for 1 minute, until the onions are translucent and the peppers are tender. Add the rice, wine, clam juice, chicken stock, saffron, and paprika, and stir well. Place the lid on the Dutch Oven and close the lid of the EGG. Cook for 12 minutes, or until the liquid is absorbed and the rice is cooked.

Add the clams, place the lid on the Dutch Oven, close the lid of the EGG, and cook for 5 minutes. Add the mussels and shrimp. Cook until the mussels are open and the shrimp are opaque. Remove the Dutch Oven.

Stir in the reserved scallops, peas, parsley, and lemon juice. Discard any unopened clams or mussels. Season with salt and pepper. Garnish with lemon wedges and serve.
Serves 6

Shrimp Fra Diavolo

You and your guests are sure to love this dish! It is made with Spicy San Marzano Tomato Sauce, but if you want it even hotter, turn up the heat by adding extra red chile flakes. Diavolo is Italian for "devil," referring to the heat and color of this red sauce.

Ingredients

1 pound spaghetti

¼ cup extra-virgin olive oil

1 pound large shrimp, peeled, deveined, and tails removed

1 cup diced tomatoes

½ cup dry white wine

3 cups Spicy San Marzano Tomato Sauce (page 200)

2 tablespoons freshly squeezed lemon juice

½ cup firmly packed chopped fresh basil

Kosher salt and freshly ground black pepper

Equipment: Porcelain coated grid, Dutch Oven
Set the EGG for direct cooking with the porcelain coated grid.
Preheat the EGG to 400°F.

Place the Dutch Oven on the grid and preheat for 10 minutes.

Cook the spaghetti according to the package directions, reserving ½ cup of the cooking water. Let the pasta cool completely and set aside. Pour the olive oil into the Dutch Oven, add the shrimp, close the lid of the EGG, and sear for 1 minute. Using a slotted spoon, transfer the cooked shrimp to a small bowl and let cool. Add the tomatoes to the Dutch Oven, close the lid of the EGG, and sauté for 1 minute. Add the white wine, close the lid of the EGG, and continue cooking until the wine is reduced by half. Add the tomato sauce and the reserved pasta water, close the lid of the EGG, and cook for 2 minutes, or until the sauce begins to simmer. Add the spaghetti and the reserved shrimp, close the lid of the EGG, and cook for 2 more minutes, or until the pasta is thoroughly heated. Remove the Dutch Oven.

Add the lemon juice and chopped basil to the pasta and sauce. Stir gently. Season with salt and pepper and serve immediately. **Serves 4**

"This is the best outdoor cooker I have ever used. Nothing else even comes close. Everything turns out perfect!" —Larry, Georgia

Maple-Smoked Salmon

This salmon gets the royal treatment. Marinated overnight and then cooked on cedar planks for a smoky flavor, it turns out moist and delicious. Horseradish is added to this marinade to give the salmon some zing. Make sure that the prepared horseradish is fresh and that you use real maple syrup to maximize the flavors.

Ingredients

Marinade
1 cup maple syrup
¼ cup prepared horseradish
¼ cup freshly squeezed lemon juice (1 to 2 lemons)

4 (5-ounce) salmon fillets
2 tablespoons canola oil
Kosher salt and freshly ground black pepper

Equipment: Porcelain coated grid, 2 cedar planks
Set the EGG for direct cooking with the porcelain coated grid.
Preheat the EGG to 400°F.

To make the marinade, use a whisk to combine the maple syrup, horseradish, and lemon juice in a small bowl. Place the fillets in a resealable plastic bag, pour the marinade over the fillets, and seal the bag tightly. Refrigerate for 24 hours, turning occasionally.

Place the cedar planks in a large pan, cover with water, and soak for 1 hour.

Remove the cedar planks from the water and place them on the grid. Close the lid of the EGG and allow the cedar planks to heat for 3 minutes. Turn the cedar planks over, close the lid of the EGG, and continue heating. Brush each cedar plank with canola oil. Remove the salmon fillets from the marinade and discard the marinade. Place 2 salmon fillets on each cedar plank and season the fillets with salt and pepper. Close the lid of the EGG and cook for 12 to 15 minutes, or until the desired doneness is reached.

Transfer the salmon fillets to a platter and serve immediately. **Serves 4**

Triple-Treat Tacos

This recipe takes tacos to a whole new level. There is something for everyone—steak, chicken, and shrimp—all served in corn tortillas. These have just the right amount of heat and smokiness. All you need is guacamole and margaritas!

Ingredients

3 ancho chile peppers
1 cup hot water
2 chipotle peppers in adobo
½ cup extra-virgin olive oil
1 teaspoon dried oregano
1 teaspoon ground cumin
1 teaspoon ground cinnamon
¼ teaspoon ground cloves
2 bay leaves
5 cloves garlic
1 teaspoon kosher salt
1 pound boneless sirloin steak, cut in half lengthwise
1 pound boneless, skinless chicken breasts
1 pound large shrimp, peeled, deveined, and
   tails removed
12 corn tortillas
½ cup corn oil
Crumbled queso fresco, minced yellow onions,
   cilantro leaves, Mexican green sauce (optional)

> **Equipment: Cast Iron Grid**
> **Set the EGG for direct cooking with the**
>   **Cast Iron Grid.**
> **Preheat the EGG to 500°F.**

Place the ancho chiles in a small bowl, pour the water over the chiles, cover the bowl with plastic wrap, and let steam for 10 minutes. Strain the chiles over a bowl,

reserving ½ cup of the water for the marinade. Place the rehydrated ancho chiles, the chipotle peppers, olive oil, reserved water from the ancho chiles, the oregano, cumin, cinnamon, cloves, bay leaves, garlic, and salt into the bowl of a food processor fitted with the steel blade. Process the ingredients until they are pureed.

Place the steak, chicken, and shrimp in 3 separate resealable plastic bags. Divide the marinade into thirds and pour one-third into each bag. Seal all of the bags tightly and refrigerate for 8 to 12 hours.

Remove the steak, chicken, and shrimp from the marinade and discard the marinade. Place the chicken on the Grid and close the lid of the EGG. Grill the chicken for 8 minutes per side, or until the juices run clear. Transfer the chicken to a rimmed sheet pan, place the steak on the Grid, and close the lid of the EGG. Cook for 4 minutes per side, or until medium-rare. Transfer the steak to the sheet pan, place the shrimp on the Grid, and close the lid of the EGG. Cook for 1 minute per side. Transfer the shrimp to the rimmed sheet pan.

Cut the steak and chicken into bite-size pieces. Cut each shrimp into small pieces (in half or in thirds, depending on the size of the shrimp). Cover the steak, chicken, and shrimp with aluminum foil until ready to serve.

Brush the corn tortillas on both sides with the corn oil. Place the tortillas on the Grid and grill for 10 seconds per side, until heated. Transfer the tortillas to a sheet of aluminum foil and keep the tortillas tightly wrapped until ready to serve.

Place the steak, chicken, and shrimp on a platter with the warm tortillas. Serve with the cheese, onions, cilantro, and sauce. **Serves 4 to 6**

Asian Marinated Flank Steak

You can easily find chili garlic sauce, one of the ingredients in this recipe, in the ethnic foods section of your local grocery store. If you like your sauce good and hot, just bump up the amount of chili garlic sauce.

Ingredients
½ cup soy sauce
½ cup pineapple juice
½ cup canola oil
½ cup sliced scallions
¼ cup chopped fresh ginger
¼ cup chopped garlic
1 tablespoon five-spice powder
1 tablespoon chili garlic sauce
1 (2-pound) flank steak

> **Equipment: Cast Iron Grid**
> **Set the EGG for direct cooking with the Cast Iron Grid.**
> **Preheat the EGG to 600°F.**

Using a whisk, mix the soy sauce, pineapple juice, canola oil, scallions, ginger, garlic, five-spice powder, and chili garlic sauce in a small bowl. Place the flank steak in a large resealable plastic bag, pour the marinade over the steak, and seal the bag tightly. Refrigerate for 24 hours, turning occasionally.

Remove the flank steak from the marinade and discard the marinade. Place the steak on the Grid. Close the lid of the EGG and grill the steak for 3 to 4 minutes on each side for medium-rare.

Transfer the flank steak to a platter and let it rest for 5 minutes. Slice and serve. **Serves 4**

All-American Burgers

This is your good old classic American hamburger. Barbecue spice is added for more flavor, but the real star is the meat, so be sure to buy the best quality available. Serve these burgers with Warm Southwestern Potato Salad (page 166) and fresh Grilled Corn with Roasted Garlic Butter (page 182).

Ingredients
1 pound ground chuck
1 pound ground round
¼ cup Basic Barbecue Rub (page 196)
Kosher salt and freshly ground black pepper
4 hamburger buns

> **Equipment: Cast Iron Grid**
> **Set the EGG for direct cooking with the Cast Iron Grid.**
> **Preheat the EGG to 650°F.**

Place the ground chuck, ground round, barbecue rub, salt, and pepper into a large bowl and combine. Form the beef mixture into 4 equal patties 1 inch thick. Place the patties on a rimmed sheet pan. Let the patties sit at room temperature for 30 minutes before grilling. Place the patties on the Grid and close the lid of the EGG. Sear for 3 minutes. Turn the burgers over, close the lid of the EGG, and sear for another 3 minutes for medium-rare. Transfer the hamburgers to a plate. Let the hamburgers rest for 5 minutes.

Place the hamburger buns on the Grid, cut side down, for 30 seconds. Transfer the hamburger buns to a platter. Place a hamburger in each bun and serve. **Serves 4**

Chutney-Glazed Beef Brisket

If not cooked properly, brisket tends to be a tough cut of meat. Topped with sweet and spicy mango chutney, this brisket is best cooked low and slow to ensure tenderness. When slicing the brisket, always be sure to slice against the grain; otherwise, the meat will be stringy. Leftover brisket is great shredded and turned into barbecue beef sandwiches. Try it with Fennel Slaw (page 90).

Ingredients

1½ cups mango chutney
1 cup apple cider vinegar
1 cup tomato sauce
½ cup ketchup
½ cup firmly packed brown sugar
1 tablespoon Worcestershire sauce
1 (6-pound) beef brisket
2 cups white vinegar
¾ cup Tricolor Pepper Rub (page 197)
2 cups Beer Mop (page 196)

Equipment: Porcelain coated grid, Grill Gripper, Plate Setter
Set the EGG for direct cooking with the porcelain coated grid.
Preheat the EGG to 200°F.

Mix the chutney, apple cider vinegar, tomato sauce, ketchup, brown sugar, and Worcestershire sauce in a medium bowl, until all the ingredients are combined, and set aside. Place the brisket in a large bowl, pour the white vinegar over the brisket, and let the brisket sit for 5 minutes. Transfer the brisket to a rimmed sheet pan and season all over with the pepper rub.

Place the brisket on the preheated grid and close the lid of the EGG. Cook for 30 minutes, mopping with the beer mop every 15 minutes. Turn the brisket over and close the lid of the EGG. Mopping every 15 minutes, cook for another 30 minutes, or until the brisket is brown. Transfer the brisket to a rimmed sheet pan lined with aluminum foil.

Using the Grill Gripper and barbecue mitts, carefully remove the grid and add the Plate Setter, legs down.

Pour the chutney mixture over the brisket, wrap with the foil, and seal tightly. Place the brisket on the Plate Setter and close the lid of the EGG. Continue to cook for 4 hours, or until the brisket is very tender. Transfer the brisket to a rimmed sheet pan and let rest for 10 minutes, still in the foil.

Remove the foil, slice the brisket against the grain, and place on a platter. Serve immediately. **Serves 8**

EGGfest Chili

This recipe was inspired by one of the original EGGheads, who was very instrumental in organizing the first EGGtoberfest. This version of the recipe is slightly elaborated. All you need is a bowl of this satisfying chili, some buttery cornbread (page 219), and a few good friends to share it with to understand what the EGG is all about.

Ingredients

6 ounces applewood-smoked bacon (about 7 slices)
2 cups diced yellow onions
2 cups diced celery
2 tablespoons minced garlic
2 pounds ground chuck
¼ cup Basic Barbecue Rub (page 196)
¼ cup chili powder
2 tablespoons ground cumin
1 teaspoon ground cinnamon
2 tablespoons unsweetened cocoa powder
2 teaspoons dried oregano
1½ cups beef stock
2 (28-ounce) cans diced tomatoes
2 (14-ounce) cans pinto beans, drained and rinsed
1 (14-ounce) can kidney beans, drained and rinsed
1 (14-ounce) can cannellini beans, drained and rinsed
1 tablespoon balsamic vinegar
Tabasco sauce
2 chipotle peppers in adobo
Grated Cheddar cheese, thinly sliced scallions, and sour cream (optional)

> **Equipment: Porcelain coated grid, Dutch Oven, Grill Gripper, Plate Setter, pecan chips**
> **Set the EGG for direct cooking with the porcelain coated grid.**
> **Preheat the EGG to 400°F.**

Place 2 cups of pecan chips in a large bowl, cover with water, and let soak for 1 hour.

Place the Dutch Oven on the grid and preheat for 10 minutes.

Add the bacon to the Dutch Oven, close the lid of the EGG, and cook until crisp. Using a slotted spoon, transfer the bacon to a small bowl lined with paper towels. Set aside. Place the onions, celery, and garlic in the Dutch Oven, close the lid of the EGG, and cook for 2 to 3 minutes, until soft. Add the ground chuck, barbecue rub, chili powder, cumin, cinnamon, cocoa powder, and oregano and stir well. Close the lid of the EGG and cook until the meat is cooked through and lightly browned. Add the beef stock, tomatoes, all the beans, and the vinegar, mixing until thoroughly combined. Season with Tabasco sauce. Add the chipotle peppers and stir gently. Remove the Dutch Oven from the grill.

Using the Grill Gripper and barbecue mitts, carefully remove the grid. Scatter the pecan chips over the coals and add the Plate Setter, legs down.

Place the uncovered Dutch Oven on the Plate Setter and close the lid of the EGG. Reduce the heat of the EGG to 300°F. Cook for 1½ to 2 hours, until the meat is thoroughly cooked and the chili has a smoky flavor. Using a slotted spoon, carefully remove the chipotles and discard. Close the lid of the EGG and continue to cook the chili uncovered for 30 minutes, or until the sauce has thickened. Remove the Dutch Oven.

Serve the chili with the cheese, scallions, and sour cream.
Serves 8 to 10

Beef Wellington

A traditional beef Wellington is a tenderloin that is coated in pâté de foie gras and duxelles, surrounded in puff pastry, and baked, but here, the pâté is omitted. Having the butcher trim the meat for you will make this dish easier to prepare. Duxelles is made by cooking mushrooms in butter with shallots and garlic until the water from the mushrooms has completely evaporated. The duxelles is then spread on the puff pastry before it is wrapped around the tenderloin and baked. Duxelles can be made with any type of mushroom.

Ingredients

1 (4 to 5-pound) beef tenderloin, trimmed and tied
¼ cup extra-virgin olive oil
1 tablespoon kosher salt
1 tablespoon freshly ground black pepper

Duxelles

4 tablespoons unsalted butter
1 pound baby bella (cremini) or small white mushrooms, finely chopped
¼ cup minced shallots
2 tablespoons minced garlic
1 tablespoon chopped fresh thyme
1 tablespoon chopped fresh flat-leaf parsley
2 large eggs
8 ounces cream cheese, at room temperature
1 tablespoon water
2 sheets puff pastry (1-pound box), thawed

Equipment: Porcelain coated grid, Plate Setter, Baking Stone, instant read thermometer
Set the EGG for direct cooking with the porcelain coated grid.
Preheat the EGG to 500°F.

Brush the tenderloin with the olive oil and season all over with the salt and pepper. Place the tenderloin on the grid and close the lid of the EGG. Sear for 2 to 3 minutes per side, until the whole tenderloin has been seared. Transfer the tenderloin to a rimmed sheet pan and let cool.

Using the Grill Gripper and barbecue mitts, carefully remove the grid and add the Plate Setter, legs down. Reduce the heat of the EGG to 425°F.

To make the duxelles, place the butter, mushrooms, shallots, garlic, and thyme in a large sauté pan on the stovetop over medium heat. Cook for 10 to 15 minutes, until all the excess liquid from the mushrooms has evaporated. Remove the pan from the heat, add the parsley, and stir well. Let cool completely. Using a wooden spoon, beat 1 of the eggs in a large bowl, then add the cheese and the cooled mushroom mixture and stir well. Set aside.

To assemble, use a whisk or fork to beat the remaining egg with the water in a small bowl, until frothy. Set aside. Unroll the 2 sheets of puff pastry onto a lightly floured surface. Overlap the 2 short ends of the pastry and, using a rolling pin, roll the 2 pastry sheets together into a 12 by 20-inch rectangle. Spread the duxelles evenly over one of the joined pastry sheets, leaving a 2-inch border on the edges. Place the whole tenderloin on the duxelles, parallel to the short end of the pastry sheet. Starting at the duxelle-coated end of the pastry, roll the pastry with the tenderloin halfway and then brush all the exposed borders with the egg wash. Continue to roll the tenderloin, using all of the puff pastry. Seal both ends by tucking the ends of the pastry under. Brush the entire pastry with the egg wash.

Transfer the tenderloin to the cold Baking Stone and close the lid of the EGG. Bake for 40 to 45 minutes, until the instant read thermometer registers 135°F. Transfer the tenderloin to a rimmed sheet pan. Let cool for 15 minutes. Slice and serve. **Serves 8**

Pork Crown Roast

The crown roast is formed using the rib section of the loin. The reason for its name is apparent because once tied in a circle, it resembles a crown. The center is usually filled with a stuffing before the roast is baked. Because of the elaborate presentation, a crown roast makes a perfect holiday or special-occasion dinner.

Ingredients

1 (8 to 9-pound) pork crown roast
½ cup Dijon mustard
1 pound ground pork-sage sausage
8 cups quartered small white mushrooms
2 cups diced yellow onions
1 cup diced celery
1 cup peeled and diced Granny Smith apple
1 cup chicken stock
1 large egg, beaten
4 cups plain croutons

Equipment: Porcelain coated grid, Dutch Oven, V-Rack, 9 by 13-inch Drip Pan, instant read thermometer
Set the EGG for direct cooking with the porcelain coated grid.
Preheat the EGG to 350°F.

Using a basting brush, cover the crown roast, both inside and outside, with the mustard and set aside. Brown the sausage, mushrooms, onions, celery, and apple in the Dutch Oven on the stovetop over medium-high heat, until caramelized. Using a slotted spoon, transfer the mixture to a medium bowl and let cool. Using a wooden spoon, stir the chicken stock and the beaten egg together in a large bowl, add the croutons, and continue to mix. Add the sausage mixture to the croutons and combine until all the ingredients are thoroughly blended.

Put the stuffing in the center of the crown roast and cover the top of the roast with aluminum foil. Place the roast in the V-Rack and put the V-Rack in the Drip Pan. Set the Drip Pan on the grid and close the lid of the EGG. Cook for 1½ hours. Remove the foil, close the lid of the EGG, and cook for 30 to 45 minutes longer, until the instant read thermometer registers 145°F. Remove the roast from the heat and let rest for 15 minutes. Slice and serve. **Serves 8**

Caribbean-Style Pork Tenderloin

A dry sherry is used in the marinade of this highly spiced dish. Sherry is a fortified wine that originated in the Andalusia region of Spain but is now made in other parts of the world. Mango nectar and hot peppers complement the sherry, giving this meat a sweet yet hot and spicy flavor.

Ingredients

Marinade
1 ancho chile pepper
1 cup hot water
1 chipotle pepper in adobo
1 teaspoon jerk seasoning
1 cup mango nectar
½ cup dry sherry
¼ cup canola oil

2 (1½ to 2-pound) pork tenderloins

Sauce
1 red bell pepper
1 large vine-ripened tomato
1 teaspoon saffron
1 teaspoon honey
1 teaspoon apple cider vinegar
5 cloves roasted garlic (page 202)
½ cup mayonnaise
¼ cup extra-virgin olive oil
Kosher salt and freshly ground black pepper

> **Equipment: Cast Iron Grid, instant read thermometer**
> Set the EGG for direct cooking with the Cast Iron Grid.
> Preheat the EGG to 400°F.

To make the marinade, place the ancho chile in a small bowl and cover with the water. Cover the bowl with plastic wrap and let the chile sit for 10 minutes. Drain and place the ancho chile, chipotle pepper, jerk seasoning, mango nectar, sherry, and canola oil in the bowl of a food processor fitted with the steel blade. Pulse for 30 seconds to blend. Place the pork tenderloins in a resealable plastic bag and pour the marinade over the pork. Seal the bag tightly and refrigerate for 8 to 12 hours, turning occasionally.

To make the sauce, place the bell pepper on the Grid and close the lid of the EGG. Grill, turning occasionally, until the pepper is roasted on all sides. Place the pepper in a resealable plastic bag and allow to steam. Place the tomato on the Grid and close the lid of the EGG. Grill for 2 to 3 minutes, until roasted and the skin begins to pull away. Place the roasted red pepper, grilled tomato, saffron, honey, vinegar, garlic, mayonnaise, and olive oil in the bowl of a food processor fitted with the steel blade. Let the food processor run until all of the ingredients are completely blended. Refrigerate until ready to serve.

Remove the tenderloins from the marinade and discard the marinade. Season the tenderloins with salt and pepper. Place the tenderloins on the Grid and close the lid of the EGG. Grill for 5 to 6 minutes per side, until the instant read thermometer registers 145°F. Transfer the pork to a rimmed sheet pan and let rest for 10 minutes.

Slice the pork. Place 2 tablespoons of sauce in the middle of each plate and top with the sliced pork. Serve immediately. **Serves 6**

Mediterranean Pork Tenderloins

This dish requires that you butterfly the pork in order to stuff it. Don't be too intimidated to try this technique. Once you have mastered it, you will find it very easy. After it is butterflied, the pork is lined with grape leaves and stuffed with a blend of rice, olives, and Mediterranean spices. Grape leaves are often used in Greece and the Middle East to wrap around food before cooking. You may not be able to find these fresh, but your local grocery store will most likely sell brined grape leaves in jars.

Ingredients
2 (1 to 1½-pound) pork tenderloins
8 to 10 grape leaves
⅓ cup white rice, cooked
½ cup julienned oil-packed sun-dried tomatoes
½ cup crumbled feta cheese (2 ounces)
¼ cup pitted kalamata olives
¼ cup pitted manzanilla olives
½ cup firmly packed fresh basil leaves
½ cup firmly packed fresh oregano leaves
4 anchovy fillets
1 tablespoon freshly squeezed lemon juice
2 tablespoons plus 2 tablespoons extra-virgin olive oil
1 tablespoon sweet paprika
Kosher salt and freshly ground black pepper

Equipment: Cast Iron Grid, instant read thermometer
Set the EGG for direct cooking with the Cast Iron Grid.
Preheat the EGG to 400°F.

Place each pork tenderloin on a cutting board and cut lengthwise three-quarters of the way through the pork. Open the tenderloins so that they lie flat. Place 4 or 5 grape leaves to cover the inside of each tenderloin.

Place the white rice, tomatoes, cheese, all the olives, the basil, oregano, anchovy fillets, lemon juice, and 2 tablespoons of the olive oil into the bowl of a food processor fitted with the steel blade. Pulse briefly about 10 times, or until the ingredients are coarsely chopped. Carefully remove the steel blade. Using a spatula, spread half of the filling on each of the tenderloins. Close the tenderloins and tie them in place with butcher's twine. Brush each tenderloin with the remaining 2 tablespoons of olive oil. Rub with the paprika and season with salt and pepper.

Place each tenderloin on the Grid and close the lid of the EGG. Grill for 7 to 8 minutes per side, until the instant read thermometer registers 145°F. Transfer the tenderloins to a rimmed sheet pan and let rest for 10 minutes. Slice and serve. **Serves 6**

Bread Pudding
with Figs & Pine Nuts

Pine nuts, the seeds harvested from pine cones, and dried figs combine to make this hearty bread pudding. To top it off, it's served with a side of caramel sauce flavored with sambuca, an Italian anise-flavored liqueur. Bread pudding can be made with any variety of dried fruits and nuts, and any leftover bread can be used in place of the challah.

Equipment: Plate Setter, oiled 10 by 15-inch cookie sheet, oiled 9 by 13-inch glass or ceramic baking dish
Set the EGG for indirect cooking with the Plate Setter, legs down.
Preheat the EGG to 350°F.

Ingredients
8 slices challah bread, 1 inch thick
2 tablespoons unsalted butter, at room temperature, plus 8 tablespoons butter, melted
2 cups whole milk
2 cups heavy cream
½ cup granulated sugar
8 large eggs, beaten
1 teaspoon vanilla extract
½ teaspoon ground cinnamon
¼ teaspoon ground nutmeg
2 cups dried figs, quartered
½ cup pine nuts

Caramel Sauce
½ cup granulated sugar
1 tablespoon light corn syrup
¼ cup water
½ cup heavy cream
1 tablespoon sambuca
2 tablespoons unsalted butter

Preheat a kitchen oven to 350°F. Spread one side of each slice of bread with the 2 tablespoons of room temperature butter. Place the bread buttered side up on the oiled cookie sheet and put the cookie sheet in the oven for 3 to 4 minutes, until the bread is lightly toasted. Let the bread cool, then cut into 1-inch cubes.

Using a wooden spoon, mix the milk, cream, sugar, the 8 tablespoons of melted butter, the eggs, vanilla, cinnamon, nutmeg, figs, and pine nuts in a large bowl and stir until completely combined. Add the bread and mix well until the bread is thoroughly coated. Cover and refrigerate for 6 to 8 hours or overnight.

Spread the bread mixture evenly in the oiled baking dish. Place the baking dish on the Plate Setter and close the lid of the EGG. Bake for 45 minutes, or until golden brown. Remove the bread pudding and let rest for 10 minutes.

To make the sauce, while the bread pudding is baking, heat the sugar, corn syrup, and water in a small heavy-bottomed saucepan on the stovetop over medium heat for 6 to 8 minutes, until it is caramel in color. Add the cream, sambuca, and butter and whisk until smooth and creamy. Remove the pan from the heat and let cool for 15 minutes, then keep warm. Serve with the bread pudding. **Serves 6**

"I cannot tell you how happy my family is with the Big Green Egg! Rain or snow, I enjoy getting it going in the middle of winter and just letting the aroma drift to my neighbors' yards." —Doug, New York

eggsclusive!

chefs & pitmasters

recipes

Grilled Island Chicken with Tropical Salsa by Lee Ann Whippen

Whippen's grilled chicken breasts are bathed for several hours in a coconut milk marinade before grilling, then topped with Tropical Salsa, turning chicken into a dish that family and guests will ask for repeatedly.

Ingredients

Marinade
1 (14-ounce) can unsweetened coconut milk
3 tablespoons minced fresh cilantro
⅛ teaspoon ground cinnamon
2 tablespoons freshly squeezed lime juice (1 to 2 limes)
1 large jalapeño, seeded and minced

6 boneless, skinless chicken breasts

Tropical Salsa
¼ cup chopped red onion
½ cup seeded and chopped tomato
½ cup chopped mango
¼ cup chopped green bell pepper
¼ cup chopped yellow bell pepper
1 tablespoon minced jalapeño
½ teaspoon kosher salt
½ teaspoon chili powder
2 tablespoons freshly squeezed lime juice (1 to 2 limes)
1 tablespoon honey

Lime wedges for garnish
Cilantro sprigs for garnish

Equipment: Cast Iron Grid, instant read thermometer
Set the EGG for direct cooking with the Cast Iron Grid.
Preheat the EGG to 350°F.

To make the marinade, using a whisk, mix the coconut milk, cilantro, cinnamon, lime juice, and jalapeño in a small bowl. Place the chicken breasts in a large shallow dish and pour the marinade over the chicken to cover. Cover the dish with plastic wrap and refrigerate for 2 hours.

To make the salsa, toss the onion, tomato, mango, green bell pepper, yellow bell pepper, jalapeño, salt, chili powder, lime juice, and honey in a medium bowl. Cover with plastic wrap and refrigerate until ready to use.

Remove the chicken breasts from the marinade and discard the marinade. Place the chicken on the Grid and close the lid of the EGG. Grill for 10 to 12 minutes per side, until the instant read thermometer reads 160°F. Transfer the chicken to a rimmed sheet pan.

Place the chicken breasts on plates and top with the salsa. Garnish each plate with lime wedges and a sprig of cilantro. **Serves 6**

Beer-Butt Chicken by Rick Browne

People *magazine dubbed Browne "The Godfather of Beer-Butt Chicken," but he humbly admits that he borrowed the technique from a barbecue contest competitor. However, Rick was the first in the country to publish the recipe and to prepare it on national television. When you try this fascinating, fun, and delicious way to cook a chicken, you'll want to serve it again and again.*

Ingredients

Rub
1 teaspoon brown sugar
1 teaspoon garlic powder
1 teaspoon onion powder
1 teaspoon dried summer savory
¼ teaspoon cayenne pepper
1 teaspoon chili powder
1 teaspoon sweet paprika
1 teaspoon dry mustard
1 tablespoon sea salt or kosher salt

1 (4 to 5-pound) chicken
1 (12-ounce) can beer
1 cup apple cider
2 tablespoons olive oil
2 tablespoons balsamic vinegar

Equipment: Porcelain coated grid, 1 (12-ounce) beer can or "Sittin' Chicken" Ceramic Roaster, 9 by 13-inch Drip Pan, spray bottle, Set the EGG for direct cooking with the porcelain coated grid. Preheat the EGG to 375°F.

To make the rub, combine the brown sugar, garlic powder, onion powder, summer savory, cayenne pepper, chili powder, paprika, mustard, and salt in a small bowl. Stir until incorporated. Apply the rub all over the chicken, even inside the cavity. Work the mixture gently into the skin and under the skin wherever possible. Cover the chicken and set aside at room temperature for 30 minutes.

Pour half of the beer into the spray bottle. Add the apple cider, olive oil, and vinegar and set aside. If using the Ceramic Roaster, pour the remaining beer into the cavity of the Roaster and slide the chicken onto the Roaster, through the tail end. If using the beer can, slide the chicken down over the can.

Place the chicken, still on the Roaster, on the grid and close the lid of the EGG. Cook, using the spray bottle to baste the chicken once or twice, for 20 minutes, or until the chicken is just beginning to brown all over. Carefully lift the chicken (still on the Roaster) into the Drip Pan and close the lid of the EGG. Cook, spraying the chicken with the basting spray several times, for 45 minutes to 1 hour, until the internal temperature of the thigh reaches 170°F and the chicken is a mahogany brown color. Using barbecue mitts, remove the chicken and present it on the Roaster to your guests. After they have reacted appropriately, remove the chicken from the Roaster. Be careful: The can and the liquid inside are very hot.

Spray the chicken once more with the basting spray, cover with foil, and let rest for 10 minutes. Carve and serve.
Serves 4

Bourbon-Brined Barbecue Turkey by Steven Raichlen

Raichlen's Bourbon-Brined Barbecue Turkey owes its superb taste and wonderfully moist meat to a generous marinade injection of chicken stock, bourbon, and butter, and a zippy spice mixture. Apple chips and natural lump charcoal add another flavor dimension. You'll be proud to bring this burnished bird to the table.

Ingredients

Injector Sauce
1 tablespoon Basic Barbecue Rub (page 196)
2 tablespoons salted butter
⅓ cup chicken stock, preferably homemade, or
  low-sodium store-bought, at room temperature
2 tablespoons bourbon

1 (8 to 10-pound) turkey
2 tablespoons plus 2 tablespoons Basic Barbecue Rub
  (page 196)
1 tablespoon unsalted butter, melted

> **Equipment: Plate Setter, Drip Pan,
> porcelain coated grid, apple chips,
> marinade injector, instant read
> thermometer**
> **Preheat the EGG to 350°F without the
> Plate Setter.**

Place the apple chips in a large bowl and cover with water. Soak for at least 1 hour. Drain and scatter over the pre-heated charcoal. Place the Plate Setter, legs up, in the EGG, set the Drip Pan on the Plate Setter, and set the grid on top.

To make the injector sauce, if the rub has any coarse bits or spices, finely grind it in a spice mill or coffee grinder so it doesn't clog the injector. Melt the butter in a small saucepan on the stovetop. Using a whisk, add the chicken stock, bourbon, and the rub and mix well. Let cool to room temperature.

Remove the neck and giblets from the turkey and reserve for another use. Remove and discard the fat just inside the cavities of the turkey. Rinse the turkey inside and out under cold running water, then blot dry inside and out with paper towels. Season the inside of the cavities with 2 tablespoons of the rub. Fill the injector with the injector sauce. To do this, push the plunger all the way down, place the tip of the needle in the sauce, and slowly draw the plunger up. The syringe will fill with sauce. Inject the sauce directly into the turkey breast, thighs, and drumsticks. Don't be surprised if a little sauce squirts out; this is okay. Discard the remainder of the injector sauce. Trussing the turkey is optional, but it will give the bird a more dignified appearance. Brush the outside of the turkey with the melted butter and sprinkle the remaining 2 tablespoons rub all over the turkey, patting it on the skin with your fingertips.

Place the turkey, breast side up, in the center of the grid, over the Drip Pan, and close the lid of the EGG. Cook the turkey until the skin is nicely browned and the meat is cooked through, about 2 to 2½ hours. To check for doneness, the instant read thermometer should be inserted in the thickest part of a thigh, not touching bone, and should register 165°F. If the wing tips start to burn, cover them loosely with aluminum foil; if the skin starts to darken too fast, cover the bird loosely with foil.

Transfer the grilled turkey to a platter, cover loosely with foil, and let the turkey rest for 10 minutes. Remove any trussing from the turkey. Carve and serve. **Serves 10**

Coffee-Rubbed Pork Tenderloin with Peach Barbecue Drizzle by Ray Lampe

If you've never used coffee in a rub, you're in for a real treat with this coffee-rubbed pork tenderloin. Quick and easy to prepare, it's served with Peach Barbecue Drizzle, which relies on peach preserves. Add grilled peaches on the side for a colorful and tasty presentation if desired. This is sure to be added to your list of favorite recipes.

Ingredients

Coffee Rub
2 tablespoons ground coffee
1 tablespoon turbinado sugar (coarse, raw sugar)
1 tablespoon chili powder
1½ teaspoons table salt
1 teaspoon freshly ground black pepper

2 (1-pound) pork tenderloins
1 to 2 tablespoons olive oil

Peach Barbecue Drizzle
1½ cups peach preserves
½ cup ketchup
2 teaspoons balsamic vinegar
2 tablespoons light brown sugar
¼ teaspoon freshly ground black pepper

Equipment: Cast Iron Grid, instant read thermometer
Set the EGG for direct cooking with the Cast Iron Grid.
Preheat the EGG to 400°F.

To make the rub, combine the coffee, sugar, chili powder, salt, and pepper in a small bowl. Mix well and set aside. Trim the fat and silver skin from the tenderloins. Brush the tenderloins with the olive oil and season liberally with the rub. Let the meat rest for 10 minutes before cooking.

To make the drizzle sauce, mix the preserves, ketchup, vinegar, brown sugar, and pepper in a small saucepan. Place the pan on the stovetop over medium heat and cook for 3 minutes. Transfer the sauce to a bowl and let cool.

Place the tenderloins on the Grid and close the lid of the EGG. Cook for 5 to 6 minutes, until browned. Turn the meat, close the lid of the EGG, and continue cooking for another 5 to 6 minutes, until the meat is brown on all sides. Cook until the instant read thermometer reads 140°F. Transfer the meat to a platter and tent loosely with aluminum foil. Let the tenderloins rest for 5 minutes.

Slice the meat thinly and serve drizzled with the sauce.
Serves 6

Smoked Beef Short Ribs by Kevin Rathbun

These smoked short ribs are a tribute to Rathbun's appetite for beef. He takes a once-lowly cut of meat and with innovative seasoning, hickory chips, and slow cooking turns it into tender, tasty fare, sure to please even the most discriminating palate. Ask the butcher to cut the short ribs 2 to 2½ inches thick, because they shrink during cooking. And be prepared for everyone to ask for second helpings.

Ingredients

Rub
1 teaspoon garlic powder
1 teaspoon onion powder
1 teaspoon smoked Spanish paprika
½ teaspoon cayenne pepper
½ teaspoon dried thyme
½ teaspoon ground coriander
1 tablespoon kosher salt

4 pounds bone-in beef short ribs, cut 2 to 2½ inches thick
16 ounces lager beer
2 cups chicken stock
2 cups white balsamic vinegar
4 tablespoons salted butter, cubed

> **Equipment: Porcelain coated grid, hickory chips, 9 by 13-inch glass or ceramic baking dish**
> **Preheat the EGG to 180° to 200°F without the grid.**

Place the hickory chips in a small bowl, cover with water, and let soak for at least 1 hour. Drain and scatter over the preheated charcoal. Using barbecue mitts, place the grid in the EGG.

To make the rub, mix the garlic powder, onion powder, paprika, cayenne pepper, thyme, coriander, and salt in a small bowl. Generously rub the short ribs with the spices.

Place the ribs on the grid and close the lid of the EGG. Let the ribs smoke for 1½ to 2 hours.

Mix the beer and the chicken stock in a large bowl and set aside. Place the vinegar in a heavy-bottomed saucepan on the stovetop over medium heat for about 15 minutes, or until the liquid has reduced by half. Set aside.

Preheat a kitchen oven to 375°F.

Once the short ribs have finished smoking, transfer the ribs to the baking dish and pour the beer and chicken stock mixture over the ribs. Cover the dish tightly with aluminum foil. Place in the preheated oven for 2½ hours, or until the ribs are fork tender.

Warm the reduced vinegar over low heat. Using a whisk, add the butter a little at a time, stirring constantly, until the butter is emulsified. Do not boil. Transfer the ribs to plates, top with the sauce, and serve immediately.
Serves 4

Brisket with Kale by Chef S. Dean Corbett

Chef Corbett's brisket is coated with a spicy dry rub and refrigerated for twenty-four hours. It is then slow cooked to "pit-barbecue tender" and served with a kale side dish that gets its delicious, sweet flavor from applewood-smoked bacon, sweet onions, and brown sugar. This is upscale comfort food.

Ingredients

Rub
¼ cup Cavender's Greek Seasoning
1 tablespoon anise seed
1 teaspoon cumin seed
1 teaspoon coriander seed
1 teaspoon fennel seed
1 teaspoon mustard seed
1 tablespoon kosher salt
1 tablespoon freshly ground black pepper

1 (5-pound) beef brisket

Kale
2 to 3 pounds kale, washed and dried
1 pound applewood-smoked bacon, minced
1 large sweet onion, chopped
1 cup rice wine vinegar
1⅛ cup (½ pound) light brown sugar
2 cups chicken stock
Kosher salt and freshly ground black pepper

Equipment: Porcelain coated grid, Grill Gripper, Plate Setter, Dutch Oven, instant read thermometer
Set the EGG for direct cooking with the porcelain coated grid.
Preheat the EGG to 275°F.

To make the rub, place the seasoning, anise seed, cumin seed, coriander seed, fennel seed, mustard seed, salt, and pepper in the bowl of a food processor fitted with the steel blade. Pulse on and off until the spices are ground. Rub the spices generously over the entire brisket. Store any extra spice mixture for another use. Put the brisket on a tray, cover with plastic wrap, and refrigerate for 24 hours.

Place the brisket on the grid. Close the lid of the EGG and cook for 30 minutes. Turn the brisket over, close the lid of the EGG, and cook for 30 minutes longer. Remove the brisket and, using the Grill Gripper and barbecue mitts, remove the grid.

Set the EGG for indirect cooking with the Plate Setter legs up and put the grid on top. Reduce the temperature to 225°F.

Place the brisket on the grid and close the lid of the EGG. Cook for about 6 hours, or until the instant read thermometer registers 190°F. Transfer to a rimmed sheet pan, cover with foil, and allow to rest briefly.

To prepare the kale, while the brisket is cooking, remove the center stalks from the kale leaves and discard. Coarsely chop the leaves. Place the bacon in the Dutch Oven on the stovetop and cook over medium heat to render the fat. Drain all but 2 tablespoons fat from the pan. Add the onion and sauté, stirring occasionally, for 5 minutes, or until the onion is tender. Add the kale and cook briefly. Add the vinegar to deglaze the pan, then add the brown sugar and chicken stock. Season with salt and pepper and stir well. Continue cooking for 1½ hours, or until the kale is wilted and flavorful.

Slice the brisket against the grain and serve hot with the kale. **Serves 8 to 10**

Pepper-Crusted Rib-Eye with Morel Cognac Cream Sauce by Ken Hess

If you're a steak lover, this tender, tasty rib-eye topped with a rich, creamy mushroom and Cognac sauce will surpass all of your expectations. When morels are not in season, substitute any available variety of mushrooms. Chopped shallots add a lovely, subtle flavor, but try ramps instead if you can find them; these wild green onions, abundant throughout the Appalachian Mountains in spring, are more readily found in produce sections today. If you don't think of yourself as a steak enthusiast, this mouthwatering combination will convert you.

Ingredients

Morel Cognac Cream Sauce
1 tablespoon unsalted butter
¼ cup morel mushrooms, quartered
¼ cup chopped shallots or ramps
1 clove garlic, minced
½ cup cognac or brandy
2 cups heavy cream
Kosher salt and freshly ground black pepper
Pinch of cayenne pepper

2 (1½-pound) bone-in rib-eye steaks
Kosher salt and freshly ground black pepper

Equipment: Cast Iron Grid, Dutch Oven or 12-inch cast iron skillet
Set the EGG for direct cooking with the Cast Iron Grid.
Preheat the EGG to 650°F.

Place the Dutch Oven on the Grid and allow to preheat.

Place the butter in the Dutch Oven and cook until slightly brown. Once the butter is brown, add the mushrooms and sauté until tender. Add the shallots and garlic and stir briefly. Carefully add the cognac—it will ignite, so add it slowly, then step away from the EGG. Allow the cognac to burn off, then stir, and close the lid of the EGG. Continue cooking until the cognac reduces by two-thirds. Add the cream, stirring constantly for 3 to 4 minutes, until the sauce thickens enough to coat the back of a wooden spoon. Season the sauce with salt and pepper (if you add the salt too early, the sauce will become too salty as it reduces). Add a pinch of cayenne or more if desired. Cayenne will cut some of the richness of the cream. Keep the sauce warm on the stovetop over low heat.

Coat both sides of the steaks with salt and pepper. Place the steaks on the Grid and close the lid of the EGG. Grill for about 6 minutes for medium-rare. When the steak is ready, transfer to a rimmed sheet pan and allow to rest.

Slice the steaks against the grain ¼ inch thick and place the slices on a platter or plates. Pour the sauce over the steaks and serve immediately. **Serves 4**

Molten Chocolate Cake by Andy Husbands

Andy Husbands's exquisite molten chocolate cake with its rich, saucy center is one of the most spectacular desserts you'll ever taste and certainly not something you would expect to cook in a grill. Fortunately, it is also one of the easiest to prepare. Serve it hot before the liquid center congeals.

Ingredients

Granulated sugar for dusting (about 1 cup)
1 cup unsalted butter
¾ cup plus 2 tablespoons bittersweet chocolate chips
4 large eggs
4 large egg yolks
1 teaspoon vanilla extract
2 cups confectioners' sugar
⅔ cup all-purpose flour
2 cups heavy cream, whipped

**Equipment: Plate Setter, 10 (8-ounce) glass or metal baking cups
Set the EGG for indirect cooking with the Plate Setter, legs down.
Preheat the EGG to 450°F.**

Spray the baking cups with cooking spray and dust the entire inside with the granulated sugar. Set aside. Place the butter and chocolate in a saucepan on the stovetop over low heat, stirring frequently, until the chocolate is melted. Set aside and let cool for 10 minutes.

Place the eggs and egg yolks in the bowl of an electric mixer. Using the whisk attachment, beat on medium speed for 3 to 4 minutes, until light and ribbony. Add the vanilla and confectioners' sugar and beat for 1 minute more. Slowly add the melted chocolate and beat for 1 minute, then add the flour and beat for 1 more minute, or until just incorporated. Fill each baking cup three-quarters full. Refrigerate for a minimum of 30 minutes and up to 24 hours.

Place the cups on the Plate Setter and close the lid of the EGG. Cook for 6 to 8 minutes, until slightly firm to the touch. The cakes should be firm but not cooked all the way through.

Immediately turn out onto individual plates and serve with whipped cream (see page 248). **Serves 10**

Chef & Pitmaster Biographies

Rick Browne is the creator, host, and executive producer of public television's *Barbecue America* and the author of a number of books, including *Grilling America* and *The Frequent Fryer,* and coauthor of *The Barbecue America Cookbook*. A writer, photographer, pitmaster, restaurant critic, and consultant, he is also a Doctor of Barbecue, holding an honorary Ph.B. (Doctor of Barbecue Philosophy) bestowed on him by the prestigious Kansas City Barbeque Society for his expertise and commitment to barbecue.

Browne serves as a spokesman for numerous corporations that have barbecue-related products and has spent many years researching barbecue across the United States and Canada by visiting festivals and barbecue restaurants and interviewing dozens of pitmasters. His work has been published in many magazines, including *Time, Newsweek, People,* and *Reader's Digest,* and he has appeared on *FOX & Friends,* the *Today* show, *Live with Regis & Kelly,* and *CNN.* **www.barbecueamerica.com**

S. Dean Corbett has polished his reputation of culinary excellence as a chef in Louisville, Kentucky's fine dining scene for more than twenty years. After turning his first restaurant, Equus, into one of the city's best restaurants, he launched Corbett's An American Place, which serves American cuisine in a beautifully restored farmhouse in northeast Louisville. Corbett's features a chef's interactive tasting room and a unique 150-year-old "wineskeller."

Chef Corbett hosts *The Secrets of Louisville Chefs Live,* a popular weekly television cooking show, as well as producing a line of gourmet products including seven sauces and three soups. He is recognized locally, giving back to the community via Equus's participation in many charity fund-raising events. Corbett is also heavily involved in efforts to support all local and regional farmers and purveyors. **www.corbettsrestaurant.com**

Ken Hess earned a degree in hotel restaurant management before starting his training at the Culinary Institute of America. He began his career at the renowned Greenbrier Hotel and Resort in West Virginia as a culinary apprentice and ultimately became the catering and barbecue chef in charge of all on-property catering facilities. He was responsible for preparing repasts ranging from eight-course meals to a barbecue buffet for fourteen hundred guests. He was proud to perform several private cooking demonstrations for distinguished patron Secretary of State Condoleezza Rice and her colleagues.

One of the Greenbrier's butchers nicknamed Hess "Hoss" after TV character Hoss Cartwright, whom he resembles, so when Hess formed his competition barbecue team it was an easy decision to name it Hoss's BBQ & Catering Company. His team has earned many coveted awards, including first place in the rib competition and Reserve Grand Champion. He credits his eclectic style to having lived in many areas of the country, picking up food traditions from each region. Chef Hess believes in keeping food simple in terms of seasonings, so that the natural taste of the food prevails. He loves smoking pizzas on his EGG, and while working at Greenbrier he often held parties at his house where chefs would gather, bringing their own ingredients and taking turns making pizzas throughout the night. **www.theonlyhossbbq.com**

Andy Husbands is a chef and the proud owner of four very popular restaurants: Tremont 647, Sister Sorrel, and Rouge in Boston, and Kestral in Providence. He is known for his commitment to locally grown fresh ingredients, as well as his inventive approach to food. Teaming up with the writer Joe Yonan, Husbands's first cookbook, *The Fearless Chef: Innovative Recipes from the Edge of American Cuisine,* became wildly successful. His honors and awards are too extensive to recount, but include being named Chef/Restaurateur of the Year in 2004 by the nation's leading hunger relief organization, Share Our Strength. In 2005 the National Pork Board recognized him as one of only five "Celebrated Chefs" in the country.

Husbands, together with some good ole friends, participates in barbecue competitions under the team name iQue BBQ. They have won numerous championships including the Yahoo Cup for "Team of the Year," a title they earned three times from the New England Barbecue Society. They were New Hampshire State Champions and Vermont State Champions, and took home the New England Regional BBQ Championship for two consecutive years. www.tremont647.com

Ray Lampe, better known as Dr. BBQ, grew up in Chicago and spent twenty-five years in his family's trucking business. He participated in barbecue competition cook-offs as a hobby for many years, and when the time came for a career change, he jumped right in to barbecue cooking and never looked back. Since then he has written five barbecue cookbooks, including *The NFL GameDay Cookbook,* with others in the works. He is the executive chef at Southern Hospitality, a New York City barbecue restaurant, and he's the featured barbecue chef at the Greenbrier Resort in West Virginia.

Lampe travels the country as the "spokeschef" for the Big Green Egg, and frequently appears as a guest chef at food-related events. He has been featured in many newspapers and magazines and has appeared on more than a dozen TV shows on the Food Network, HGTV, CNN, and the Discovery Channel. www.drbbq.com

Steven Raichlen is a multi-award-winning author, journalist, teacher, and television host. His best-selling books and public television shows—*Primal Grill* and *Barbecue University*—have redefined American barbecue. Raichlen's twenty-eight books include *The Barbecue Bible, How to Grill,* and *BBQ USA,* and they have been translated into fifteen languages. His work has appeared in major food and travel magazines, including *National Geographic Traveler, Food & Wine,* and *Bon Appetit.*

Raichlen founded Barbecue University, which now takes place at the Broadmoor resort in Colorado Springs. He has lectured on the history of barbecue at the Smithsonian Institution, the Library of Congress, and the National Press Club, and hosts a French TV show called *Le Maitre du Grill.* www.barbecuebible.com

Kevin Rathbun is a widely acclaimed chef and restaurateur with a history of fine dining and entertainment that runs in his family. His mother spent thirty-five years operating fine restaurants in and around Kansas City, and his father, a jazz musician, entertained patrons at night. At the Rathbun home, steak was nightly fare and dinner was always a formal production with china, crystal, silver, and friends, followed by jam sessions that continued into the wee hours of the morning.

After gaining years of experience working with many famous chefs in top restaurants and serving as Corporate Chef of the renowned Buckhead Life Restaurant Group in Atlanta, Rathbun opened Rathbun's in Atlanta in 2004. *Esquire* magazine soon named it one of the Top New Restaurants in the Country. He has since added a second restaurant, Krog Bar, and, most recently, Kevin Rathbun Steak, which pays homage to the big-league steakhouses and continues his Kansas City heritage. Rathbun's awards, honors, TV appearances, and print feature stories are legendary, and include the *Today* show, Food Network's *Iron Chef America, USA TODAY,* and the *Wall Street Journal.* He admits that in his next life he would pursue his passion for designing restaurants. www.kevinrathbunsteak.com

Lee Ann Whippen is a food expert extraordinaire who has been involved in every aspect of food preparation. President, owner, and pitmaster of Wood Chick's BBQ Restaurants & Catering Company in Chesapeake, Virginia, she is a former newspaper food columnist who spent fifteen years in hotel catering and management. She is a longtime barbecue competitor who has won multiple state grand championships, and as a Kansas City Barbeque Society–certified judge, she has tasted untold amounts of barbecued ribs, brisket, and other entries from the country's top-notch competitors. A popular guest with radio and TV hosts, as well as newspaper editors, Whippen was named the 2008 "Food Network Throwdown Champ" over Bobby Flay for Best Barbecue Pork. She has appeared on the *Today* show and VERSUS Network and has been featured in *People* magazine. www.woodchicksbbq.com

Acknowledgments

This book is dedicated to a very special couple, Jack and Edie Fischer, without whose love and support the Big Green Egg business might not have existed, and hence this book would not have been written.

It's been said it takes a village to raise a child; the same is true for publishing a cookbook. Many, many people lent their talents to this project, nurturing and incubating the newest "EGG" until it was ready to hatch into this beautiful book. Throughout the nearly two-year undertaking, the team has been immersed in everything EGG, the best part of which was tasting, and tasting again, some of the best food to ever grace a plate.

The Big Green Egg Company wishes to thank and gratefully acknowledge all of the following who have been instrumental in developing the Big Green Egg Cookbook.

First and foremost, we recognize Ed Fisher, president and founder of the Big Green Egg Company, whose thirty-five years of dedication provided the reason for writing and producing this cookbook. His vision, passion, and unbridled enthusiasm for the EGG have helped it become the best and fastest-growing outdoor cooking appliance in the United States and beyond. It might be said that he is, at least indirectly, responsible for putting some pretty awesome meals on dinner tables across the country.

Jodi Burson, marketing manager for the company, assumed overall responsibility for the creation and production of this book, guiding its direction and implementation. Understanding the vital role this comprehensive work would play in providing assistance to existing and future EGG owners, Jodi enthusiastically supported and was involved in every aspect of bringing it to fruition. She also had the enviable task of chief recipe taster.

The Big Green Egg staff is a close-knit family whose members make invaluable contributions to the company's success on a daily basis. Of course, they are all experienced EGGheads, so it is not surprising that since the book's inception they have been involved in and excited about the project, and have eagerly contributed their favorite recipes and ideas, managed to do a bit of tasting, offered encouragement, and prodded the team to deliver the finished book more quickly because they couldn't wait for it to be finished.

Donna Myers, after assisting the Big Green Egg Company for years with marketing as president of DHM Group, Inc., developed the idea and concept for the cookbook. Her vision was to share the exciting history of the EGG and the company with both new and experienced EGG owners and provide them a wealth of recipes designed specifically for the ceramic cooker. Donna pulled together the team that ultimately made the book a reality and supervised it from beginning to end. Patty Ross, DHM Group office manager, kept all the details in order. She spent countless hours distributing copies of many versions of the manuscript, tracking down information, attending to the many scheduling requirements, and ensuring that everything went smoothly. Donna Myers passed away in 2011, and the barbecue industry lost one of its leading advocates and its most knowledgeable friend.

Many thanks go to our publisher at Andrews McMeel Publishing, Kirsty Melville. Her extensive experience in the cookbook field guided the entire team as the book took shape. Andrews McMeel cookbook editor Jean Lucas maintained a strong liaison with the recipe development team and packager throughout the many months of book development.

Book packager Jennifer Barry creatively designed and produced the book, which was a considerable undertaking. Jennifer was responsible for turning the extensive information, recipes, and photographs into book format, as well as overseeing production, photography, and editing, with the ultimate goal of making the book attractive and user-friendly for readers. Assisting her were production artist Kristen Hall, designer Leslie Barry, copyeditor Leslie Evans, and Editcetera editorial services, all of whom helped in innumerable ways to bring the work to completion.

Sara Levy, recipe author, with tremendous creativity, energy, and culinary talent, developed the incredible array of innovative recipes, from appetizers to entrées to desserts, which showcased every aspect of cooking in the Big Green Egg and used EGGcessories™ that are available to enhance EGG cooking. Sara, with her accomplished assistants, Bree Williams and Bryan Hartness, was responsible for recipe testing to ensure each dish turned out perfectly every time and was also the food stylist who produced the picture-perfect food for photography. The hard work and dedication over many months by Sara and her assistants contributed enormously to the quality of the Big Green Egg Cookbook.

Lisa Mayer skillfully wrote the entire front end of the book, a labor of love considering her twenty-year knowledge of the barbecue industry, her familiarity with Big Green Egg as a company, and her fondness for cooking in the EGG. She helped explain the uniqueness of the EGG as a cooker and the phenomenon of the Big Green Egg Company, and translated the enthusiasm of its users and fans into text!

Mark O'Tyson, our talented food photographer, created photographs of more than one hundred of the recipes, which are sure to make readers want to fire up the coals and start cooking in their EGGs. Each dish is showcased with mouthwatering appeal thanks to his creative eye. Mark was aided by his assistant Scott Moore, who was truly a jack-of-all-trades. He did a great job scouring for last-minute props and maneuvering EGGs, backdrops, and other equipment in and out of the set. He kept the entire crew "fed and watered" and was ready to lend a helping hand wherever needed.

A number of highly recognized chefs and barbecue celebrities generously shared some of their favorite EGG recipes for the book. Their recipes, in our special Chefs & Pitmasters chapter, are ones that they serve to their restaurant patrons, highlight in their own cookbooks and newsletters, or feature on their national television shows.

Karen Adler, president of Pig Out Publications, author of numerous books on outdoor cooking, and one of the two BBQ Queens, gave us her invaluable counsel in the early stages of planning the book. She guided us regarding efficiencies, encouraged us when we were uncertain about a direction, and cautioned us when we veered off course.

Special thanks go to the EGGheads™, who have been such a major factor in the success of the Big Green Egg. Their ideas, recipes, enthusiasm, camaraderie, and total dedication to "The Ultimate Cooking Experience" constantly inspire us, and we are truly grateful for their support over the past three decades. The wonderful recipes that many of our EGGhead™ friends have shared with us were the inspiration for the classic recipes found in the EGGhead Recipes chapter. We owe them tremendous thanks for their contributions, which planted the seed for this book long ago.

Very special recognition and appreciation goes to Brenda Miller and her late husband, Bill. They were two of the earliest EGGheads and most vocal and involved supporters of the EGG and the company. Bill developed the original Big Green Egg Forum, Brenda played an important role in launching the first EGGtoberfest celebration, and together they initiated the idea of using the distinctive EGG words such as EGGstraordinary and EGGcessories. Today Brenda continues on as a legendary Big Green Egg employee.

Metric Conversions & Equivalents

Metric Conversion Formulas

To Convert	Multiply
Ounces to grams	Ounces by 28.35
Pounds to kilograms	Pounds by .454
Teaspoons to milliliters	Teaspoons by 4.93
Tablespoons to milliliters	Tablespoons by 14.79
Fluid ounces to milliliters	Fluid ounces by 29.57
Cups to milliliters	Cups by 236.59
Cups to liters	Cups by .236
Pints to liters	Pints by .473
Quarts to liters	Quarts by .946
Gallons to liters	Gallons by 3.785
Inches to centimeters	Inches by 2.54

Approximate Metric Equivalents

Volume

¼ teaspoon	1 milliliter
½ teaspoon	2.5 milliliters
¾ teaspoon	4 milliliters
1 teaspoon	5 milliliters
1¼ teaspoons	6 milliliters
1½ teaspoons	7.5 milliliters
1¾ teaspoons	8.5 milliliters
2 teaspoons	10 milliliters
1 tablespoon (½ fluid ounce)	15 milliliters
2 tablespoons (1 fluid ounce)	30 milliliters
¼ cup	60 milliliters
⅓ cup	80 milliliters
½ cup (4 fluid ounces)	120 milliliters
⅔ cup	160 milliliters
¾ cup	180 milliliters
1 cup (8 fluid ounces)	240 milliliters
1¼ cups	300 milliliters
1½ cups (12 fluid ounces)	360 milliliters
1⅔ cups	400 milliliters
2 cups (1 pint)	460 milliliters
3 cups	700 milliliters
4 cups (1 quart)	.95 liter
1 quart plus ¼ cup	1 liter
4 quarts (1 gallon)	3.8 liters

Information compiled from a variety of sources, including *Recipes into Type* by Joan Whitman and Dolores Simon (Newton, MA: Biscuit Books, 2000); *The New Food Lover's Companion* by Sharon Tyler Herbst (Hauppauge, NY: Barron's, 1995); and *Rosemary Brown's Big Kitchen Instruction Book* (Kansas City, MO: Andrews McMeel, 1998).

Approximate Metric Equivalents

Weight

¼ ounce	7 grams
½ ounce	14 grams
¾ ounce	21 grams
1 ounce	28 grams
1¼ ounces	35 grams
1½ ounces	42.5 grams
1⅔ ounces	45 grams
2 ounces	57 grams
3 ounces	85 grams
4 ounces (¼ pound)	113 grams
5 ounces	142 grams
6 ounces	170 grams
7 ounces	198 grams
8 ounces (½ pound)	227 grams
16 ounces (1 pound)	454 grams
35.25 ounces (2.2 pounds)	1 kilogram

Length

⅛ inch	3 millimeters
¼ inch	6 millimeters
½ inch	1¼ centimeters
1 inch	2½ centimeters
2 inches	5 centimeters
2½ inches	6 centimeters
4 inches	10 centimeters
5 inches	13 centimeters
6 inches	15¼ centimeters
12 inches (1 foot)	30 centimeters

Oven Temperatures

Description	°F	°C	British Gas Mark
Very cool	200°	95°	0
Very cool	225°	110°	¼
Very cool	250°	120°	½
Cool	275°	135°	1
Cool	300°	150°	2
Warm	325°	165°	3
Moderate	350°	175°	4
Moderately hot	375°	190°	5
Fairly hot	400°	200°	6
Hot	425°	220°	7
Very hot	450°	230°	8
Very hot	475°	245°	9

To convert Fahrenheit to Celsius, subtract 32 from Fahrenheit, multiply the result by 5, then divide by 9.

Common Ingredients & Their Approximate Equivalents

1 cup uncooked white rice = 185 grams

1 cup all-purpose flour = 140 grams

1 stick butter (4 ounces • ½ cup • 8 tablespoons)
    = 110 grams

1 cup butter (8 ounces • 2 sticks • 16 tablespoons)
    = 220 grams

1 cup brown sugar, firmly packed = 225 grams

1 cup granulated sugar = 200 grams

Index